THE BOOK OF SACRAMENTAL MAGIC

THE BOOK OF SACRAMENTAL MAGIC
A Guide to Christian Ritual Ceremony

by
Stephen Mandes Thomas

AEON

First published in 2025 by
Aeon Books

Copyright © 2025 by Stephen Mandes Thomas

The right of Stephen Mandes Thomas to be identified as the author of this work has been asserted in accordance with §§ 77 and 78 of the Copyright Design and Patents Act 1988.

All rights reserved. No part of this publication may be reproduced, stored in a retrieval system, or transmitted, in any form or by any means, electronic, mechanical, photocopying, recording, or otherwise, without the prior written permission of the publisher.

British Library Cataloguing in Publication Data

A C.I.P. for this book is available from the British Library

ISBN-13: 978-1-80152-192-5

Typeset by Medlar Publishing Solutions Pvt Ltd, India

www.aeonbooks.co.uk

CONTENTS

INTRODUCTION ix

PART I: FUNDAMENTALS OF PRACTICE

LESSON 1
Sacraments and sacramentals 3

LESSON 2
A guide to magical philosophy 11

LESSON 3
Resolving binaries 29

LESSON 4
A prayer rule 33

PART II: FOUNDATIONS OF MAGICAL PRACTICE

Introduction — 41

LESSON 1
Esoteric Christian theology — 43

LESSON 2
Banishing — 57

LESSON 3
Meditation — 63

LESSON 4
The Confiteor — 67

LESSON 5
The initiation of the rosary — 75

PART III: SACRAMENTAL THEURGY

Introduction — 93

LESSON 1
Opening a magical temple — 95

LESSON 2
The kyrie energetic practice — 101

LESSON 3
Working with the saints and angels — 105

LESSON 4
Consecrations and the devotion to the Three Hearts — 111

PART IV: SACRAMENTAL THAUMATURGY

Introduction — 123

LESSON 1
The principles of effective magic — 125

LESSON 2
Sacred things: the sacramentals of the Church — 137

LESSON 3
Traditional sacramentals — 141

LESSON 4
Natural sacramentals — 155

LESSON 5
Novenas, psalms, and other prayers — 161

LESSON 6
The magic of the psalms — 167

PART V: THE SACRAMENTS

Introduction — 173

A rite of self-dedication — 177

A home mass — 181

The home mass: instructions — 185

Baking bread for the home mass — 199

The remaining sacraments — 203

Afterword — 217

PART VI: APPENDIXES

APPENDIX 1
A prayer book — 221

APPENDIX 2
The saints — 229

APPENDIX 3
Sources and further reading — 237

ACKNOWLEDGEMENTS — 241

INDEX — 243

INTRODUCTION

Growing up as a Catholic in rural Pennsylvania, there were three things that were obvious to me about my religion. The first was that it was magical. Crucifixes, pictures of saints, blessed rosaries, and scapulars all had a kind of special power. Every kid knew that they could drive away ghosts and vampires, and even the adults seemed to know it. The sign of the cross could do that too, and so could the little collection of rose petals, blessed by a priest on the feast of Saint Therese, that I kept in my dresser drawer. Invisible spirits watched over us, angels of God and ghosts of the exalted Dead.

And then there was the special ritual every Sunday, where the man dressed up in robes like Merlin recited the magical formula over the crackers and wine, and turned them into the body of a living God, which we'd then eat amid the scent of incense smoke and the sound of a congregation singing off key. All of this was clearly magic. The odd thing about it for me, though, was that nobody else seemed to think of it that way. These were just things that you did.

The second obvious thing was that it was full of rules. Now some of these were clearly good rules, such as the ones that said we shouldn't steal things or hurt people, and that if we did we'd have to make up for it. Others seemed rather arbitrary, such as the rule that we shouldn't eat meat on Fridays in Lent, that we should genuflect before sitting down in church, or that it was okay to leave mass right after communion if the Steelers had an early game that Sunday.

And then there were the *other* rules. These were the rules that if you happened to have grown up in a different Church, well, once you died you would be tortured, in Hell, forever. And also that if one spent too much time swearing or fighting and happened to die before running into a priest, you would be tortured, in Hell, forever. Or if you spent too much time thinking about the girls you'd be tortured. Forever. Actually there was quite a great number of things that could get you tortured until Forever.

And that leads to the third thing about it, which was that it had once been far more magical, but that at some point in the past most of the magic had been lost. The rules had been preserved, especially the bad ones. Actually, the whole point of the rules seemed to be to cover over the magic. Well, that was the point of the bad rules, anyway, especially the worst ones. The better rules worked together with the magic. I remember well the first time I followed the rule that said you had to confess your sins to a priest. I was seven or eight years old, and after he pronounced the formula of absolution I walked out of the confessional feeling as though I were surrounded by a cloud of glowing light. That priest was a good priest, though. There were other priests with whom it would not have been nearly so good for an eight-year-old boy to spend any time alone. We learned about them later.

Each of these three realizations, however, was also a question. It seemed obvious to me that our tradition was magical, but it didn't seem obvious to anyone else. At least, no one talked about it that way. Sacred images, holy water, church on Sunday—these were just things that we did. Was it really magic?

And then there were the rules. Like I said, some were very good, but others were quite destructive. I remember learning about the concept of "mortal sin" as a young boy and lying awake in bed at night, terrified that I was going to go to Hell. And of course, we were told that the magic would stop working if you didn't follow the rules—even the worst ones. Was that really true?

And, finally, it was just so very clear that we had lost something. Really it seemed that we were living in the ruins of a tradition. Take our church, for example. It was a new construction, built in the 1970s. Its shape could be described as an auditorium inside of a spaceship built in the Soviet Union. But I had heard that it was different before, darker, built of stone, filled with side altars dedicated to various saints. Or consider the angels. We were all told that we had guardian angels, and these sounded very interesting, and sometimes we were told about other angels as well. But most of the angels that we actually saw, in pictures and in statues, were chubby little babies with wings, not worth a second thought after one reached the age of ten. I lived with my grandparents, who were born in the 1930s, and they remembered an older way of talking about angels. To them, angels weren't little cartoon babies but exalted spirits who governed the universe at the command of God. I never heard about such things from priests or religion teachers, though. That was another one of those things that we'd gotten rid of. I heard about many things like this, like legends of an ancient time when the gods still walked on the Earth. Whatever magic we had left, it was only a small remnant of what they'd had before. Where did it all go?

Eventually, after the usual way of things, the rules became too much for me to bear, and the magic faded more and more. In my teenage years I quit going to church. and quit believing in much of anything. In my twenties I tried to go back, only to discover that what little of the magic remained had been almost completely lost. I was living in Oregon then, far from home, and felt the need to reconnect to at least something that might be familiar. And so I went to the local Catholic church. This was a wooden building that looked like a log cabin. In the center was a large wooden cross, with no Christ on it. There were no statues and no pictures of any angel or any saint. Over the cross were two large projectors, on which the words of the bad hymns appeared when the band started up. The band, of course, was an acoustic rock band, and by the third time the guitarist struck his open G chord I was quite ready to leave. Whatever magic had remained was gone. Many of the rules were gone, too, both the better ones and the worse ones. All that remained was a way to kill an hour or two on Sunday. My questions, it seemed, would never be answered.

And so for years I wandered in a kind of spiritual darkness. This was the early 2000s, and atheism was very popular then, if you remember. Indeed, it seemed that atheists were everywhere, especially on the internet, and attacks on "religion" were a constant thing. Especially if you spent your time with people who thought of themselves as smart or educated, it was not a safe thing to admit to believing in God, and especially not to being any sort of Christian.

I never became an atheist myself. The trouble with atheism, it seemed to me, wasn't the question of how many gods there might or might not be. The trouble was their philosophy of materialism. Materialism insists that nothing exists but matter and energy. To the materialists, as I understood their argument, our minds were nothing but illusions, and all of our experiences of thought, emotion, memory, and imagination were, in fact, nothing but the activity of our brains. Fair enough. The trouble with that argument, it seemed to me, was that there was no physical means for discovering a mind. You could take a picture of every single thing that ever happened in a brain during its entire life and never discover a mind. That is, if you didn't have a brain yourself, you'd have no reason to think that someone else was having mental experiences which you could never see yourself but which went along with everything that happened in that brain. You'd just be looking at physical processes, like water flowing in a creek, trees growing in a forest, or lightning flashing in the clouds. From there, I reasoned that there was no reason to believe that creeks or forests or storm clouds lacked minds, and I still think that. Of course, it's no great leap from creeks and forests to the world as a whole. And so, by grappling with the arguments of the atheists, I discovered the soul of the world, that great power revered throughout the ancient world and not forgotten even by Christians until very recently. This was god enough for me for some time.

But is that really enough? For some it has been. For the ancient Stoics, for example. For people like Pliny the Elder, the great Roman naturalist, as for other Stoics of his time, the world was either the only god or at least the only god worth talking about. In my twenties I was unaware of Stoics and knew of "Pliny the Elder" only as the name of a very strong beer brewed somewhere in Arizona. The Stoic teachings on virtue and self-control were totally foreign to my mind and my world. And so my god was Nature, but for me that just meant license to do whatever I felt like at any given moment, the way that rivers and storm clouds do. At the end of the day, it wasn't enough. Like most people who live entirely according to their impulses, I found myself at age twenty-nine with no money and no job, with most of my bridges burned, and little hope for the future. I needed something more than a vague belief in the god of Nature, and every possible way forward seemed closed to me.

And so I decided to turn to magic.

I'd dabbled a bit with witchcraft in my teenage years, as many did in the 1990s, that lost golden age of shopping mall Celts and Hot

Topic Wiccans. I never got very far with it. It was desperation that led me back to it, more than a decade later. I found a book of lessons in "high magick" online and duly downloaded it from a pirate website. (Please don't do that.)

Not the most auspicious of beginnings, but God works with the tools he has available. I supposed that I would be worshiping the Moon and calling down the gods of the ancient Celts. I quickly discovered, very much to my dismay, that the magical tradition being taught in the book was something called the "Golden Dawn," and that, rather than the gods of the ancient Celts or any such thing, I would be working with the Christian archangels, Hebrew names of God out of the Old Testament, and even Jesus Christ himself! At the time, I found the very word "angel" so nauseating I couldn't even say it out loud. But I was desperate, and I persevered.

And something happened. The first thing was quite simply that, overnight, after my very first practice of the very first lesson in "high magick," everything changed. I mean everything. My sleep cycle, which was then on a 3 am to noon rotation, normalized, and the next day I woke up in the morning, for the first time in a great long while. My cravings for alcohol and nicotine dried up and nearly vanished. I found it easy to take up a daily exercise routine of running and yoga, and to eat nourishing food. I even started making small amounts of money.

I continued to work through the book, and my practice of magic deepened. A few weeks after I started, I performed the Lesser Banishing Ritual of the Pentagram for the first time. Those experienced with magic will know that this includes invoking four archangels, those awful beings I'd so dreaded having to deal with. But I did the ritual, and they appeared: neither the dreadful powers I'd feared nor the saccharine little babies that are so common in bad art, but powerful, wise and yet gentle beings. I mixed up the names of two of them, and I felt their amusement. I also felt a strange sense of recognition, as though I'd done this before, long ago. They remembered me well, and were pleased that I'd found my way back.

But there was more. The pentagram ritual opens with the names of God in Hebrew. As a child I had loved God, that is, the God with whom I'd been raised. Later I came to fear and despise him, and not without good reason, since I'd been told so many times that he was planning on sending me to Hell. But in the invocation of God in the rituals of the Golden Dawn, I found again the powerful, loving, and merciful God of my childhood. This was a God who spoke the very stars to light and saw that they were good, not a God who tortured people until Forever for minor infractions.

In this way, I resolved two of the questions of my childhood. The Christian tradition was indeed a magical tradition. And the endless lists of rules were, if not irrelevant, nowhere near as important as I'd been told. But one more question remained.

As I continued to practice magic, I felt a strange pull back to the religion of my childhood. I began to explore the sacred music and art of the Christian tradition—the masses of Adrian Willaert and Giovanni Palestrina, the majesty of the gothic cathedrals, the talismanic paintings of Botticelli and the other Renaissance masters. And here I found the answer to my third question. Where did the magic go? It was abandoned, and in some cases destroyed, by the very people who had been charged with preserving it.

The story of how that happened is long and involved, and not something I want to go into in detail here. One thing that is worth noting, however, is that much of the destruction that happened was accidental. The Second Vatican Council is a critical moment, of course, but many of the attendees of that council weren't trying to destroy the old magic, but were often looking for liberation from the worst of the old rules. Hence the declarations of that council that "The church rejects nothing that is true and holy" in other religions, the favorable statements made toward Protestants, and the lifting of the anathemas between the Catholic and Orthodox Churches. And Vatican II wasn't the only attack on the old magic, but only the most recent. Prior to Vatican II there was the Devotional Revolution of the 1800s, which sought to scour the Church of anything other than prayer and obedience. Prior to the Devotional Revolution, the Council of Trent and other works of the early modern period did their best to snuff out practices of magic and divination that had been widespread throughout the Christian world.

It's not my purpose to condemn the past, but rather to propose something new. The purpose of this book is to present a complete system of sacramental Christian magic. I start from the principles of the Western Magical Tradition, which is the tradition of magic which has come down to us from antiquity, and has been modified and developed through the Middle Ages, the Renaissance, and the modern period. The book as a whole and the system of practice it teaches is intended to be a way to engage with the deep magic of the Christian tradition, without becoming mired in the problems which have beset that tradition.

I suspect that there are two sorts of people who will be drawn to this work. The first are believing members of sacramental Christian Churches, especially the Catholic and Anglican Churches—perhaps the Lutheran as well—who love their traditions but feel that they have lost something, and want that something back. The second are practicing ceremonial magicians, esotericists and occultists who feel called to the traditional religion of the Western world, but find in the established Churches only empty forms and arbitrary rules. And there is a third group of people, possibly the largest, who fall somewhere in between those two poles.

The perspective of this book

I should note that this book is not intended as an attack on the Catholic Church or any other Church. There is little in the practices given herein that will offend an orthodox believer. With that said, I will tell you that my own take on theology and traditional Christian mythology is different from that of any orthodox Church that I'm aware of. My philosophical perspective is informed above all by the tradition called Neoplatonism. In that I'm not actually very different from the mainstream Churches: Dionysius the Areopagite, Augustine of Hippo, and Thomas Aquinas are just a few names among many prominent Catholic theologians who were strongly influenced by Neoplatonism. There is a difference, though, in my own perspective, and that has to do with the way that I read the Christian Scriptures and the other stories and articles of the faith. I approach the stories of the Christian religion as revealed in the Holy Scriptures in the same way that the ancient pagan Neoplatonists approached the myths of their own tradition. Before we go on, it may be helpful to give an example of what that looks like.

In the ancient myth, Saturn, the son of Uranus, god of the sky, overthrew and castrated his own father, and became king of the gods. Having learned that one of his children would overthrow him in turn, he devoured them as they were born. Eventually he was tricked into swallowing a stone in place of Jupiter, and was overthrown in turn. This is a rather grisly myth, and makes of Saturn a rather grisly God. It was for that reason, actually, that Plato proposed banning the teaching of myths from his ideal city: He reasoned that since the gods were good by their very nature, young and unformed minds shouldn't be exposed to stories of them castrating their parents and eating one another. It's a reasonable point, you have to admit.

After Plato, however, came other philosophers, who agreed with his perspective but wanted to continue to worship their old gods and tell their old stories. But the problem remained: How to understand a god like Saturn, a god who was good, and indeed had been the king who reigned during the Golden Age of mankind, but who could also have done such awful things? They found the answer in an allegorical interpretation of myth. Saturn, they said, is the Divine Mind. He is said to eat his own children because when we eat something, we unite it to our very being, and in the Divine Mind, all things are one. He is said to "castrate his own father" only to teach us that his father Uranus is the "first god" who created our universe, but our universe is the only one of its kind. There is no "multiverse" for the Neoplatonists. So it is said that Saturn removes the ability of his father to make more universes, to teach us that there is only one universe, and there will never be another one. Moreover, none of these things were understood as historical events that really happened. Instead, they were stories which presented eternal truths in a form the human mind could comprehend. As the philosopher Sallust wrote, "These things never happened, but always are."

So far, so good. The trouble was that the old problem still remained, because the average believing pagan didn't spend their time poring through the tomes of the philosophers to learn the allegorical interpretations of their myths, but continued to believe and worship as they always had. The question of how this might have gone on had the pagan world continued is an interesting one, but it will have to be left for another universe to answer.

In this book, I have employed the same sort of allegorical interpretation to the Christian myths. In this, again, I'm not doing anything entirely new. The allegorical was one of the four different ways that the traditional Christian world interpreted its Scriptures, along with the literal, the moral, and the anagogical. Nor do I necessarily deny the historical reality of any of the events of the Scriptures. To be quite honest, I don't know whether they happened the way that we're told or not. I think that some of them almost certainly did, and in this I include the life, death, and resurrection of Jesus Christ. There's really no reason to think that he didn't return after his death, unless you've already decided ahead of time that no one returns after they die. But that's nonsense. Almost everyone knows someone who has died, and if you talk to enough people, you'll find that a great many of them have had at least one encounter with at least one person after their death. The differences between my approach and that of the more mainstream Churches is that I'm far less interested in these stories as histories than as allegories—stories which present eternal truths in a way that the human mind can grasp. The man Jesus of Nazareth almost certainly died on the Cross, descended into Hell, returned on the third day, and ascended into Heaven, where He is seated at the right hand of the Father. But it is more important to understand that the Eternal Man is always descending through the universe as far as the absolute limit of reality, and returning back to the absolute Source of existence, and that this is the nature of the Eternal Man, which is also the Divine Mind or Word of God.

Moreover, while many of my own beliefs are no different from that of ordinary Catholic or Orthodox Christians, some of them are well outside the bounds of accepted belief in any mainstream Church. When this comes up in this book I've tried to make it clear, and if you prefer to hold to the opinions of one of the mainstream Churches, you should just ignore those parts.

How to use this book

This book is divided into five parts. The first four are organized into lessons, usually four or five. Of these lessons, some are knowledge lectures, which discuss topics like magical philosophy or sacramental theology. Others are practical lessons. These are divided into two types. Some are daily practices, while others are specialized practices meant to be performed either on specific occasions or as needed. Each practical lesson will contain Notes for Practice, explaining how and when the practice is to be performed.

The first two parts establish the foundations of practice. In the lessons contained in these two parts we cover magical philosophy and the esoteric interpretation of the Christian story. We then provide a basic prayer rule and teach the most important magical rituals and techniques of meditation.

The third and fourth parts are concerned with practical magic. Here we discuss the foundations of magic in the sense of causing changes both in ourselves and in the outside world. There are additional rituals to learn, of course, and we teach the invocation of saints and the use of the sacramentals, those great magical tools of the Christian religion.

The fifth part is concerned with the sacraments. For some, there either is no church available or is no church acceptable which can provide these. Others may simply wish to have access to the sacraments on their own, in addition to what they get from their regular church. The central part of this section is a home mass, which can be performed by anybody. We also cover the remaining six sacraments, all of which can be modified for home use. Following the fifth part, a number of appendixes are given, including a prayer book, a short list of saints, and notes for further reading and exploration.

When working through the lessons, it is important to read each one slowly and carefully. If the lesson is a knowledge lecture, reread as many times as necessary to make sure you've understood. If the lesson is a daily practice, you should do your best to memorize it, and then start practice as soon as you can. Be prepared to spend anywhere from two weeks to two months working with a specific practice before you proceed on to the next one. This isn't a race: You will get more out of each lesson if you take more time with it than you need than if you take less time.

At the end of each part of the book, you should pause to reflect on your journey so far. What sorts of changes have you noted in yourself and in your life since you began this work? What sorts of changes would you like to see that haven't manifested yet? After this, take some time to look through the lessons in the next part and make sure it's something you want to undertake. This book is designed so that each part is a self-contained unit: If you just learn the very basic practices in the first part, you will have gained a set of valuable spiritual tools that you will be able to rely on for the rest of your life. Just as there are no points for rushing through a lesson, there are also no points for pushing yourself into practices that you are either not ready for or uninterested in: Be honest with yourself, and only proceed to a particular part if you really feel called to the work presented.

One tool that will be very helpful for evaluating your progress is a *journal*. An actual pen and a physical notebook are best, but you can type your notes out if you really want to. The point is to have a way to keep track of your progress and keep from deluding yourself. You may start with a bit of freeform journaling about your own spiritual practice, why you began working with this book and what you hope to gain out of it, and maybe some notes on your own religious or spiritual beliefs. Later, you will use your journal on a daily basis to record your experiences in meditation.

PART I

FUNDAMENTALS OF PRACTICE

LESSON 1

Sacraments and sacramentals

Knowledge lecture

Magic in the Christian tradition takes a number of different forms. Many people are familiar with the grimoires, which are books of magic, such as Cornelius Agrippa's *Three Books of Occult Philosophy*, the *Arbatel of Magic*, or Francis Bardon's *The Magus*. These sorts of books present detailed accounts of the magical universe as well as ritual methods of summoning spirits and creating magical images in order to bring about particular effects in the world. Very often these books work with the tradition of astrological magic. That is, they are derived from the old theory that everything on the Earth reflects the patterns of the stars in the heavens. The stars and planets, then, become their primary source of power.

Some people think that astrological magic is forbidden to Catholics or to Christians generally, but this isn't the case. In fact, no less an authority than Saint Albertus Magnus wrote a treatise on the proper use of astrological images. With that said, this book is not going to focus on astrology or astrological magic. In a future volume, we are going to explore astrological magic in detail. In this work, however, we are going to limit our focus to the traditional forms of magic practiced by believing Christians throughout the Western world: the sacraments and the sacramentals.

What is a sacramental?

I'm going to start by offering a simple definition of a sacramental, which is entirely correct but which some readers will not like one bit.

A sacramental is any type of Christian ritual magic aside from the Seven Sacraments of the church.

In order to make that definition work, we're going to have to define magic. Here again, I'm going to present a definition which will not please everyone:

Magic is the art and science of causing changes in consciousness in accordance with will.

This is the definition given by Dion Fortune, one of the great occultists of the twentieth century. Fortune was a ceremonial magician and a devout Anglican. In her writings, she makes it clear that she saw the sacraments and rituals of the Church as among the greatest of all works of magic.

It's important to consider the words used in this definition of magic, and to understand what it is saying and what it isn't saying. Let's go through it one piece at a time, and then circle back around to discussing the sacramentals.

First, magic is said to be an art and a science. Consider, first, what it means for something to be an "art." Think of music, poetry, painting, or even martial arts. Each of these separate disciplines shares a few things in common. On the one hand, each of them has certain principles which *must* be learned in order for the art to be effective. If you want to play music, you need to learn what a note is, what chords and scales are, and how these things are combined to produce songs. And it is not enough simply to learn these things intellectually. You have to learn them by practice. You can read a thousand books of music theory, and you will never learn how to play even one note on a guitar until you pick up that same guitar and play it. And if you want to be any good at all, you will have to practice playing it every single day.

All arts are like that. Martial artists need to learn the principles of fighting, how to punch, how to throw, how to roll. And then they need to practice. Writers need to write, and painters need to paint.

Magic is the same. There are principles which can be learned, but you will only become good at magic by practicing it every single day. As with other arts, there are basic drills that can be practiced on a daily basis, and we will come to those in time.

Magic is also a science. What are sciences? Sciences are fields of knowledge which grow by the means of observation and experimentation. Every science has a body of knowledge, and you can learn the basics of it by picking up an introductory textbook. This body of knowledge, however, is always provisional and subject to change if new observations provide new information and different experiences yield different results. True, many scientists often forget this, especially when dealing with the public, but the foundation of science is this very idea that every theory is subject to revision if another theory is found to be more useful.

It may surprise you to learn that magic is the same. The fixation on magical books in popular culture and among magicians themselves—who are often no wiser in this way than other scientists—may lead you to think that magic is something that was discovered once and for all time at some point in the distant past. But this isn't the case. Like other sciences, magic uses models of reality that are found to be useful. If other models work better, we can use those instead. Like other sciences, magic requires experimentation, and its guidepost is the useful. If something works, it works, and if it doesn't, it doesn't—no matter what you might have read in a book.

The object of magic is said to be "changes in consciousness." For consciousness, we can understand everything that we experience as conscious beings. Thought, emotion, perception, willpower, memory, energy—all of these things are aspects of consciousness. The aim of magic is to produce changes in these things—to transform sorrow into joy, for example, or weakness into strength, loss into love, isolation into connection.

Of course, another way to say the word "consciousness" is with that older and more exalted word, *soul*. It's become popular in recent years to debate whether or not we "have souls." I always find this amusing, because it assumes that the soul is some kind of external object we carry around with us, like a handbag. It would be more accurate to think of the body as something we carry around with us—or, really, as something we are carried around in. The soul is our consciousness: the sum total of our thoughts, emotions, memories, actions, experiences, and states of mind. We do not "have" souls. We are souls.

Notice, based on this definition, what magic cannot do and does not do. Levitating objects and throwing fireballs from your hands are not changes in consciousness, but changes in matter. That doesn't mean that they are impossible. But they aren't accomplished by magic, but by technology. Magic doesn't do the things technology does.

Finally, let's look at the last part of the definition, "in accordance with will." Consciousness changes all the time, as anyone who's been alive long enough to have even a single memory knows. But most of the changes in consciousness that we experience are caused by forces or people outside of ourselves, often very much against our will, and a great many of them are simply random. If you are walking down the street and it suddenly begins to rain, you're likely to experience a change in consciousness, and possibly a very drastic one if the rain is severe enough. But this isn't magic, as your will was not involved. (Whether or not someone else's will was involved is a question we can leave for another time.) One of the aims of practicing magic is to take control of this process of change, which is happening all around us, all the time.

Notice, though, that the definition doesn't say precisely whose will is being changed. Many magical traditions simply focus on getting what you want at any given time. At best, this is simply the way that most people live all the time anyway, and people like this use magic to give themselves an edge over others. At worst, this leads to enslavement to the desires, which is something we'll be discussing as we continue.

Other magical traditions take a more exalted view of the matter, and focus on the magician's True Will. This is the idea of a higher purpose which is above and often independent of the shifting desires that we all experience from day to day.

In magical Christianity, we accept the concept of the True Will, but we go further. The True Will of every magician and of every person is nothing more or less than the Will of God Himself, made manifest in that person. Each of us is, in our very existence, an act of God, and God does not act without purpose. And so, when we use magic to produce changes in our consciousness, our aim is to do so in accordance with the Will of God, which is also our own True Will.

And so we see that magic is the art and science of causing changes in consciousness in accordance with will. We have also seen that "consciousness" is the same thing as "the soul," and that the "will" with which we are acting in accordance is, ultimately, the Will of God. And so let me offer another definition:

Sacramental magic is the Christian art and science of causing changes in the soul in accordance with the Will of God.

Now, let's circle back around and use this understanding of magic to look at one of the most common of the sacramentals, the sign of the cross. This is a very simple ritual, performed by Catholic, Orthodox, and other Christians on a daily basis, and often more than that. Its form is a simple gesture, accompanied by the words, "In the Name of the Father, and of the Son, and of the Holy Spirit. Amen."

Simply by saying the words, we are reminded of the Holy Trinity. Whatever thoughts or feelings had occupied our minds are interrupted, and the mind turns toward God. Now, the nature of the mind is such that everything within it is connected through association to a vast network of ideas, memories, and meanings. When we connect to God, even briefly, we are reminded of His will for us—His love, His commandments, His way of life. Even when it is performed in a quick and perfunctory manner, the sign of the cross can produce an immediate change in the consciousness of the person making the sign and in others around them. When it is performed slowly, reverently, and with attention, it can produce very great changes.

All of the sacramentals can be understood in this way. They are one of the two great forms of magic of the Christian tradition. The other form of magic, of course, is the sacraments.

Sacramentals and sacraments

How do the sacramentals differ from the sacraments? Both are types of magic. That is, both are rituals designed to produce specific changes in consciousness, which is to say, in the soul. But the sacraments are very special rituals. In the first case, there are only seven of them—no more, and no less. The number of sacramentals, on the other hand, is potentially unlimited. They also differ in the way that they work. In technical terms, the sacraments are said to work *ex opere operato*. This is a Latin phrase meaning "from the working worked." What it means in practice is that a sacrament *always* works, provided it is performed properly. Specifically, a sacrament needs only three things to function: the correct form, the correct matter, and the correct intention. Provided all of these are present, it doesn't matter who is performing the sacrament; it works by its own power, in the same way that the engine of your car starts when you turn the key in the ignition.

The sacramentals are different. Like the sacraments, they are magical rituals. Unlike the sacraments, the sacramentals draw their power from the operator. In technical terms, they work *ex opere operantis*, from the work of the worker. What that means in practice is that the energy that powers a sacramental comes directly from the magician himself. Make no mistake: magic always works. If you consecrate a sacramental, you will empower it in certain ways. But its power will be drawn from the state of your own soul, your consciousness, at the time.

More on sacramentals

In general, we can divide the sacramentals into three categories:

1. Rituals meant to produce changes in your own state of consciousness
2. Blessings of objects, places, or other things outside of yourself, and the use of those same objects
3. Prayers meant to bring about some particular effect in the world.

The best-known example of the first category is the sign of the cross, which we have discussed already. As we will see as we continue, with the aid of a few simple magical techniques, the sign of the cross can be expanded into a powerful work of protective magic. Other examples of category 1 sacramentals range from simple practices like the Angelus prayer, to more in-depth workings like the Stations of the Cross, and extended devotions like the total consecration to Mary.

Holy water is probably the best known of the category 2 sacramentals. It is less well known that holy water is designed for specific purposes. In the traditional blessing, which prevailed throughout the Catholic world until the "reforms" of the 1960s, holy water was intentionally blessed and empowered both in order to drive away evil spirits and restore physical health. Other examples of category 2 sacramentals include blessed incense, candles, salt, oil, and saints' medals.

Category 3 sacramentals have, like all forms of traditional Christian magic, become unfortunately less common these days. One example still commonly practiced is the blessing of the throat on the Feast of Saint Blaise. During this ritual, consecrated candles are placed in a cross form over the throat, and a prayer said which is intended to protect the Christian from the illnesses of the throat which are common during wintertime. Note that this also demonstrates the way that the three categories lead into one another, as the throat blessing makes use of consecrated candles and is accompanied by the sign of the cross. Other examples of category 3 sacramentals include novenas to saints, the use of the psalms in magic, and specific prayers like the Memorarae.

In the pages that follow, we are going to explore all three forms of the sacramentals. We will start with a series of basic ritual practices, designed to attune you to the work of Christian ceremonial magic, purify your soul, and charge your energetic body with magical energies. We will continue with general instructions for each type of sacramental. A range of traditional sacramentals will be given. We will also include lists of additional sacramentals of each type, and suggestions for creating new sacramentals, all your own.

The sacraments

And what of the sacraments themselves?

As described above, the sacraments require the appropriate matter, form, and intention. In a number of cases, the "matter" for the sacrament includes a priest who has received the sacrament of holy orders. This means that, for those of us who are not ordained to the priesthood, those sacraments are technically off-limits. This includes the most important sacrament of all, the holy Eucharist. It can be disheartening to learn this, as it seems to mean that many of the most powerful and sacred rites of the Church will remain unavailable to anyone who can't find someone to ordain them to the priesthood. Fortunately, this need not necessarily be the case.

Above all, the sacraments are magical rituals. Magic, as we have seen, is a science, and the magicians of the world are always at work expanding our understanding of how magic works through trial and error. This may be surprising to some people, who assume that magic is something handed down from ages long past. Many people suppose that we don't understand the principles that make magic work, but that we must simply accept the authority of ancient books, especially those written in Latin. Oddly enough, this description actually does apply to much of the mainstream Church, which regularly abuses and destroys its own rituals because it can no longer understand how they function and is no longer willing to accept the authority of people who did understand (and wrote in Latin). But it doesn't apply to the magical tradition. Over the course of centuries, the principles of magic have been painstakingly assembled and reassembled and tested through trial and error, and that work continues to this day.

The result is that we now have a basic but perfectly functional understanding of the principles of magic. And the principles of magic are the same under all circumstances. The same principles that we use to perform or consecrate sacramentals can also be used to celebrate all seven sacraments. There are many practicing magicians and occultists who would like to have access to the sacraments, especially the Eucharist, but who lack either a Church which would accept them or a Church which they could accept.

And that's where magic comes in. The sacraments are very special rituals, but rituals nonetheless. In every case, it is possible for a layperson to perform them. The difference is that, in these cases, the sacraments themselves effectively become sacramentals. At least in theory, they don't have quite the same power as they would were they to be performed by an ordained priest, but I can attest from experience that they do, nevertheless, have power. We will conclude this book by presenting forms of all seven sacraments which can be used by anybody, under any circumstances.

The question will naturally arise: What are these principles of magic? We will answer that in the next chapter of this book.

LESSON 2

A guide to magical philosophy

Knowledge lecture

What is it that makes magic work?

Let's restate the question, bearing in mind our definition of magic.

How is it that we are able to produce changes in consciousness in accordance with will?

This is a simple question, and so it may be surprising that the answer requires us to describe the nature of the universe itself.

On reflection, that shouldn't be too surprising. According to the materialist philosophy which dominates modern culture and modern science, magic doesn't work and it can't work. But it goes beyond that. Materialism teaches that only matter and energy exist. Consciousness is what is called an "epiphenomenon" of the brain. That's a fancy word which means "a thing which shouldn't exist because it doesn't do anything, and so we can act as though it didn't exist." Will, meanwhile, is simply an illusion, something we like to think about but which has no basis in reality. According to materialism, then, magic doesn't work because there is no consciousness which can be changed and there is no will which can change it.

And so we can see that in order to establish how magic works, we first have to have a model of the universe which has room for magic in it.

The planes of being

The foundation of the magical model of the universe is the concept of the planes of being. At its most basic, this is the idea that the different sorts of things that we encounter in our experience of the universe are all real, and that they relate to one another in a very specific way.

Consider your own experience of the world, at this moment. You hold a physical object in your hand, and you're seated on a physical chair. The room you're in has a feeling to it; bright and happy, dull and gray, sad and lonely, whatever the case may be. Perhaps the book does, too. As you read, images form in your mind; perhaps you hear the words as you read them as though read by an unseen narrator, perhaps you picture the scenes described. Perhaps you imagine setting this book down, picking up a whole lemon, and taking a great big bite out of it. As you read the words, munching on your lemon, cold lemon juice dribbling down your chin, you understand the meaning behind them. Oh, and did I mention that you exist at all? Take a moment to think about what that looks like. Before you have any of these experiences—seeing these words on the page, feeling the seat under your butt, taking another juicy bite out of that lemon—you have the mere fact of your ability to have experiences.

The thing to notice is that all of these different things are precisely that: different. Material objects like books and rooms and chairs are not the same sort of thing as the way it feels to sit in a room and read a book. The way it feels to sit in a particular room and read is not the same thing as the mental images that you experience when you read a book or imagine eating a whole lemon. Mental images are not the same things as the meanings you derive from the words that you perceive on the page. And meaning is not the same as mere existence. These are not simply five different things, they are five different *types* of things.

In magical philosophy we call these types of things the planes of being. This is the foundation of the magical worldview. The different types of things in the universe are all real. Moreover, they have a very specific relationship to one another. They aren't strewn about the cosmos at random, but rather are arranged into an ordered hierarchy, like a stack of pancakes on a plate. Every plane acts on the plane below it, and it also reacts upon the plane above it.

We didn't invent this idea, by the way. In technical philosophical language, the concept of the planes of being is what is called a "layered ontology." "Layered ontology" is a fancy way of saying "planes of being."

And so we have our first Law of Magic: **The Law of the Planes**.

How do we understand this concept from, not simply a magical perspective, but a Christian magical perspective?

The Law of the Planes tells us that the whole of the universe created by God is organized into a series of different levels. At the very highest level is God Himself and the great spiritual powers like the Seraphim and Cherubim. At the lowest level is matter. God Himself relates to the planes in three different ways. He occupies the highest plane. He is also, at the same time, present throughout all the planes. And before this, he is both above and outside of all the planes.

You might be surprised to learn that this idea of a layered universe is very much within the Christian tradition. It wouldn't be correct to say that every theologian has subscribed to a layered ontology, but many have, including many of the greatest. While no mainstream Church that I'm aware of uses the specific term "planes of being," the idea of a layered universe is very much part of the mainstream Christian tradition. It can be found in the writings of Thomas Aquinas as well as Dionysius the Areopagite, and also in other, more esoterically inclined thinkers like the Renaissance philosopher (and priest) Marsilio Ficino. The model of the planes we will use in this course is very simple, and is derived from Ficino.

We will go through the planes one at a time, and explain their nature.

The planes of being

> Because the most perfect unity is found in the highest summit of things, God, and because with each reality so much the more it is one, so much the greater is its power and dignity, it follows that, to the extent that things be further away from the First Principle, so much greater is the diversity and variety found in them. Therefore it is necessary that the process of emanation from God derive unity from this principle, and be multiplied according to the lowliness of

things, where it comes to its end. (Saint Thomas Aquinas, *Summa Contra Gentiles*)

The brief passage from Thomas Aquinas, above, is our guide to understanding the planes of being. Following Marsilio Ficino, we will divide them into five. Please note that other ways of modeling the planes exist, and work equally well in other contexts. The test of a model is not so much its accuracy as its usefulness.

First plane: The Plane of Unity, also called the Divine Plane. This is the special plane of God Himself, which we can know only through the various Names of God given in the Holy Scriptures.

Second plane: The Intellectual Plane. This is the plane of the patterns of meaning which shape the material world. It is especially the plane of angels and saints.

Third plane: The Astral Plane. This is the plane of consciousness. All ordinary thinking takes place on the astral plane. It is also the plane of spirits, whether good, evil, or neutral. Finally, it is the plane where the subtle forces that shape our world emerge, especially the forces of astrology.

Fourth plane: The Energetic Plane. This is the plane of the "life force." Not well understood in modern Western thought, the life force is the vital power which gives life to every living being and binds the world of Nature together. Everything in Nature has a life energy. In other traditions, this energy is called qi, ki, prana, and so on.

Fifth plane: The Material Plane. This is the plane of ordinary matter that we experience.

The Plane of Unity or the Divine Plane. The first plane is the plane reserved for God Himself. Please remember that it isn't God as such: God comes before all of the planes, and he is also present to all of them. Both in the writings of Dionysius the Areopagite and the mystical tradition of the Kabbalah, the Plane of Unity is seen as the plane of the *names of God*. In his treatise, *On the Divine Names*, Dionysius discusses many of these names, including the Good, Life, Light, Beauty, Truth, and Wisdom. Each of these is a name of God, not separate gods. In Dionysius' thought, each of these names represents a kind of activity of God. These activities are not really separate from one another—but to us they appear to be. It's as though "The Good" were at once one of God's names, and something that God is doing. But, in a way that it's very hard or impossible for the human mind to grasp,

"The Good" isn't truly separate from God's other names, such as Life, Wisdom, and so on. All spiritual power ultimately begins on the Plane of Unity, and descends through the Planes of Being as far as the last of things.

The Intellectual Plane. After the Plane of Unity, this is the hardest for us to understand. Part of the reason has to do with language. In common English, the "intellect" means the thinking mind, and "an intellectual" is someone who spends a lot of time thinking about things and trying to learn things. But that isn't what is meant here. Instead, the Intellectual Plane is the plane of patterns of force and activity which shape our material world. To know something on the Intellectual Plane is to know it immediately and entirely, without any separation between the knower and the object of knowledge.

There are two types of beings who inhabit the Intellectual Plane. The first are eternal spirits, and the second are exalted human beings. We know the first group as angels, and the second group as saints.

On angels. Angels are spiritual beings created by God in order to govern the world, and for other tasks as well. In the Christian tradition, the angels are divided into nine hierarchies or choirs, and these nine are organized into three groups of three. The angels at each level are given a different task. The following description of them is derived from Dionysius' work *The Celestial Hierarchy* and the writings of Dom Gueranger in *The Liturgical Year*:

Seraphim—Exalted, fiery spirits with six wings.
Cherubim—Powerful beings depicted with four faces: one of a man, one of a lion, one of an eagle, and one of an ox.
Thrones—Beings depicted as wheels with many eyes, that pull the chariot of God.

It can be very difficult to understand the work of the three highest of the angelic hierarchies, as they are very far removed from the world of our experience. It is said that the Thrones act as the very throne of God, which is driven by the Cherubim, while the Seraphim sing the praises of God and purify the thoughts of those who stand before His throne. These ideas should not be taken literally: there are no wheels or eyes or faces at the height of the Intellectual Plane. Instead, they should be understood as images which reveal something about the reality toward which they point. You may find it very rewarding to contemplate them in meditation.

The work of the next six choirs is easier to understand:

Dominations—These preside over the government of the entire universe.
Virtues—These angels watch over the course of Nature's laws, the preservation of species, and the movements of the heavens.
Powers—The powers hold evil spirits in check.
Principalities—Govern the human race as a whole and all large social groups, such as nations, cultures, Churches, and so on.
Archangels—These govern smaller groups like families and command the next order, the angels.
Angels—These include the guardian angels who are set over every individual human soul.

Note that the term "archangel" has a second meaning as well. It can also refer to any angel, from any hierarchy, who is in command of a group of angels, or who is set over a particular force like a planet or one of the elements of Nature.

On saints. The word "saint" is a title, meaning "holy person," and it can refer to anybody in Heaven. When we address the angels, we add the word "Saint" to their name in the same way that we refer to someone on Earth as "Mister" or "Doctor" or "General." But it especially refers to those human beings who have transcended life on Earth and now dwell in Heaven with God. In the terms we're using here, the saints are human beings who have developed, through the grace of God and their own spiritual practice, the ability to live on the Intellectual Plane and are now able to participate in the Will of God in the shaping of the world of human affairs.

Now, there is some disagreement between the mainstream Churches and the esoteric tradition on exactly how this happens. The Catholic Church teaches that most of us, when we die, are not yet ready to enter into Heaven. And so our souls go to another place, called Purgatory, where we work through the consequences of our sins. After a time in Purgatory, we are then given entrance into Heaven.

The esoteric teaching is similar, but with a big exception. We believe that if a soul at death is not ready to enter into Heaven it enters into a spiritual world, which is similar to Purgatory. But after a certain time—perhaps a short time, perhaps a very long time—it returns to life on Earth to "try again." A part of every person's next life or incarnation will include working out the consequences of their failures in the previous life.

In practice, this amounts to much the same thing: Everyone agrees that most souls have not yet completed the work of spiritual development necessary to enter into Heaven, and that we need to spend a certain amount of time after death working out the consequences of our sins. But we disagree quite strongly on exactly *where* we do this. In this book I don't plan to tell you what to believe about these things. You're an adult, and you can make up your own mind.

But let's return to the saints.

Every saint is set over some specific area of life on Earth. This can be a particular nation or ethnicity, as Saint Patrick is the patron of the Irish, Saint Andrew, the patron of the Scottish, and so on. It can be an occupation or way of life, as Saint George is the patron saint of soldiers and Saint Luke is the patron saint of doctors. It can even be something harmful, such as a natural disaster or disease. Saint Dymphna is called upon to help people struggling with mental illness; Saint Blaise protects against sore throats; and Saint Therese of Lisieux helps alcoholics.

It is because the saints have established themselves on the Intellectual Plane that they are able to participate in the government of things on Earth. It's important to understand this, so that we know what we are doing when we pray to the saints. Many Catholic and Orthodox Christians will tell you that we don't directly pray to the saints, but instead "ask them to pray to God for us." In the esoteric tradition, we see this as a metaphor. God's power is always creating reality, always emanating down the planes from even beyond the Plane of Unity. At the Intellectual Plane of existence, there is neither time nor space. And so when a saint "prays for us," it isn't the same as when we pray. They don't go into a separate room, light a candle, and hope that God is listening. They are immediately present to God. But each of them is also connected with that part of God's activities which ultimately goes on to create the things of this world of which that saint is a patron.

You can think of it as light passing through a prism. At the Plane of Unity, the light is colorless. The prism is the Intellectual Plane. Here the light appears to divide into a rainbow of many different colors. When the light hits a wall, one part will appear purple, another orange, another red, and so on. Of course, these colors aren't really separate; it's all one light. In our actual world, it's as though the "light" of God "divides" and creates the separate things that we experience, from a forest to a career as a doctor to the nation of Ireland. The saints are like particles which dwell in one particular ray of light. The great advantage of working with the saints is that they were human once, and so it is easy for us to understand them and for them to relate to us. When we pray to them, they help us attune ourselves to the particular "ray" of God, which is the "ray" that they themselves participate in. That is what we mean when we say the saints "pray for us." As such, we always close our prayers to the saints with the words "Pray for us," or, in Latin, *Ora pro nobis*.

Always remember that this is just a metaphor, describing realities that are beyond our human ability to understand.

Our Lady. As we have seen, the highest of the angels are exalted far beyond ordinary human beings, even beyond the universe itself! And yet, it is the teaching of the Christian tradition that one human being is set above even the highest of the angels. This is the Blessed Virgin Mary, called Queen of the Angels, and Queen of Heaven and Earth. We will discuss her in greater detail later on. For now, it's important to know that she is set above every other angel and saint. In magical terms, she is set at the summit of the Intellectual Plane. Perhaps she can even be said to be set above the Plane of Unity, at the unimaginable border between the Plane of Unity and the primordial infinity of God.

All of those things I am calling the "powers" or "energies" or "activities" of God are called graces, and Our Lady is given the power to dispense the graces of God wherever she sees fit. You will do very well indeed to cultivate a relationship with her if you do not already have one. Start today.

The Astral Plane

As we have seen, the Intellectual Plane is not actually the plane of thinking that we normally call "intellect." Instead, thought in the ordinary sense is part of the Astral Plane. In fact, the Astral Plane is the plane of all ordinary consciousness. Thought, imagination, dreams and visions, memory, emotion, and sensation are all part of the Astral Plane.

The Astral Plane is also the plane of spirits. This includes the angels and saints, at least much of the time. The proper habitation of angels and saints is the Intellectual Plane, but when we encounter them we usually do so through the Astral Plane as a medium. This is simply because it is much easier for us to perceive the Astral Plane. The Astral

Plane also includes ghosts, which are human spirits that are attached to the material plane for various reasons; Nature spirits; and evil spirits such as demons. In this course we won't be working with any of these.

Finally, the Astral Plane is a plane of subtle forces that shape human consciousness. In traditional magical theory, we model these forces using sets of categories such as the seven planets of traditional astrology and the four elements of traditional physics. The forces of the Astral Plane also include the forces and cycles of history and culture that shape human life. A musical fad or a political movement, the sort that sweeps people up without them really being aware of it, is an Astral Plane phenomenon. The well-known generational theory of historical cycles discovered by Neil Howe and William Strauss is also an example of the cyclical forces of the astral plane.

That leads us to an important point: According to magical philosophy, our minds are not limited to our bodies. Instead, they are part of the Astral Plane, and they are participants or cells in larger collective minds. Each of us participates in many different collectives, all at once. Families, businesses, parishes, cultures, nations, and eras all have their own collective mind. Some of these large-scale astral phenomena persist over time, such as the collective mind of a nation or culture. Some appear at specific moments, like tides, and recede again like the tides. If you've ever looked at a picture of yourself from twenty years ago and wondered what you were thinking wearing those clothes, which seemed so cool or trendy then but are now embarrassing, you've seen one of these astral tides at work.

Magical power is derived from the planes above the Astral, but the Astral Plane is primarily the plane on which magic operates. Remember our definition of magic: the art and science of causing changes in consciousness. All ordinary consciousness is astral in nature.

Finally, while this model of the planes will work well for our needs, it should be noted that every plane can be divided even further. This is especially important with respect to the Astral Plane. The Astral Plane can be divided into Higher, Middle, and Lower levels. These correspond to different levels of consciousness. Ordinary waking consciousness and ordinary thoughts are largely of the Middle Astral Plane. This is the sort of consciousness you experience when you get out of bed, yawn, put on your slippers and make a cup of coffee. Above this, we have the Higher Astral Plane. This is the plane of higher forms of thought, and especially of spirituality and love. If, instead of simply rolling out of bed in the morning, you begin by saying a prayer, and then telling your spouse and your children good morning and that you love them, you begin your day by attuning yourself to the Higher Astral Plane. The Lower Astral Plane is the plane of negative thoughts and emotions, especially anger, fear, envy, uncontrolled lust, and hatred. If you begin your day by being angry at the Sun for having risen and then immediately reaching for your cell phone to look at the latest bad news on social media, you begin your day by attuning yourself to the Lower Astral Plane. It's very important to avoid this, because, of course, another name for the Lower Astral Plane is Hell.

The Energetic Plane

As I mentioned above, the Western world at present has only a limited understanding of this plane, but it is much discussed in other traditions. The Energetic Plane is the plane of subtle forces which maintain life on Earth and weave every life together. Have you ever felt "electrified" when walking into a crowd waiting for a concert to start? Or have you ever walked into a building and noticed that it had very "bad vibes," and perhaps afterwards felt depressed or simply "drained"? Those were experiences of the Energetic Plane.

There are many methods of working directly with the Energetic Plane, such as those taught in the traditions of yoga, qigong, and certain Asian martial arts. In this course, we will work with the Energetic Plane in a few ways. First, you are encouraged to spend time every day in Nature. Exposure to sunlight and fresh air and the radiating energy of plants and natural features like rocks and rivers will strengthen your energetic body. Second, we will learn how to make use of certain natural substances such as incense, salt, and water, in order to benefit from their particular energies. Finally, some of the practices we will learn will allow divine power to descend down the planes of being to change the energy of certain objects, places—and ourselves.

The Material Plane

This is the plane of the ordinary matter and energy that we experience. If you want to learn more details about it, you can pick up any introductory physics textbook.

For our purposes, the most important thing to understand about the Material Plane relates to another magical law, called the Law of Correspondences. According to this way of looking at things, every substance in the Material Plane is said to correspond to forces on the higher planes. In an earlier time, Christians called this the "Great Chain of Being." Everything in the universe was thought to descend in an ordered way from God, through the ranks of angels and spirits, and down into the natural world of humans, animals, plants, and minerals.

The Law of Correspondences is critical to magic, and natural magic in particular. Every stone, herb, plant, and animal corresponds to one of the traditional seven planets and one of the four elements. Knowing this, we can make use of those substances in order to invoke the power of the planet or the element to which it corresponds.

For example, roses correspond to the planet Venus, which is the planet that governs love and romance. Knowing this, we can use roses as part of a magical working intended to bring love into our lives.

The Devil and evil spirits

Finally, it remains to say something more about the Devil, evil spirits, and evil magic. As noted above, these are all primarily phenomena of the Astral Plane, particularly the Lower Astral Plane. However, in another sense, the Devil and the demons are said to dwell at a level of being which is even below the material. This is what is meant when it is said that the Devil has been "cast into Hell." Notice that, whenever we encounter the material world, we never encounter matter all by itself. It's always formed into an object, whether a blade of grass or a kitchen table. Natural objects are formed by God and have a natural life energy, as we've discussed. Man-made objects can be designed in ways to both purify their energetic environment and elevate the mind to the Higher Astral and even the Intellectual Plane, or they can pollute the energetic environment and cause us to descend to the Lower Astral. Or they can do nothing much at all.

In any case, every object that we encounter has some kind of order to it; that's why we are able to call it an object: a book, a candle, a cat, a blade of grass. Below this is what is sometimes called the sub-natural, or the level of Chaos. At this level of being, there is no order, no harmony, no pattern, no symmetry. The esoteric tradition teaches that, though the influence of the evil spirits extends as far as the Lower Astral Plane, their proper habitation is below even the material world, at the level of Chaos.

The human microcosm

In magical philosophy, the universe as a whole is sometimes called the macrocosm, and the individual human being, the microcosm. These words mean "great universe" and "little universe." The point is that every person is a reflection in miniature of the entire universe. What this means is that each of us functions on every level of being. The planes are not places "out there" which we can visit, but realities which are always present within us. Let's explore this, starting, in this case, from the bottom, and working our way back up.

The physical body. This one is simple. The Physical Plane in the human microcosm is the physical body. You're already familiar with this, but it's worth keeping two things in mind.

First, the body is not the same as its matter. We're using the term "Physical Plane" because it's familiar, but it would be more accurate to say "Corporeal Plane," because what we're really talking about is the plane of bodies. The truth is that we never really encounter "matter" as such—we always encounter specific forms of matter. These forms are bodies, including our own.

Second, it's important to understand our proper relationship to our bodies.

We sometimes talk about the body as a prison house of the soul, or as the tomb of the soul. This is because, in our current condition, our souls reside within our bodies, and we can't get out of them. It's not that the body is evil as such. It's that, as spiritual beings, we're supposed to be free of matter, and able to work and shape it. Instead, we've become trapped inside of it, like a painter stuck to his own canvas. But the body is meant to be the form with which we work, not the place in which we're stuck. We're like people under house arrest—we don't hate our homes or think they're evil, but we'd like to be able to leave when we choose!

Part of the point of magical training is to restore our proper relationship with our bodies insofar as this is possible in this lifetime. We won't get to the point where we can be totally free of them, not while we are still alive. We can, however, learn to perceive and understand our true selves as something beyond the body—which has great advantages when the body passes away!

The energetic body. In the esoteric lore of the Western world, the energetic body is often referred to as the "spirit." And this can be a major source of confusion, because we also use the word "spirit" to mean "immortal soul," and also to mean "ghost or other disembodied entity," and also to mean "personal vitality." Oh, and it also means "booze." It's very important to keep these distinctions in mind when you're reading magical texts, including this one. Sometimes a spirit is not a spirit.

The role of the spirit in this sense is to mediate between the Physical Plane and the Astral Plane. As some of the old writers say, it sometimes behaves like body and sometimes like soul. That is because it has qualities of both, and it is what allows the soul to come into contact with the body.

The energetic structure of each human being can be understood as having two parts. The first part is the aura, which is a sphere or oval which extends outward about three feet to the sides, above the head, and below the feet. This is sometimes called the "sphere of sensation," as it is the medium through which we encounter the outside world and onto which we project the contents of our own minds like images on a TV screen.

The second part is the subtle body itself. This consists of three major energy centers, which are connected by a central column or channel. Now, there are many smaller energy centers, and each of the three can be further subdivided. For our purposes, however, it is enough to speak of the three centers by themselves. Each energy center is home to one of the three "spirits." In this case, "spirit" means "energy," not "immortal soul" or "shot of whiskey." Each of these energy centers has its function and also its particular virtue.

The head forms the first energetic center. This is the center of the animal spirit, where the data gathered through the senses is transmitted to the soul. Its virtue is *Clarity*, or correct perception and correct understanding.

The heart is the second energetic center. This is the center of the vital spirit, which is the source of life. The heart is seen as a kind of sun in the body, radiating light, warmth, and vital energy. Its virtue is *Charity*, which is the use of the life and the life force in the service of God and our fellow man.

The abdomen, sometimes simply called "the liver" in some earlier writings, is the third energetic center. This is the center of the natural spirit, which rules the digestion and elimination of food and the reproduction of the species. Its virtue is *Chastity*, which means the correct use of the forces of generation.

The astral body. This is what we usually mean by the word "soul." The astral body in man consists of the entirety of our conscious experience. Every thought, every emotion, every desire, and every sensation is part of the astral plane. What this means is that, most of the time, our perceptions are actually perceptions of the astral plane. We don't actually sense anything with our physical or energetic bodies. Instead, these structures relay information to our mind, which is to say, to our astral body, where the information is compiled into images that we can understand.

Like the energetic body, the astral body has a structure. This can be thought of as the anatomy of the soul. Remember that we said that the energetic body or spirit is the medium between the physical body and the astral body or soul. Each one of the parts of the energetic body corresponds to a part of the soul. It can be said that the spirits house a different part of the soul.

Like the spirits, the parts of the soul also have their proper virtue. There is a difference, however. Within the soul, there are two levels of virtue. The first level consists of the *natural virtues*. Also called the "cardinal virtues," these were the four highest virtues as understood by the pagan Graeco-Roman world. Above the natural virtues are the supernatural virtues. These are the three additional virtues that require supernatural grace and that Christianity introduced to the world.

The three parts of the soul are called *nous*, *thymos*, and *epithymia*. These are Greek words, and this discussion of the soul derives ultimately from the *Republic* of Plato.

The nous. The nous is housed in the head, and it is the part of our soul that thinks. Like the soul as a whole, it is divided into three separate levels. The lowest level of the nous is opinion. This is the power of the mind that allows us to look at the information given to us by our senses and sort it into categories: "That shape of a four-legged animal is a cat; that one is a squirrel; that one is a dog."

The next level is reason. Much of what passes for reason at the present time consists of simply repeating other peoples' opinions, and so it's important to understand that this is not what is meant here. Reason is the capacity of our minds to think their own thoughts.

Above the reason is nous properly so called. This is the level at which the soul reaches beyond itself, beyond the Astral Plane, to contact the Intellectual Plane. The nous in this sense is sometimes called the "eye of the soul," because it is able, when it is clear, to directly perceive spiritual realities. This capacity of the human soul has been largely forgotten by mainstream Christianity in the Western world. At best, we have the concept of "intuition" to describe the work of the nous, but this is very often mixed up with the idea of "instinct." An understanding of the nous was, however, preserved in the Christian East, and we can learn a great deal from our Eastern cousins on this subject.

The natural virtue of the nous is wisdom, which consists of knowledge and the understanding of its use.

The supernatural virtue of the nous is faith, which is defined as "the assent of the intellect to the truths of the Christian faith." Remember, when you consider this definition, that intellect is another name for nous, and that the nous is called the "eye of the soul."

The thymos. The thymos is housed in the heart. "Thymos" is a Greek word which has no exact English translation. It is often translated as "spirit," just in case you wanted to be confused further. "Spirit," in this context, does not mean "immortal soul." Instead, it is what we mean when we say that someone is in "high spirits," or that they have "team spirit," or speak of a "spirited" horse or dog. The best way to understand the thymos is to think of it as the *will*. It is also the seat of social emotions. At its worst, the thymos wants to be the top dog in the pack, regardless of what it takes to get there. At its best, the thymos directs its natural desire for power into a desire to serve mankind and to imbue those placed below it with the love of Christ.

The natural virtue of the thymos is fortitude, which is the ability of the will to pursue its tasks to completion without shrinking away in fear or turning aside for pleasure.

The supernatural virtue of the thymos is charity, which is defined as "willing the good of another." Keep in mind that "The Good" is one of the names of God Himself, and that we become good only by participating in the life of God.

The epithymia. The epithymia is housed in the abdomen. Epithymia means "appetite" in Greek, and its location in the area of the digestive system and the genitals tells you most of what you need to know about its role. This is the seat of all of our desires. It's important to note that our desires are not evil, any more than our body itself is evil. It's just that, as our soul is not supposed to be ruled by the body, our reason and our will are not supposed to be ruled by our appetites.

The natural virtue of the epithymia is temperance, which is the ability to control our desires, rather than being controlled by them.

The supernatural virtue of the epithymia is hope, which is the direction of all of our desires toward our proper home in Heaven.

The aura. The aura has an astral as well as an energetic level to it. At the energetic level, the aura can be thought of as a sphere of protective energies, corresponding to the "weiqi field" of traditional Chinese medicine. At the astral level, the aura is still visualized as a sphere, and it is understood as a kind of screen, on which images are projected. Some of these images rise from within the soul. Others are perceptions of things outside the soul. It's as though it were a transparent, flat, circular TV screen with images appearing on both sides. The images on the outside are perceptions of the substance of the Astral Plane. The images on the inside are the works of the imagination. Both sets of images are useful and necessary—but we begin our work stuck in a situation where we can't tell which images come from where. And it doesn't help that our culture teaches us that all of the images are internal to us. They are not, but the work of discovering which images are internal, which are external, and how to switch off either the internal screen (so that we can see things outside) or the external screen (so that we can focus on our own images) is another critical part of the work of magical training.

The natural virtue of the aura is justice, which is the right relationship between all parts of a whole.

There is no supernatural virtue of the aura; instead, at this level, all of the natural virtues correspond to the aura while the supernatural virtues take up their places in the nous, thymos, and epithymia.

A properly ordered soul is, in the imagery given to us by Plato and adopted in the Middle Ages, like an ideal kingdom. The nous is king, reigning with the authority of God, with whom he is always present. The thymos is like the knights or warrior class, who follow a code of honor and chivalry and serve the king in the interests of the kingdom as a whole. The epithymia is like the workers and the peasantry, who offer their service willingly to the king and the nobility in exchange for justice and protection.

The intellectual body. As we have seen, the word "intellect" in Greek is nous, and the Greek Orthodox Church as well as the Eastern Orthodox Churches make it a central focus of their prayer life and their philosophy in general. The Eastern Churches teach that the nous is a faculty different from the mind, more in line with what we sometimes mean by "heart," as in the phrase, "Listen with your heart." They sometimes use the term "the eye of the soul," for the nous is able to perceive spiritual realities directly.

The esoteric doctrinal perspective is nearly identical to the Orthodox—appropriately enough, since we're ultimately drawing on many of the same sources. The Intellectual Plane in man can be called the intellect or nous, and it is the highest part of the soul—the part that reaches above the level of the Astral Plane, to perceive the realities of the Intellectual Plane.

The idea of the evolution of the soul is central to many systems of Western esotericism. According to this way of looking at things, human beings in general are able to function on three planes—the physical, the energetic, and the astral. We have fully formed bodies on all of these planes. But we don't yet have a body or form on the Intellectual Plane. Instead, we're in the process of developing an intellectual body from the rudimentary intellect in our souls. Sainthood, according to this way of thinking, is what happens when we complete this work and gain the ability to function on the Intellectual Plane.

Remember that the Physical and Energetic Planes are limited by both space and time, and the Astral Plane is limited by time but not by space. On the Intellectual Plane, there is no time. Those human souls who have come to reside there thus abide outside the confines of time, in the Aeviternal Realm.

The Divine Plane. The Divine Plane is the plane of the names of God. If we are barely awake to the Intellectual Plane, still less are we able to even fathom the Divine Plane. We perceive it, for the most part, second or third hand, through the patterns of the Intellectual Plane and their images on the Astral Plane.

But we are not totally estranged from it—if we were, we could have no contact with divinity. The Divine Plane manifests within us as the mere fact of our existence, which itself is an eternal act of God. It is by the Divine and within the Divine that we live and move and have our being.

Macrocosm, microcosm, and mesocosm

And so we see that the Five Planes of Being and their subdivisions manifest in the universe as a whole, and in the individual human being. They also manifest in an intermediate way, in things larger than individual humans but smaller than the universe.

Every country, nation, and culture; every religion, Church and parish, and equally every forest, every mountain chain and bioregion has its own manifestation on every one of these planes. Each is like a small world unto itself, nested within larger worlds and containing still smaller worlds.

If you've ever driven across the United States, you've seen this principle in action. Everywhere, the land, the climate, the people, and the culture differ. People talk differently, act differently, and think differently. The mountains, the trees, the animals, and the sky, too, talk differently, act differently, and—think differently.

Each region shares in its own larger form, a mesocosm, extending downward into matter and upward to the Divine Plane. Each of these is a world, home to smaller worlds, nested in larger worlds, downward to the individual human souls and upwards to the universe as a whole.

This is critical for understanding magic, and for understanding people. Every mesocosm is a different geographic location—that's its physical body. Each also has its energetic body: that is, there is a particular way that it *feels* to be in a certain place, or around certain people, that has nothing to do with the weather.

In every place, the culture is different—different patterns of speech and dress, different histories, different myths and legends, different heroes. This is the astral body. Above the astral plane, each culture also differs in its *values*. This is something that many of us have a hard time with, because we just wish that those darned yankees up in New England, or those darned rednecks in Appalachia, or those lousy Southerners, or those idiots out on the Left Coast, would just get with the program. But they never will, because values and patterns of meaning are functions of the Intellectual Plane. Those lousy people in those other lousy places don't share our values because they participate in a different intellectual body from the one we do. Indeed, every human culture has its own particular angels, exalted beings from the order of Principalities, that watch over and guide it.

And we know, we must know, that in each region and in every mesocosm, the spirit of God is present, manifesting differently, under different names in different ways, in order to show forth the glory of God as a whole. If we were willing to remember that, maybe we would also be willing to leave each other in peace.

LESSON 3

Resolving binaries

Practical exercise

Our lives are lived, as we have seen, primarily on the Astral Plane. We sense the Physical and Energetic Planes, even if we don't always realize it with the latter. We get inklings in this life of the Intellectual and Spiritual Planes. But all the faculties of human experience, from sense to emotion, imagination and reason, are of the Astral Plane. As such, it is critically important to train our minds, in order that we may spend our time on the upper reaches of the Astral Plane and not descend into the Hell which is the Lower Astral.

The practice of resolving binaries is a traditional one in many magical societies, and you will find it very helpful on your journey. The practice itself is quite simple. Every day when you're reading or listening to the news, watch for moments when you are told that there are only two options available. Very often, especially in these highly polarized times, you will be told that one and only one of these options is the correct one, and the other will surely lead to ruin. This is called *binary thinking*, and it is endemic in our present culture.

Consider what you've already learned about the nature of the magical cosmos. We have seen that the universe has its beginning as the one divides into two. The two further divide into two more, and two more, onward through the orders of being, terminating finally in the infinite chaos which is the true Hell at the bottom of reality. As such, it is clear that the constant presentation of two and only two options is a way of making chaos manifest.

The English word "Devil" comes from the Greek word *Diabolos*, which means "the divider." As we shall see, what orthodox Christianity terms "the Devil" actually covers a wide range of spiritual powers, some far worse than others. It is the devil as the divider that is at work in the constant fixation on binary thinking.

We have also seen that God is both Unity and Trinity, both at the same time. This also teaches us something: We never encounter God as the absolute unity that He is to Himself. We encounter God, rather, as the Trinity, which is the Unity of the Three Persons. As the Devil is the divider, the Holy Trinity is the uniter, for it is by the power of the three that the two are resolved back into one. This principle will allow us to overcome binary thinking, which is usually inflicted upon us by someone outside of ourselves with the deliberate intention of stifling our minds, manipulating our behavior, and dividing us against our fellow man. As the Trinity overcomes the Devil, we will overcome binary thinking by *ternary thinking*.

Begin this practice today. Every time you encounter a binary presented to you during your day, whether in a news report, a podcast, or a blog; a novel or a television program; or just in the words of another person: stop. First, figure out what the two options being presented are. Then take some time to think through each option, as charitably as you can. That is: Usually one option will be presented as good, and the second as evil. Instead, consider each one on its own terms. What are the reasons for supporting it? Why might someone else see it as good, even if you see it as evil? You can simply think this through, or you can do whatever research is necessary until you fully understand the issue on its own terms.

Once you have done this, you will take the critical step: *Come up with a third option*. This third option may be a compromise between the two you were given, as gray is a compromise between black and white. It may be a more extreme form of one of the two, like a darker shade of black or a lighter shade of white. Or it may be a different option altogether, as red, blue, and green are neither white nor black. Think this third option through, until you can make a case for it. You don't have to agree with it, though you might. Though you might support it, you shouldn't then go around presenting it to people as the one and only option, against which all others will lead only to disaster. Your goal is only to rise out of the chaos of the binary, and into the unity of the ternary.

You may have heard of the three enemies which the Christian faces in this life, called the World, the Flesh, and the Devil. Now, by the World is not meant, obviously, the physical world, or the living world of Nature. The "World" is our age and our culture—and, in fact, it is every age and every culture. This is because what we call "culture" is a set of automatic habits, ways of thinking, and ways of acting that we learn when we are too young to question, understand, or form our own opinions. We need culture. Without it we couldn't find food or clothing or shelter. We couldn't even speak. And yet, because it keeps us from thinking our own thoughts, culture becomes an enemy of the soul on its journey of spiritual evolution. The World is, thus, both a necessary help to our existence and an adversary we must overcome.

By the Flesh is meant our physical bodies, but especially the passions which keep us in subjection to them. Like the World, we need our bodies, and their passions: Without them we wouldn't even bother to breathe, let alone to eat, to drink water, or to reproduce! And yet, our natural condition, especially in our youth, is one in which our higher faculties of will, reason, and intuition are effectively slaves to our passions. We care more for eating, drinking and pleasure than for spiritual development. The Flesh is, thus, both a necessary condition for our existence, and an adversary we must overcome.

We have already looked at the meaning of the word "Devil." This is that power of division which separates us from the highest things, and ultimately leads the soul downward, into incarnation in matter, into imprisonment in the body, with the emotional life governed by the body's passions and the mental life governed by the scripts and programs of our culture. And yet, without this descent into matter, we could not rise again to the world of spirit. And we have to believe that God is no fool; if he created beings who would, in the metaphor of the book of Genesis, "disobey his commands" and descend into matter, it can only be because he intended that they would do so. Therefore the Devil is a necessary precondition for our existence, and the greatest of the adversaries which we must overcome.

The practice of resolving binaries is a weapon against all three of these enemies. By allowing us to discover new modes of thinking and to see the patterns behind the thoughts we have been given by our culture, it allows us to overcome the World. By freeing us from the binary, which is a reactionary mode of thinking designed to arouse our passions and overcome our reason, it allows us to overcome the Flesh. By resolving the division of the binary into the unity of the ternary, it allows us to overcome the Devil.

Do this practice every day while you are working through this book. Eventually it will become your habitual way of thinking. This will have the great advantage of freeing you from this very common form of manipulation. Unfortunately, it won't make you very popular with people who are stuck in their binaries. But if you want to be popular, this probably isn't the book for you.

LESSON 4

A prayer rule

Daily practice

Prayer is foundational to the Christian life, and indeed to the spiritual life of any tradition. Most people know this, and everyone either prays or claims to pray.

That said, it is important to understand what prayer is and is not, and what it can and cannot do.

Prayer is not a means of changing God's mind or forcing God to do anything for us. We cannot compel God or any of the beings who exist at a higher level of being than ourselves—not the angels, not the saints, not the intelligences that govern astrological and other subtle forces. We can't even change them.

What we can do is elevate our own consciousness to theirs, and that is the purpose of prayer. Remember our image of God as a point at the center of a circle. From that point radiate many lines, along which are found the saints, the angels, and other higher beings. We ourselves live at the circumference of the circle. By prayer, we effectively grab ahold of one of the lines and find ourselves drawn upward and inward, closer to the center.

In another sense, however, the center of the circle that is God is not somewhere else, but is *everywhere* in the universe. In one sense we have departed from God. In another sense, we make use of prayer and sacramental ritual to return to God. In still a third sense, we have never left the presence of God, and, when we pray, we simply make ourselves aware of what we've already known all along: that it is in God that we live and move and have our being, and we cannot be parted from Him.

For our purposes, we can divide prayer into three forms: liturgical prayer, extemporaneous prayer, and contemplative prayer.

Liturgical prayer simply means prayer that follows a formula. The best-known liturgical prayer, of course, is the Our Father, which was given to us by Jesus himself. The Hail Mary is a close second. The sacramental Christian tradition has an immense wealth of liturgical prayers. Some are directed to one of the persons of the Holy Trinity, or to all three; others are directed toward the Virgin Mary or one of the other saints or angels. Many are intended to have specific effects. For example, with regard to Marian prayers, the Hail Mary is a general invocation of Mary, while the Hail Holy Queen is a prayer of praise to her, and the Memorare is a call for her help. All of these have their uses, and the use of liturgical prayer in general is precisely that it gives us a simple formula with which we can pray. It's important to have a set of liturgical prayers memorized that you can recite when the occasion calls for it.

Extemporaneous prayer is what we do when we call on God, a saint, or angel, without using a specific formula. This can be a harder thing for some people than liturgical prayer, but it's also an important skill to develop. We begin our relationship with God and with the saints through liturgical prayer, but we deepen it through extemporaneous prayer. We shouldn't think of these as two different things, really, because most of the time we're going to practice them together. We'll see how this works momentarily. But first, let's talk about the third form of prayer.

Contemplative prayer is both simpler and more difficult than the other two. To practice contemplation simply means to sit quietly in the presence of God or of the saint that we have invoked, without speaking or thinking, but taking note of whatever comes into our thoughts or our awareness.

These three can be thought of as three parts of a conversation. Liturgical prayer is formulaic. It is equivalent to dialing a phone number and saying "Hello" when the person you've called picks up. You do this the same way every time. Extemporaneous prayer is your part of the conversation. This is when you tell the other person what you're calling about. Depending on circumstances, this may be the longest part of the conversation, the shortest part, or it may be barely there at all. "I just called to hear your voice." Contemplative meditation, finally, is the other person's part of the conversation. This is when we stop talking and start listening.

Instructions for practice: a basic prayer rule

There's a very good chance that if you're reading this, you already know how to pray. While you are working through this book, you should adopt a daily prayer rule. "Prayer rule" simply means a schedule of prayer that you will follow. At minimum, you should make time for prayer every morning and every night. What this looks like is up to you. The Catholic, Anglican, and many other Churches have a tradition of prayers for the various times of the day, typically varying depending on the season of the year. If that idea appeals to you. A daily rosary, the Jesus Prayer, the Angelus, or chanting the psalms are also good options. I recommend that you get a suitable prayer book and follow its guidelines, saying the appropriate prayers, depending on your tradition and your sensibilities, and I leave the choice of a selection to you.

If you don't have a prayer rule, you may make use of the following.

In the morning

Begin by making the sign of the cross. Then say the Our Father, three Hail Marys, and the Glory Be. Say these slowly and reverently.

After this, simply sit for a time in silent contemplation. Don't try to do anything during this time. Let go of thought, and simply rest in the divine presence. If this is unfamiliar, you may use rhythmic breathing to induce a state of calm. How to do this will be described at the end of this part of the book.

You have invoked the grace of God the Father as instructed by Our Lord, the intercession of the Blessed Mother, and the power and presence of the entire Holy Trinity. Take a moment to allow yourself to settle in to the feeling of connection to this power which is above all human conception.

Now, move into extemporaneous prayer. This is a good time to talk to God about the day ahead of you, reviewing the challenges you will face and your hopes for the day, and asking for his grace, his strength, and his presence. Concentrate especially on things that you wish to accomplish and virtues that you wish to develop. You can also take the time here to pray for other people in your life.

Chances are very good there are additional saints that you are working with. Now is a good time to get in touch. You may be a working parent asking for the strength of Saint Joseph, a pet owner asking for Saint Francis to watch over your cat or dog, or someone with a family member dealing with cancer asking for the intercession of Saint Peregrine—or all of the above. You may also wish to speak with one or more saints and ask for their presence in your life, or thank them for their blessings. Either way, now is a good time to check in, say hello, and make any special requests you might have.

In the morning it's always a good idea to say the Guardian Angel prayer:

> Angel of God, my guardian dear,
> To Whom God's love commits me here,
> Ever this day be at my side,
> To light, and guard, and rule, and guide.

After this, you can close with a suitable prayer. I recommend the Fatima Prayer, the Prayer of Saint Francis, or the Prayer of the Holy Spirit. All of these can be found in the appendixes to this book.

At night

Before you retire for bed, make the sign of the cross, and repeat the sequence of the Our Father, three Hail Marys, and Glory Be.

After this, take a moment to again close your eyes and enter into silent contemplation, using rhythmic breathing if you like. It will help if you're away from bright electric lights, and from any sort of TV or your cell phone. Say a prayer asking for guidance, and review the events of your day. While you're doing this, ask yourself three questions, and ask for God and your guardian angel to guide you in answering them:

What are you grateful for today? Come up with at least five different things. Some days are hard, some are miserable, and at least one is the worst day of your life. Even on these days, you will find something you are grateful for. It may be something as simple as a cup of coffee, or the fact that things aren't even worse than they already are. Take a moment to give thanks for these things.

What have you accomplished today? In the morning, you reviewed your plan for the day, and asked for the guidance of God, the Blessed Virgin, and the saints who are your friends and guides on the journey. How have you developed in virtue, or accomplished your goals? Take a moment to feel both the satisfaction of accomplishment and the awareness that you couldn't have done it without help from above.

How have you fallen short today? Some days are good, others are great, and at least one is the best day of your life. Even on these days, you will find something that you could have done better. Take a moment to understand what you did wrong, and ask for help in doing things better tomorrow.

Close with a suitable prayer or set of prayers. You can repeat the guardian angel prayer—of course, substituting the word "night" for "day." You can also invoke any saints or angels you wish to ask for protection while you're sleeping, or to repeat any prayers of intercession.

A final closing prayer for the day might be any of those from the morning. I often say the Serenity Prayer at this time, as there really is no day that doesn't merit it:

> God grant me the serenity
> To accept the things I cannot change
> Courage to change the things I can
> And wisdom to know the difference.

As your spiritual practice grows, your prayer rule will grow and change. As we discussed above, you may find a prayer book or traditional prayer rule you like to follow, or you may find a particular devotion or chaplet that works well for you—either right now, or always. Allow your prayer rule to develop, and ask your guardian angel to guide you. The only thing you can do wrong in this work is nothing at all.

Whether you choose this or another prayer rule, you should spend at least two weeks working with it every day before you continue on to the next part of the book.

Rhythmic breathing

Many people are familiar with Eastern methods of meditation, which focus on the breath, and with practices such as qigong or pranayama, which direct the breath toward specific ends. If you have a preferred method of breathwork that you like to use to prepare for meditation, you may use that during your time of prayer.

If you aren't familiar with any particular method of rhythmic breathing, you may find the following practice helpful. First, place your attention in your abdomen, about an inch below your navel. When you inhale, this area should expand, while your chest remains relatively still. If you have any doubts of this, place one hand on your abdomen and the other on your breastbone. Inhale, slowly, in such a way that only the lower hand moves.

Once you've mastered the ability to breathe deeply in this way, you can move to rhythmic breathing. Inhale slowly for a count of four. Now, retain the breath for a count of four. While you do this, do not close your throat, but keep it open, using only the muscles of your diaphragm to do the work. Exhale for a count of four, and then hold the lungs empty for another count of four.

Remember that the word "spiritus" also means "breath." It is by the Holy Spirit that we live and breathe, and when we contemplate our breath in this way, we connect to that divine life within us.

Notes for practice

You should begin your daily prayer rule as soon as possible, and be prepared to stick with it through the remainder of this book. Once you have practiced every day for at least one month, you may move on to the next part of this book.

PART II

FOUNDATIONS OF MAGICAL PRACTICE

Introduction

The previous part laid the groundwork for our practice by introducing magical philosophy and a way of thinking designed to begin the work of elevating the soul above the Astral Plane and toward the Intellectual Plane.

In this part our work truly begins. We will start by retelling the Christian story from the point of view of magical and esoteric philosophy. I invite you to read through this part once, before you proceed to the practical work. Please note that it is not presented as a statement of doctrines which you must accept and believe, but, rather, as a perspective which you may find helpful.

From here, we continue onward and provide a foundation of magical practice. This includes instructions in meditation and basic ritual practice. By the end of this part, you will have a full set of magical and spiritual tools, that will be enough for many people for a lifetime.

LESSON 1

Esoteric Christian theology

Knowledge lecture

Every Christian denomination has its own interpretation of the sacred stories of our tradition. Some insist on a literal interpretation, reading the Scriptures as a history text. Others add to this literal interpretation other layers of meaning, called anagogical and typological.

From the differences in interpretation of Scripture arise different accounts of theology, which is to say, of the nature of God and His relationship to Creation. All of these differ from one another. The differences are sometimes minor, and sometimes dramatic.

The esoteric tradition has its own interpretation of Scripture and its own theology. Of its theology you have already learned much in the chapters on magical philosophy. We now turn to Scripture.

At the heart of the Christian tradition is a great story. This is the story of the Creation of the universe by God; the Creation of man in the image of God; the Fall of Man; the incarnation of Christ; his death on the Cross; his resurrection and ascent into Heaven; and his Second Coming at the End of Time.

We see this great story, firstly and most importantly, as *myth*. It is important to understand what this means. A myth is not a falsehood or fable. It is not even a fable which is not true but in which we can find some sort of guidance or meaning. The definition of myth given to us by the ancient philosophers is this:

Myths are stories of things that never *happened*, but always *are*.
What does it mean for something to happen?
It means that it takes place in the world of Time.
If something always *is*, it takes place outside of Time, in the world of Being.

A myth, then, teaches us something about the eternal processes that lie outside of Time and shape the world of Time itself. We technically call these patterns "aeviternal," to distinguish their existence from the true eternity of God Himself. Aeviternal things never happen, because they are not found in the world of Time. They are found in the world of Being, and they always are. Myths express these aeviternal truths in a form which the human mind can grasp most easily: a story.

Now, this doesn't mean that the events recorded in Scriptures didn't happen in time. They may well have happened, exactly as the ancient writers declared that they did. Our perspective is not that they didn't happen, but that the fact that they *happened* is less important than the fact that they *always are*.

And so let us explore the Christian story from the perspective of the mythic interpretation and magical philosophy.

A cautionary note

The following is not presented as a set of doctrines in which you must believe. That is important, so let's repeat it. *This is not a set of doctrines in which you must believe.* As another adept wrote of her own book of doctrine, "This is intended to train the mind, not to inform it." Our intention is to present a set of images which can guide your understanding and provide material for meditation.

It has another purpose as well. There are many people who feel strongly inspired by traditional Christian practices, but who cannot accept traditional Christian doctrine. Many magicians, occultists, and people involved in alternative spirituality have had the experience of Jesus, Mary, the angels, and saints working miracles in their lives. When I say "miracles," be aware that I'm not talking about filling up anyone's bank account with money or getting all the hot chicks. Anyone can do that. It takes a divine power and only a divine power to turn addiction into sobriety, to turn a dissolute slacker into a productive citizen, or a permanent bachelor into a loving father. At the same time, many of us, whether involved explicitly in magic, or in spiritual practices derived from other traditions like Buddhism or Hinduism, or spiritual fellowships like Twelve Step recovery programs, have seen the same sorts of miracles performed by non-Christian powers. Understand well: The devil cannot do these things. He can fill your bank account; he can help you seduce women; but he cannot humble the proud, sober the addict, or turn dissipation into discipline. Only good can work good.

These experiences immediately put the lie to any claims made by any particular Church or religion to have a monopoly on truth. God cannot be caged, and He is not caged.

How, then, are we to understand the great story of Christianity? How are we to understand the Fall of Man, the incarnation of Christ, His death on the Cross, and his resurrection?

The following is an attempt to answer these questions. Let me repeat for the third time: This is not a set of doctrines in which you must believe. It is a set of ideas with which you can engage.

That said, let us start where we must start. In the beginning …

Creation

> In the Beginning, when God began to create the Heavens and the Earth, the Earth was without form and void, and darkness was upon the face of the Deep; and the Spirit of God was moving over the face of the waters.

We begin with God, who is prior to all creation, as we have seen. God is the First Principle, meaning that He is the cause of existence for everything which comes after Him.

Following God, there is chaos. This is the Earth, "without form" and "void." This is the "darkness upon the face of the deep." The sea is often an image of the primordial chaos.

The chaos is called "Earth," not because it is the Earth we know—it doesn't even have a shape, let alone day and night—but because it is a sort of matter. In particular, it is the first matter, out of which everything is formed.

> And God said, "Let there be light"; and there was light. And God saw that the light was good; and God separated the light from the darkness. God called the light Day, and the darkness he called Night. And there was evening and there was morning, one day.

From the monad or one, which is God, we have the dyad or two, which is light and darkness. Now, consider the nature of a dyad. The dyad is two, but, being two, the dyad contains both one and two. The one within the dyad is light, which most closely resembles the Primordial One. The two within the dyad is two itself, the principle of division. Now, this two also contains one and two; and the third two contains one and two; and the fourth; and so on, unto infinity. And what is that infinity to which it leads? Nothing other than the primordial Chaos.

Thus we see that the path of division is the way of descent into matter. This is the way of following the dyad into further dyads, all the way to infinity. The path of union, then, is the way of ascent toward spirit. This is the way of following the monad within each dyad, climbing ever upward, toward God. Notice that the primordial Chaos remains always out of reach. To an even greater extent, God also remains, ultimately, out of reach. There is always further to go, up or down.

The creation of man

> On the Sixth Day, He created Man. Male and female created He them, in His Own Image created He them.

Or, after another way:

> The Lord God formed man of dust from the ground, and breathed into his nostrils the breath of life; and man became a living being. And later, the Lord God caused a deep sleep to fall upon the man, and while he slept took one of his ribs and closed up its place with flesh; and the rib which the Lord God had taken from the man he made into a woman and brought her to the man.

And so we have two different accounts of the creation of Mankind. These two do not contradict one another. We are to understand that, in one sense, the form of Man comes late in the sequence of Creation. God first brings forth land, which is the mineral creation; and then plants and trees, the vegetable creation; and then the animal creation. Only after these things are accomplished can the form of Man come into being.

This is a model of the journey of ascent. Every soul, sinking into matter, must rise through the orders of being, finally completing its journey in the return to the divine world.

There is a reason that it must be so. The Eternal Man is nothing other than Christ Himself, true man and true God. And Christ is the divine mind. To be truly the divine mind, Christ must know all things. And to truly know is to know by experience. Christ is thus present to all things, knowing all things, experiencing all things, suffering all things. This is how we may know that the path of ascent is always present to all beings, no matter how low they have sunk: Because Christ is always present to them, urging them upward.

Now, even as Man comes last in the order of Creation, he also comes first. All visible and sensible things are shaped and governed by the invisible and intelligible ideas. This is what is meant by "The Lord created the Heavens and the Earth." The Earth refers, here, to sensible things, and the Heavens to intelligible things.

In the second account in Genesis, we learn of the Idea of Man, and of his structure. "Male and female created He them, in his own image created He them." By the male is signified the nous or intellect, and by the female, the psyche or soul. By the image of God, the presence within man of the divine monad.

The man and the woman are not two individuals, but one, the archetypal human being. Each person has within him Adam, and Eve, and the image of God.

* * *

> Now the serpent was more subtle than any other wild creature that the Lord God had made. He said to the woman, "Did God say, 'You shall not eat of any tree of the garden'?"
>
> And the woman said to the serpent, "We may eat of the fruit of the trees of the garden; but God said, 'You shall not eat of the fruit of the tree which is in the midst of the garden, neither shall you touch it, lest you die.'"
>
> But the serpent said to the woman, "You will not die. For God knows that when you eat of it your eyes will be opened, and you

> will be like God, knowing good and evil." So when the woman saw that the tree was good for food, and that it was a delight to the eyes, and that the tree was to be desired to make one wise, she took of its fruit and ate; and she also gave some to her husband, and he ate.
>
> Then the eyes of both were opened, and they knew that they were naked; and they sewed fig leaves together and made themselves aprons.

Within the soul, the serpent signifies the desiring part or appetite, and it now turns toward the material creation. This is why it is said that the tree is "good for food" and a "delight to the eyes." And the serpent which sheds its skin and goes through the Earth is the image of the life lived in the world of life and death, generation and corruption.

The serpent also represents that which is outside of the soul and toward which the soul looks: In this case, rather than keeping its eye fixed on the heavenly world of God and the angels, it finds itself tempted by the things of the material world. Thus the soul turns toward its lower parts, the appetites, which are bound up with the body and material things. It then draws after it the nous. Every part is now drawn into material creation. The human being, formerly altogether spiritual, now "makes itself an apron," which is to say, it clothes itself in a material body. At first, the human being sews for itself an apron of fig leaves; later, God himself will create for them garments of skins. This signifies both the descent into matter, and it also hints at the process of ascent back to Spirit, as the fig leaves give way to animal skins. But for now, the process of descent is complete; Man, entirely spiritual and eternal, now sinks into Matter and begins his long pilgrimage through the world of death and time.

And the fruit of the Tree will indeed make him wise. But that comes later.

> Then the Lord God said, "Behold, the man has become like one of us, knowing good and evil; and now, lest he put forth his hand and take also of the tree of life, and eat, and live for ever"—therefore the Lord God sent him forth from the garden of Eden, to till the ground from which he was taken. He drove out the man; and at the east of the garden of Eden he placed the cherubim, and a flaming sword which turned every way, to guard the way to the tree of life.

It is said that, at this time, Sin and Death entered the world. In ancient writing and iconography these are proper nouns, names. It could as well be said that the human being, Adam-Eve, enters the world of Sin and Death. By sin is signified karma, actions which bind us to matter. By Death is signified death as we commonly understand it, but two other things. The first is Death himself, or Hades. The second is the Underworld over which Hades presides, which is also called Hades. In early Christian writings and to this day in the Eastern Church, "Hell" and "Hades" are distinct, and so are Death and Lucifer. Entering into the world of sin, mankind is subject to Hades, the ruler of the world of the dead.

Here is the secret teaching, which was at the heart of the ancient mysteries:

We are all, already in the world of the Dead.

The descent into Hades is also the descent into the material body. The soil wherein the dead are buried is the mineral kingdom, the kingdom of raw matter, whose ruler is Death. When we depart our bodies at death our spirits abide for a time as ghosts in the Underworld, and then return to material bodies, again and again and again. As the ancients wrote, *Soma* is *sema*: The body itself is the tomb. This will go on until we can become free. But how? Let us return to our story.

The incarnation

On Earth, ages pass, and many generations are begotten.

> Abraham was the father of Isaac, and Isaac the father of Jacob, and Jacob the father of Judah and his brothers, and Judah the father of Perez and Zerah by Tamar, and Perez the father of Hezron, and Hezron the father of Ram, and Ram the father of Ammin'adab, and Ammin'adab the father of Nahshon, and Nahshon the father of Salmon, and Salmon the father of Bo'az by Rahab, and Bo'az the father of Obed by Ruth, and Obed the father of Jesse, and Jesse the father of David the king.
>
> And David was the father of Solomon by the wife of Uri'ah and Solomon the father of Rehobo'am, and Rehobo'am the father of Abi'jah, and Abi'jah the father of Asa, and Asa the father of Jehosh'aphat, and Jehosh'aphat the father of Joram, and Joram the father of Uzzi'ah, and Uzzi'ah the father of Jotham, and Jotham the father of Ahaz, and Ahaz the father of Hezeki'ah, and Hezeki'ah

> the father of Manas'seh, and Manas'seh the father of Amos, and Amos the father of Josi'ah, and Josi'ah the father of Jechoni'ah and his brothers, at the time of the deportation to Babylon.
>
> And after the deportation to Babylon: Jechoni'ah was the father of She-al'ti-el, and She-al'ti-el the father of Zerub'babel, and Zerub'babel the father of Abi'ud, and Abi'ud the father of Eli'akim, and Eli'akim the father of Azor, and Azor the father of Zadok, and Zadok the father of Achim, and Achim the father of Eli'ud, and Eli'ud the father of Elea'zar, and Elea'zar the father of Matthan, and Matthan the father of Jacob, and Jacob the father of Joseph the husband of Mary, of whom Jesus was born, who is called Christ.

In the genealogy is, perhaps, signified a literal genealogy, or perhaps not. Its inner meaning is the cycle of reincarnation. Abraham begins the process of return by assent to divine commandment. In his willingness to give Isaac to God is signified the turning of the soul toward spiritual things; in God's freeing of Isaac, the beginning of the end of subjection to the rule of Death. In the genealogy that follows we see the long cycle of reincarnation that continues from the beginning of a spiritual journey to its culmination. Abraham is Adam, or a participant in the Human Idea which is called Adam-Eve and sometimes, in Kabbalistic writings, Adam Cadmon.

> And in the sixth month, the angel Gabriel was sent from God into a city of Galilee, called Nazareth,
> To a virgin espoused to a man whose name was Joseph, of the house of David; and the virgin's name was Mary.
> And the angel being come in, said unto her: Hail, full of grace, the Lord is with thee: blessed art thou among women.
> Who having heard, was troubled at his saying, and thought with herself what manner of salutation this should be.
> And the angel said to her: Fear not, Mary, for thou hast found grace with God.
> Behold thou shalt conceive in thy womb, and shalt bring forth a son; and thou shalt call his name Jesus.
>
> He shall be great, and shall be called the Son of the most High; and the Lord God shall give unto him the throne of David his father; and he shall reign in the house of Jacob for ever.

> And of his kingdom there shall be no end.
> And Mary said to the angel: How shall this be done, because I know not man?
> And the angel answering, said to her: The Holy Ghost shall come upon thee, and the power of the most High shall overshadow thee. And therefore also the Holy which shall be born of thee shall be called the Son of God.

Before we get to Jesus, we have to start with Mary. Here are some of Mary's titles: Immaculate Conception, Model for Christians, Virgin Pure, Mother of God, the New Eve.

By the New Eve we understand that Mary *is* Eve. The complete human Being is called Adam-Eve, and is also called Mary-Jesus. The journey from Adam-Eve to Mary-Jesus through the stories of kingship, exile, conquest, and redemption found in the Old Testament is the archetype of the journey of the human soul. This is why she is called "model for Christians." Turning toward matter, the soul descends into matter. Assenting to divine command, it begins its conquest of matter. Purified and divinized, it is born free of karma: this is the Immaculate Conception. The soul may now "give birth" to the Christ, which is to the nous, the higher part of the spirit which is above soul. This is why she is called "virgin," because she signifies the soul which has turned its gaze away from the things of generation in the material creation and toward the eternal things of the noetic (intellectual) and divine realms.

As Mary is the New Eve, Jesus is the New Adam. As Eve is born of Adam's rib, Jesus is born of Mary's womb. Neither has a second parent. Eve is called "wife of Adam" to signify that Adam-Eve represents the soul in its downward journey into materiality. But Jesus is called "son of Mary" to signify that here the soul is on its upward journey, away from generation.

The serpent, meanwhile, who tempted our first parents, is now replaced by Saint Joseph, the guardian of the Holy Family. Saint Joseph represents the strength of the soul, the part called the thymos, which is now put into the service of the nous, rather than acting as a willing conspirator with the appetites. In addition to being guardian of the Holy Family, Saint Joseph is also the patron of the Universal Church. Now, the Universal Church is more than a particular human institution. The Church as a whole includes all of the true particular Churches, and from our perspective that very much includes the esoteric, the magical, and Gnostic traditions. Remember that the Church is also called "the body of Christ." Real bodies have many parts, and truly resemble forests more than statues. As such, the Universal Church represents the redemption of the body and of matter as a whole. This is the ultimate purpose both of Adam-Eve's descent into matter and the incarnation of Christ through the Holy Spirit and the Virgin Mary.

> In those days a decree went out from Caesar Augustus that all the world should be enrolled. This was the first enrollment, when Quirin'i-us was governor of Syria. And all went to be enrolled, each to his own city. And Joseph also went up from Galilee, from the city of Nazareth, to Judea, to the city of David, which is called Bethlehem, because he was of the house and lineage of David, to be enrolled with Mary, his betrothed, who was with child. And while they were there, the time came for her to be delivered. And she gave birth to her first-born son and wrapped him in swaddling cloths, and laid him in a manger, because there was no place for them in the inn.

We come now to the birth of Christ. The author, Luke, begins with a census. It is critical to understand this: in ancient times the census was not a mere bureaucratic venture. Every ancient city had its census every three or ten years. During this time, all of the citizens would return and offer repentance for their sins to the God of their city. An Athenian returns to Athens, and repents of his sins to Athena and Poseidon; a Spartan returns to Sparta, and repents to Zeus; and so on. Every city has its particular God.

But now the census is to survey "the entire world." What this means is the particular God is, in fact, the God of Gods, the God of the whole world.

He is born in a manger, with animals; and this is also called a cave. By the cave is signified the material order, and his birth there signifies the beginning of the return journey from the material creation to the spiritual order. By the animals it is signified that the soul which descends into matter descends at least as far as the level of the beasts, though some say lower, to the level of vegetables; and others say lower still, all the way to the mineral creation. Perhaps it depends on the soul.

In ancient times, it was said that animals could speak at midnight on Christmas; this is to signify that the noetic power is present in the animal creation as well, and the animals are also on the journey of return.

The Cross

> For our sake he was crucified under Pontius Pilate, he suffered death and was buried, and rose again on the third day in accordance with the Scriptures. He ascended into Heaven and is seated at the right hand of the Father.

Jesus, which is to say, the awakened nous in the Human Being, returns to the Garden, which is now called Gethsemene. And he ascends the Tree of Life, which is the Cross. Descending, he breaks open the doors of Hades, so that all who follow after Him may no longer die. This is to indicate that He descends even as far as the very last of things, and rises again to the First Principle. This is the journey of return, which is given to every being whatsoever, for Christ is always present to them, upholding and sustaining their very being, closer than their own minds.

The Cross is the Tree of Life, and the Way of the Cross is itself the journey of return. This is called the "narrow way," for it is given to only a few, and "crucifixion." To return, finally, the God, we must die to ourselves and to all the things of this world. We must suffer as he suffered: And because he is the mind within all things, he has suffered all things. We, therefore, ourselves, must know all things as he knows all things, and suffer all things as he suffered all things. A lifetime is insufficient: We must return and return again, at times rising higher, at times falling back, but always moving as if in a spiral upward toward Heaven. At the last we must finally give ourselves entirely to the will of God and be purified of everything which binds us to matter.

Now, let us remember what in earlier and wiser times was known to all. The cross on which he was crucified was made from the wood of the Tree of Life itself. And the Place of the Skull is the resting place of our first parents; the skull is Adam's skull.

Of the three members of the soul, the nous is the highest, and its place in the subtle anatomy is in the skull. Here at the Place of the Skull, He dies upon the Tree of Life.

He descends into Hell. And there he comes in triumph; the gate of Hell is broken, and its inmates are released.

"Take up your cross and follow me," He tells us. By sacrifice, bind yourself to the Tree of Life. Descend from the nous in your head to the passions burning in the hellfire of your belly, and release the energy and the will that you have bound up there in the following of earthly things. Do this, die to this world, and you will be reborn, even as He is reborn.

The Second Coming

And I saw a great white throne, and him that sat on it, from whose face the earth and the heaven fled away; and there was found no place for them. And I saw the dead, small and great, stand before God; and the books were opened: and another book was opened, which is the book of life: and the dead were judged out of those things which were written in the books, according to their works. And the sea gave up the dead which were in it; and Death and Hades delivered up the dead which were in them: and they were judged every man according to their works. And Death and Hades were cast into the lake of fire. This is the second death. And whosoever was not found written in the book of life was cast into the lake of fire.

And he shewed me a pure river of water of life, clear as crystal, proceeding out of the throne of God and of the Lamb. In the midst of the street of it, and on either side of the river, was there the tree of life, which bare twelve manner of fruits, and yielded her fruit every month: and the leaves of the tree were for the healing of the nations. And there shall be no more curse: but the throne of God and of the Lamb shall be in it; and his servants shall serve him: And they shall see his face; and his name shall be in their foreheads. And there shall be no night there; and they need no candle, neither light of the sun; for the Lord God giveth them light: and they shall reign for ever and ever.

The ancients imagined the planes as corresponding to the structure of the universe itself. At the center lies the Earth, representing the Material Plane. Between the Earth and the Moon, we find the Energetic Plane. At the Moon, the Astral Plane begins, divided into seven layers for each of the seven planets of the ancient world, that is, the Moon, Mercury, Venus, the Sun, Mars, Jupiter, and Saturn. Every planet runs its course in a great sphere, each nested within the sphere above.

Beyond Saturn we find the sphere of the fixed stars. The stars, gathered into constellations, represent the Intellectual Plane. Of these the most important are the twelve signs of the Zodiac. These ring the sphere of the stars like a city wall. Each of the signs is a gate in that wall, and of the gates there are three in the East, three in the South, three in the West, three in the North.

What lies beyond the gate of the stars?

Here we have the source of all life, the First Sphere, called by the ancients Primum Mobile, the First Turning. This is the Divine Plane, which is the source of all things. This is the True Sun which illumines the Eternal City of the Intellectual Plane, not visibly, but spiritually. There all see Him in His own proper place, and not in another, and contemplate Him as He truly is.

And the river which rushes forth from the city is the stream of pure life descending from God into manifestation. Its visible image is nothing other than the Milky Way itself, which was called in ancient times the River of Souls. It is given to each soul to return to the city by one of the twelve gates, which are the twelve signs, and which are also the twelve tribes of Israel, the twelve apostles, and the twelve gods of Olympos.

But when? Revelation is the story of an ending to the world, coming at some point in time. But we have already learned that myth takes place always, and beyond time: it is no more subject to the future than it is to the past. It is given for every soul, when released from the body, to stand before God. The judgment always is, and those whose names are written in the Book of Life return through their proper gate to the heavenly city, and abide no longer in the realm of time. But we know them, for they are established in the Intellectual Plane with the angels of God and govern and shape the realms below. But for the rest of us it is given to abide as spirits in the Astral Plane and, after a time, to return to this realm, to begin the work again.

From this perspective, the Second Coming is not something which will happen in time, at some future date. It is something which is always happening. The exalted dead have already awakened to the New Heaven and the New Earth.

And we have been taught how we may join them: *Take up your cross and follow me.*

LESSON 2

Banishing

Daily practice

There is a core set of practices which must be learned before any advanced magic can be undertaken. Of these, the most important is banishing, which is foundational to any magical work.

But what is banishing? It is sometimes presented as a magical sterilization of a given space. There is a certain truth to this, but it isn't the whole truth. Banishing is a ritual act which is intended to clear the Astral and Energetic Planes in a given area, and the astral and energetic bodies of the magician, of unwanted energies. It does this not merely by driving unwanted energies away, but by calling in balancing and healing spiritual forces.

Most traditions of contemporary magic make a particular banishing ritual central to their system. The Golden Dawn uses the Banishing Ritual of the Pentagram. Thelemites use a related ritual called the Star Ruby; Wiccans "cast a circle" and "call the quarters." Each of these rituals is effective on its own, but also contains within it a great deal of the symbolic structure on which its particular system of magic depends. For our purposes, we are going to going to need our own banishing ritual, which is rooted in the Christian tradition. Fortunately, such a ritual is already available. It is practiced by Christians around the world every day, and its power has been known since ancient times.

I'm talking, of course, about the sign of the cross.

The use of the cross as a protective symbol is well known and attested from the earliest days of Christianity. A story from the lives of the saints will help illustrate the point.

Long ago there was a sorcerer named Cyprian who fell in love with a Christian woman, a virgin named Justina, and desired to possess her. Cyprian was a great wizard who had learned all the sorceries of the ancient world, and he cast a love spell on the young woman. But Justina, becoming aware of Cyprian's magical attack, made the sign of the cross, and the spell fell apart. Cyprian tried it again, and again, but every time Justina made the sign of the cross, and Cyprian's spells came to nothing. Ultimately, Cyprian gave up working with evil magic and became a Christian. Today, many honor him as the patron saint of Christian magic.

Like Justina, and like countless Christians throughout the ages, we can make use of the sign of the cross to purify our auras and our personal space, and to drive off evil spirits, unbalancing energies and evil magic.

Before banishing: a simple scanning exercise

First, take a moment to sit up straight, and close your eyes. Now place your attention at the top of your head, and move it by slow degrees downward, along the back of your head, your face, your neck and shoulders. Then move on to scan your torso, your upper chest and arms, the region of your rib cage, your abdomen, your bladder and genital area, and on down over your hips, through your legs and into your feet. Do this quickly for now. The goal isn't to change anything, but only to find out what is there. Take note of anywhere you are holding tension. Take note of your thoughts and your emotions. Are you feeling happy? Sad? Anxious? All three, depending on where in your body you look? Are your shoulders hiked or relaxed? Is your breathing deep or shallow, slow or rapid?

Also ask yourself how the quality of energy around you feels. You may not be used to answering a question like that: If so, simply ask yourself how it feels to be in the place you are in. Does it feel calm? Frantic? Is there a sense of buzzing electricity around you? Does it feel clean? Dirty?

For all of these questions, don't try to find the right answer. If you're sitting on a couch that feels filthy, your shoulders are pulled forward, your neck hurts and you're filled with anxiety, that is okay. If you're on a pew in a church that feels tranquil and holy, your body relaxed and your breath settled in your bellow, that's okay too. The point isn't to get the right answer, but to discover the true answer.

Read the instructions again, and do the scanning exercise right now.

The Banishing Sign of the Cross

The following ritual can be performed at any time, but it is best done before meditation or any act of magic or blessing.

Step 1. Imagine a brilliant point of light located at an infinite distance above your head. Know that this light is not God the Father, but is, rather, the closest that a human mind can come to comprehending the power of God the Father.

Step 2. Now, imagine a column of light descending from that remote point down through the cosmos, finally coming to rest at the crown of your head. Reach up with your right hand, and draw the light to your forehead. Vibrate* the words "IN NOMINE PATRIS."

* To "vibrate" means to chant in such a way that your voice creates a noticeable buzzing in your body, or in the space around you. If you're working with a specific part of the body, as in the point of light at the forehead, you should feel the buzzing there. Some people find this very easy to do; others struggle. If you're of the latter persuasion, just sing or chant the words, and imagine you can feel the vibration in your body.

Step 3. Draw your hand to your heart. As you do, bow your head, and imagine the column of light descending down, through the center line of your body, and all the way into the heart of the Earth. Vibrate ET FILII.

Step 4. Draw your hand up and out to your left shoulder, and then your right shoulder. As you do so, visualize another line of white light rising up from the heart of the Earth, meeting the first at your heart, and then extending outward to either direction in infinite space. Vibrate ET SPIRITU SANCTI.

Step 5. Bring both of your hands together at your heart. Imagine a sphere of golden light at your heart. Vibrate the word AMEN. As you do so, imagine that sphere expanding outward in every direction, until it surrounds you on all sides. Know that you are surrounded and protected by the Light Divine.

Step 6. Say the Our Father, three Hail Marys, and Glory Be.

Step 7. After the prayers, make the sign of the cross again. This time, though, you can do so more quickly, closer the way that people ordinarily do—though you should always pray with a reverent attitude. You will find, even if you rush through it, you will reconnect to the energy of the fuller ritual, so that any time you make the sign of the cross in daily life, it will have an added power and majesty.

Explanation and notes

In traditional Christian philosophy the creative power of God is said to have three parts or movements. These movements are called abiding, proceeding, and returning. Abiding means remaining in stillness. Proceeding is the work of God's creative activity going forth into the universe. Dionysius compares this with light—not the visible light of our world, but the eternal Light of the Divine. This is the "light that shineth in the darkness, and the darkness could not grasp it." The third movement is returning, a word which can also be translated, very importantly, as "conversion." This is the process whereby all created things return to God, who is their source and origin.

At the same time, the Trinity is never truly divided, and all three persons are always present at the same time, in all three movements.

This is the special meaning of the "descent of the Holy Ghost" on the apostles at Pentecost. In one sense, the Spirit is said to "descend." At the same time, it is not so much that the Spirit goes anywhere as it is that the apostles themselves, through their continuous work of prayer, have elevated their own souls to the level at which the Spirit can be perceived—that's why the Spirit descends on their heads, meaning the highest part of the souls. In another sense, the Spirit is the force which drives their prayer, leading them in the work of conversion.

Each of these movements is the special work of one of the three persons of the Holy Trinity. God the Father abides eternally in stillness. He speaks his Word, and his Son goes forth in the work of Creation. And all of Creation works ever to return to God, through the power of the Holy Spirit. At the same time, the Trinity is never separated; the Father, in another sense, goes forth and returns; the Son abides and returns; the Spirit abides and proceeds.

Spiritual practices can be compared to technology, but in an important sense they are not a technology. God's power or energy is not a force like electricity that we can manipulate at will. It isn't even that of a sentient animal like a horse or a dog who can be trained to follow commands. God's energy, with which we are working here, is God Himself manifest; it is alive and personal in a higher way than ourselves. You should see the Banishing Sign of the Cross not so much as a technique as a prayer. All prayer involves an element of thought. Most of the time, we think in words, as when a person silently prays "Our Father, who art in Heaven …" In this case, we are thinking in images—the light, the cross, the sphere. It is still a prayer.

As a prayer it will always be answered. "Who among you, if your son asked for bread, would give him a stone?" God is a loving Father. But he must be approached with reverence and respect. Neither the Holy Trinity nor the saints and angels are subject to our command.

Instructions for practice: daily banishing

Every day for the next two weeks, take some time to perform the scanning exercise, and then the Banishing Sign of the Cross. Afterwards, perform the scanning exercise again. After that, you can go directly into your daily cycle of prayer.

You should set aside a particular place and a time where you can do this work. If that place is a corner of your bedroom, or your living room couch, that's fine. You'll find that it will be best if you can do the work when natural darkness allows you to make use of candlelight; incense is also helpful if you enjoy it.

LESSON 3

Meditation

Daily practice

The term "meditation" has gone through a number of changes in the last century or two. At one time, it was associated with prayer and the study of the Scriptures, the lives of the saints, and the writings of holy people. Later, it became something exotic, a strange Eastern practice associated with mystic yogis and wandering kung fu monks. Now, finally, it's come to be a therapeutic practice recommended by nearly every doctor and psychotherapist in the Western world.

The Christian tradition has its own form of meditation—in fact, it has several different forms. In this book, we are going to focus on one of these, which is called *lectio divina* or "divine reading." We are also going to learn another, but that will come later.

The practice of lectio divina

Preparation. The first thing we are going to need is, of course, something to read. Fortunately, Christianity is very much a text-based religion, and you have a range of options, in addition to the Scriptures themselves. You may start with the Gospels, or with a spiritual text like

The Imitation of Christ or *True Devotion to the Blessed Virgin Mary*. You will also want a notebook or journal and a pen.

Step 1. Begin with the Banishing Ritual of the Cross.

Step 2. Proceed with your usual daily prayers, and then say a prayer to the Holy Spirit, in order that you may be guided in your meditation:

> Come Holy Spirit, fill the hearts of thy faithful, and enkindle in them the fire of thy love.
>
> O God who did instruct the hearts of the apostles by the Holy Spirit, grant in that same Spirit that I may be guided toward thy wisdom in this practice of divine meditation.

Step 3. Slowly and carefully read the text that you have in mind.

Step 4. Look for a theme. If you happen to have suffered through public education, the idea of searching for a "theme" in literature might sound off-putting. In this case, we're not trying to figure out the topic, the moral, or the "main idea" of our text. Not at all. What you want to do is to find *something* in the text that jumps out at you. It can be anything, for any reason.

Let's say, for example, that you chose to read the first chapter of the Gospel of Matthew. This book begins with a lengthy genealogy of Jesus Christ, demonstrating his descent from Abraham and David. Suppose, then, that the idea of a *genealogy* itself is what jumps out at you. Why? It doesn't matter; what matters is that you've found something.

Step 5. Now it's time to meditate. Begin by relaxing your body and calming your spirit, using the method of rhythmic breathing given in Lesson 4: Prayer, in the first part of this book.

Step 6. Now, bring your theme to mind. *Genealogy*. What does it mean? Why is it important? The genealogy of Christ. Turn it over in your mind. Why is it important? What does it signify?

It might occur to you that Jesus is called the son of David, and David, the son of Abraham. In this way he is being connected with these previous patriarchs, so that his mission is in some sense similar to theirs. That might lead you to think, what was it that they did? Abraham was the first called by God, and the opening incident in his story is God rejecting the sacrifice of his son Isaac. David, meanwhile, was the youngest of the sons of Jesse, and a shepherd. At the opening of his story he is chosen by God when his brothers are rejected, and then overthrows the giant Goliath and becomes king of Israel.

Is there something that unites these three figures, then? Does Christ, like Abraham, inaugurate a new era of God's relationship with His people, and change the nature of sacrifice? Is he, like David, a shepherd, but one who rises to conquer the forces of darkness, and become king? What does this say about Christ and His mission?

You will also want to bear in mind all that you have learned thus far about magical philosophy and esoteric Christianity. We hold, for example, that the soul begins its journey in the presence of God, and then descends through the Intellectual and Astral Planes, into incarnation in matter. It then does the work of rising back up from material incarnation, through the height of the Astral and Intellectual Planes, returning ultimately to the presence of God. In the genealogy of Christ, do we see a parallel to the esoteric genealogy of the soul? Is the work of Abraham akin to the establishment of the Christian world as a seed among the ideas of the Intellectual Plane? Is the establishment of David's rule in Israel akin to the creation of a coherent form on the Astral Plane? The Babylonian Captivity, then, is equivalent to our final descent of the soul into matter, in which it finds itself imprisoned. And it is then that it can begin its great journey of return, in which the seed of Abraham finally flowers in Christ, the Everlasting Man, as He returns to His Father in Heaven.

Or maybe you will think something completely different. That's okay. No, it's better than okay: That's the work before you. Take a single theme as the germ of a thought. It needn't be the theme we've presented here. Perhaps you'd rather meditate on the concept of fourteen generations, or on the specific patriarchs named, or on the importance of Christ being named the son of David. It doesn't matter. What matters is that, for a set period of time, you follow that thought out as far as you can.

Step 7. Once you feel that you have extracted as much as you can from your theme, or from no less than ten minutes, release your thoughts. Offer a prayer of thanks to God, and if it is appropriate, take a moment to consider how you can apply the ideas you've encountered in your own life. Close your meditation with a suitable prayer.

Step 8. This is a very important step. *Write down everything that you came up with in meditation.* You don't have to write out all your thoughts exactly as they came to you, but you will want to write down everything important.

This concludes your meditation.

Notes for practice

If you are pressed for time, you can do the reading at one time, and the meditation on the reading at another time. Many people find that it works best to read at night and meditate in the morning. You may find this a very easy way to incorporate lectio divina into your daily prayer rule. At night, after your prayers, do your reading. In the morning, begin by practicing the Banishing Ritual of the Cross, and then proceeding through the cycle of daily prayers, rhythmic breathing, and then onto the period of meditation.

It's worth noting that many older books are deliberately written in short, often numbered paragraphs, which makes discursive meditation very easy. (You'd almost think that was the point.) Particularly good works include *The Imitation of Christ* by Thomas a Kempis, *True Devotion to the Blessed Virgin Mary*, by Louis de Montfort, and *The Interior Castle*, by St Teresa of Avila.

Other texts from within the tradition of Christian magic also make very good resources for discursive meditation. Esoteric works such as the *Rosicrucian Cosmo-Conception of Max Heindel*, *The Science of the Sacraments* by Dion Fortune, or *Three Books of Occult Philosophy* by Heinrich Cornelius Agrippa are good choices.

Oh, and you might also consider meditating your way through the opening chapters of this book, especially if you've found the subject of magical philosophy confusing in any way. In fact, I strongly recommend it.

You should be prepared to continue your practice of lectio divina for the whole length of time you are working through this book. For now, you should practice lectio divina on a daily basis for at least a month before you proceed on to the next lesson.

LESSON 4

The Confiteor

The word "Confiteor" simply means "I confess" in Latin; it is the first part of the traditional confession of sins in the Roman Catholic Church. "The Confiteor" has come to be the name for the general confession, prayed by the faithful at the beginning of every mass.

This general confession, prayed sincerely and reverently, has a great deal of power all by itself. In the following practice, we are going to modify the traditional Confiteor in order to turn it into a potent magical ritual of purification.

The nature of sin

Too often, the concept of "sin" is treated as a legal matter, consisting in breaking rules. These rules may be wise and good, or they may be arbitrary, or they may make no sense at all. The problem is that we've broken them, and unless we perform a certain set of actions, we're going to be in big trouble!

This way of looking at sin may have been a useful metaphor at one time. Much of the Christian tradition works that way. God isn't *really* an old man who sits on a throne in the sky and rules the world like a medieval lord. Instead, this is a metaphor, which allows us to represent

God to our minds and provides an easy way to explain how He works to children and people new to religion. Sometimes in the past, certain ideas were exaggerated, such as the torments of Hell, for reasons which may have been very good at the time but which are harmful now. In other cases, certain rules were introduced simply based on the cultural fashions of the time, but were preserved when those fashions changed. The trouble is that we've now taken these simplifications as literal descriptions of how the spiritual world works.

But does that mean that we can ignore sin, or disregard the entirety of Christian moral teaching as something "outdated," a "relic of the past" which we have outgrown?

Absolutely not. Morality consists in the development of virtue, and to become virtuous is the central task of every human being. In the magical life in particular it is critically important.

So what is sin, from a magical perspective?

Many people know that in Greek, the language of the New Testament, the word for sin is *hamartia*. Hamartia means "to miss the target." This gives us a starting point. Sin as hamartia is a failure to reach our spiritual target.

The target, of course, is God himself. But we aren't God, and never will be, so does that mean that we exist in a state of perpetual hamartia? No: Our target is the divine version of ourselves. We become divine through union with God, but we don't become God Himself. We become participants in His divinity, a process called "divinization."

Imagine wandering through a snowy forest on a winter's night, so cold you can barely move your limbs. Suddenly you come across a fire. As you gradually draw closer, your limbs begin to thaw, your teeth stop chattering, you even find yourself loosening the buttons on your coat. No matter how close to the fire you come, you never become fire yourself. But you do become warm. And then you become hot. And then you catch fire yourself. This is divinization.

And sin? Sin is everything which draws us away from that divine self, like a man retreating from the fire, back into the frozen wood.

The evolution of the soul

In order to draw near to God, we must become like God, and the nature of God is *unity*. God is the perfect unity at the absolute summit of existence. The opposite of unity is chaos, the condition of total fragmentation and division at the bottom of reality. Thus, we become divine and participate in the divinity of God by achieving unity in our souls and in our relationships.

Now, it is important to understand that God has no true opposite. God, in His own being, stands outside of the universe, and transcends both unity and chaos, existence and nonexistence. It's more correct to say that unity is the first manifestation of God that our minds can understand. But we can leave this aside for right now. For now, what we need to understand is that our work is to draw closer to God and to become more like Him.

The constant work of uniting ourselves with God is what is called, in the esoteric tradition, "the evolution of the soul." Some critics of magic and occultism have taken this for a selfish end, since self-development is so critical. But this misses the point that the purpose of self-development is not self-indulgence, but union with the will of God.

God is also called the Good Itself, because all goodness is participation in the life of the Holy Trinity. Each of us has our own particular good, which is our way of participating in the goodness of God and thus becoming the best possible version of ourselves. This best form of our self is called our "higher self." Opposed to it is the "lower self," which is what is also called the ego. The lower self is the set of often conflicting passions, desires, and habitual thoughts and behaviors which trap us in the world of matter and keep us from becoming what we are meant to be. Sin or evil is everything which diverts us from that good and causes us to turn away from our soul's evolution, toward the division and fragmentation of chaos and nonexistence. It is the presence of disunity and division in the soul.

The higher self is truly the complete version of ourselves, in which all of our various parts are united under our eternal spirit and under the God who dwells within us. And yet, when we look to ourselves, considering our thoughts, our feelings, our reactions, our behavior, we find that there is much that is foreign, and much that is in conflict. Our passions war with our reason; our actions are determined by others or by our culture; our decisions do not serve our higher good.

This brings us back, finally, to the confession of sins.

The purpose of this practice is to restore us to a condition of unity. It does so in three ways. First, by purifying our souls of everything that is foreign to them. This restores unity in the soul. Second, by purifying our relationships. This restores unity in the larger collective souls in which we participate. Finally and most importantly, by restoring our relationship with God. In a final sense, this is a relationship that can never be broken; to be totally disconnected from God is to cease to exist entirely. But existence and nonexistence are really a kind of spectrum. Good is more real than evil, unity more real than chaos. By restoring our relationship with God, we literally become more real.

In the work of practical magic, this kind of purification practice is *critical*. Any time we work magic, we are causing changes in ourselves and our world. Before we do this, we need to make sure that we are the kinds of people who can cause the right sorts of changes. And we need to make sure that we are as much *ourselves* as possible, so that we can produce the right sorts of outcomes.

The Seven Deadly Sins

The traditional model of the Seven Deadly Sins provides an excellent guide to behaviors which pull us away from our soul's evolution. Each one of these is a pattern, which becomes a habit as we continue to engage in it.

Pride: Pride is the elevation of the lower self in place of the higher self. Pride refuses to apologize for bad behavior, because the lower self fears the loss of status that would result, as a dog fears to be lower in a pack. Above all, pride is the belief that we can achieve our good without God, the Good Itself, when, in fact, we are able to have anything only by opening ourselves to the goodness of God.

Lust: Lust is not the desire for sex, but enslavement to that desire. The desire for sex is a passion, and our passions are not evil in themselves—but we are meant to rule our passions, and not to be ruled by them. At its most benign, lust is simply a distraction; at its worst, lust is extremely destructive indeed.

Greed: Greed is similar to lust. Where lust enslaves our souls to the desire for sex, greed enslaves us to the desire for material comfort. We all need some measure of comfort and security in order to live, but this, too, is meant to serve our spiritual needs and our soul's evolution.

Envy: Envy is the desire to have the blessings which have been given to another. Rather than praying for blessings for ourselves, or committing ourselves to work for the things we need or want, envy simply resents another person for having them. When we envy, we direct negative energy at another person's goods, and we curse both them and ourselves. In this way, envy destroys our relationships.

Wrath: Wrath is the direction of destructive energies, physically or otherwise, at others or at ourselves. Wrath is not the same as anger. Like all the passions, anger is natural. Anger at injustice is, indeed, an appropriate response. But wrath responds either to real or to perceived injustice with destructiveness. It is like trying to put out a fire in your kitchen by setting a fire in your bathroom: Instead of working to heal a broken situation and restore chaos to unity, wrath simply expands the force of destruction.

Sloth: Sloth is unwillingness to work for our good, material or, especially, spiritual. Sloth would rather sleep than meditate, check social media than write a book, browse the internet than clean the kitchen, watch football than go to church. Eventually sloth mires us in stagnation, so that no unity is left in us.

Gluttony: Gluttony enslaves us to the desire for food or drink in the same way that lust enslaves us to the desire for sex and greed enslaves us to material comfort. At its most benign, gluttony has three chocolates instead of just one, and we suffer a sugar crash half an hour later. At its worst, gluttony ends in alcoholism, drug addiction, or morbid obesity.

By each of these sins, we harm both ourselves and others. Relationship is unity: Our relationship with others and the unity of the parts of our soul are ways in which we participate in the primal unity of the Holy Trinity. When we destroy our relationships, external and internal, through sin, we fall further and further from the unity that is God.

The Confiteor ritual

Preparation: Make a list. Especially the first time you do this, it is best to focus on one particular sin or group of sins at a time. If it's been years, or decades, since you've considered your own failings, and you try to go through everything, you're going to be at this a very long time. It can be very helpful to list out your sins beforehand, so that you can focus on one or a few at a time.

Step 1. Begin by performing a banishing ritual, followed by the Our Father, three Hail Marys, and the Glory Be. In the future, you can perform the Confiteor at any time, but the first few times you perform it, you should do so as part of your formal practice.

Step 2. Relax your body, and use rhythmic breathing to enter into meditation.

Now, call to mind your sins. In some cases, these will be general patterns of bad behavior and mistakes. Every time you do this, expect a few specific things to come to mind. Things you've heard about times you were lazy or neglectful, drinking or playing video games when you should have been getting work done. In each of these cases, take a moment to imagine the situation from the perspective of the other people who were involved. Understand how your actions affected them, and how, even if they hurt you, they could not have done any different, given the circumstances. Forgive them, and ask God to forgive them. Many times, of course, you will be the one affected by your actions. Commit to forgiving yourself, and asking God to forgive you.

Step 3. Say a Confiteor prayer. I've provided three examples, and encourage you to choose the one that best suits your needs and your practice. Each will work, but the symbolism is slightly different.

The Roman Catholic Confiteor

I confess to almighty God, to blessed Mary ever Virgin, [to blessed Saint Michael the Archangel, to blessed John the Baptist, to the holy apostles Peter and Paul,] and all the saints, that I have greatly sinned in thought, word, and deed: through my fault, through my fault, through my most grievous fault. (Strike your heart center three times while saying this.) Therefore I pray blessed Mary ever Virgin, blessed Michael the Archangel, blessed John the Baptist, the holy Apostles Peter and Paul, and all the saints, to pray for me to the Lord our God.

Note: During the part in brackets [ ], you may substitute other saints, such as those of your particular tradition or the patron saints of yourself, your family, and your craft or trade.

The Anglican general confession

Almighty and most merciful Father; we have erred, and strayed from thy ways like lost sheep. We have followed too much the devices and desires of our own heart. We have offended against thy holy laws. We have left undone those things which we ought to have done; And we have done those things which we ought not to have done; And there is no health in us. But thou, O Lord, have mercy upon us, miserable offenders.

Spare thou them, O God, which confess their faults. Restore thou them that are penitent; According to thy promises declared unto mankind in Christ Jesus our Lord. And grant, O most merciful Father, for his sake; That we may hereafter live a godly, righteous and sober life. To the Glory of thy holy Name. Amen.

The liberal Catholic Confiteor

O Lord, Thou hast created us to be immortal and made us to be an image of Thine own eternity; yet often we forget the glory of our heritage and wander from the path which leads to righteousness. But Thou, O Lord, hast made us for Thyself and our hearts are ever restless till they find their rest in Thee. Look with the eyes of Thy love upon our manifold imperfections and pardon all our shortcomings, that we may be filled with the brightness of the everlasting light and become the unspotted mirror of Thy power and the image of Thy goodness; through Christ our Lord. Amen.

Step 4. Now, imagine a tiny light, like a candle flame, at the very center of your heart. This light is the grace of God within you, the healing mercy of Christ within you. Imagine it slowly expanding. It fills your heart, bringing warmth, healing, and blessing. It expands outward, filling your body, your head, your arms and your legs, healing and blessing every part of you. It expands, filling your aura, until you feel yourself surrounded by a sphere of holy fire. From there, it extends outward, bringing the healing mercy of God to every single person who has been harmed by your sins.

Do this slowly, and allow yourself to forgive others, to forgive yourself, and be forgiven by God. Know that God loves you in this moment, precisely as you are.

Step 5. For a time, take a moment and simply rest in the healing mercy of God. When you are ready, rise to your feet. Say the words:

May Almighty God have mercy on us, forgive us our sins, and lead us to everlasting life. Amen.

This concludes the ritual.

Notes for practice

For now, you should practice the Confiteor ritual at least once a week. Some people, when they're new to this work, are eager to pile on practices until half their life is devoted to magic and spirituality, but this isn't always helpful. Instead, you should use the Confiteor ritual in place of another practice, rather than in addition to it. Lectio divina or the rosary will wait until tomorrow.

Later, we will incorporate the Confiteor into other sorts of practices. For now, keep it to once a week, and let the effects radiate out into your life.

Once you have spent at least one month working with the Banishing Ritual of the Cross and lectio divina on a daily basis, and have practiced the Confiteor at least one time, you may proceed to the next part of this book.

LESSON 5

The initiation of the rosary

Practical lesson

After the sign of the cross, the rosary may be the best known of Catholic sacramentals. Catholics around the world pray the rosary every day, and various saints and even apparitions of Our Lady have recommended the practice, if not commanded it.

A very great deal has been written about the rosary over the centuries. Despite this, it still has depths which have never been explored in print. And despite both its age and its simplicity, it continues to reveal new secrets to nearly everyone who practices it regularly. Many spiritual graces have been promised to those who pray the rosary daily.

For our purposes, the rosary is of great practical value, for a number of reasons. First, the rosary begins with prayer, and proceeds to every form of meditation. By the time you work your way around a set of rosary beads, you will have worked with active, discursive, and contemplative meditation, and even an element of sensory meditation. Second and even more importantly, the fifteen Mysteries of the rosary present the entire work of the Christian spiritual life and the entire journey of the development of the human soul. As such, the simple practice of praying all fifteen Mysteries over the course of three days functions as an initiation into the Christian Mysteries. This initiation can then be repeated again and again, with its power deepening every time.

How to pray the rosary

Preparation. All you need for this practice is a strand of rosary beads. These are not at all hard to find; you can find one for a few dollars on the internet or at your local thrift store. But if you don't have one or for some reason can't get access to one, don't worry: you can say all the prayers all on your own.

We are going to work through the rosary from the cross around the circle of beads, one at a time.

Step 1. At the cross, say the Apostles' Creed. At least for now, you should do this even if you don't exactly believe in it—it's more helpful to push yourself beyond your comfort zone, and to think about how you can understand prayers like the Apostles' Creed, than simply to come up with your own thing. Later, you can use a creed that may work better for you. Some alternatives will be given in the appendixes.

The Apostles' Creed

> I believe in God,
> the Father almighty,
> Creator of Heaven and Earth,
> and in Jesus Christ, his only Son, our Lord,
> who was conceived by the Holy Spirit,
> born of the Virgin Mary,
> suffered under Pontius Pilate,
> was crucified, died and was buried;
> he descended into hell;
> on the third day he rose again from the dead;
> he ascended into heaven,
> and is seated at the right hand of God the Father almighty;
> from there he will come to judge the living and the dead.
>
> I believe in the Holy Spirit,
> the holy catholic Church,
> the communion of saints,
> the forgiveness of sins,

the resurrection of the body,
and life everlasting.

Amen.

Step 2. Above the cross you will find a set of five beads: one single bead, a set of three beads, and another single bead. At the first single bead, pray the Our Father. At the set of three beads, pray one Hail Mary each, for a total of three. At the final single bead, pray the Glory Be.

Understand that each of the three Hail Marys is a prayer for one of the three higher Christian virtues of faith, charity, and hope. Each of these is also connected with the three primary energy centers in the human body: Faith is the supreme virtue of the head, the center of the intellectual spirit; charity of the heart, the center of the vital spirit; hope is the supreme virtue of the abdomen, the center of the animal spirit.

Step 3. You will now encounter five sets of ten beads each, with single beads dividing them. Now the Rosary proper begins, and we will begin to pray the Mysteries. For each of these sets of ten, perform the following steps:

Follow the following steps for the remaining beads. These come in sets of ten, with one bead, usually larger or of a different color, dividing them.

Step 1. Read the text of the Mystery, out loud if you are working with a group, silently if by yourself.

Step 2. Close your eyes, calm your breathing, and enter into meditation. Visualize the scene described in the Mystery text as clearly as you possibly can. Notice what you see, hear, and feel.

For example, the first joyous Mystery is the Annunciation. See Mary, a young woman, living in ancient Israel. If you already know this or if you find it interesting, you can research the time and place, so that you can imagine with historical accuracy the details of the scene, but this isn't necessary. You can also imagine her situation as occurring in your own time or as whatever set of images your mind presents to you under the title "ancient Israel." If you have an image or icon of the visitation, that may work as a guide to visualization.

Imagine the archangel Gabriel appearing before her, a majestic being, one of the great powers who watch over the universe. And here he presents himself to a woman living in a remote province of the Roman

Empire, the mighty bowing before the low. In a voice which is more powerful than the thunder, closer than the thoughts of her own mind, he greets her:

> Hail, fullness of grace! The Lord is with thee. Blessed art thou among women.

And he tells her,

> You will conceive a child and you will call his name Jesus, because he will save his people from their sins. He will be great, and the Son of the Most High.

But how? she wonders, for the day of her marriage is far off yet. And the answer comes:

> The Holy Spirit will come upon you, and the power of the Most High will overshadow you. And therefore your child will be the Son of God.

Perhaps she pauses, seeing by the archangel's power the enormity of what has been proposed. And then she tells him,

> Behold the handmaiden of the Lord; be it done unto me according to thy word.

Step 3. Now, consider the subject of the Mystery through using the tool of discursive meditation. As always, keep in mind everything you know from traditional theology and everything you've learned from the magical and esoteric traditions. Something will jump out at you. Spend a few minutes, and follow it down to its conclusion. Keep in mind also the spiritual fruits of each Mystery: in this case, that is humility.

Step 4. Now, release both the imagination and the reasoning mind, but let the sense of them remain. Move on to say the following prayers:

The Our Father
Ten Hail Marys
The Glory Be

As you pray the Hail Marys, let your hands move across the beads, to track their number. Try not to think about anything else while you are praying. Instead, enter fully into the words, as though you were speaking them yourself to Mary as to another person in the room, each time saying them as though for the first time.

Step 5. Continue through the full circle of the rosary, praying each Mystery in the same way. When you reach the end, conclude by saying the Hail Holy Queen:

> Hail, Holy Queen, Mother of Mercy,
> our life, our sweetness and our hope!
> To thee do we cry, poor banished children of Eve.
> To thee do we send up our sighs,
> mourning and weeping in this valley of tears.
>
> Cast, then, O most gracious Advocate,
> thine eyes of mercy toward us,
> and at the end of this, our exile,
> show unto us the blessed fruit of thy womb, Jesus.
> O clement, O loving, O sweet Virgin Mary.
>
> Amen.
>
> Pray for us, O Holy Mother of God.
> That we may be made worthy of the promises of Christ.

Over the course of three days, work your way through the joyful, the sorrowful, and the glorious Mysteries. Visualize the Mysteries as intensely as you can, and allow them to transform you. After the third day, you may return to your usual practice of daily meditation, or you may either alternate it with the rosary or substitute the rosary in its place. As previously noted, the rosary can be prayed over and over again, deepening in power every time.

The cycle of the joyful, sorrowful, and glorious Mysteries closely parallels the whole process of spiritual development. At the beginning, the work of magic and spirituality is exciting, delightful, joyous: we welcome it like Mary saying yes to God and receiving the Lord Jesus in her womb. But after a while, the work of daily spiritual practice starts to feel like drudgery. The rituals that light up our minds when we first practiced them start to become routine; the idea of performing the same meditation again and again feels like dragging ourselves through the desert. Or like being sacrificed on a cross. But if we can persevere through this time—if, that is, we can "take up our cross" and follow after Christ—then everything comes around again. Our joy is resurrected, and it is all the more joyful for having come back to us; in our achievements, we receive a crown of glory, like Mary ascending into Heaven.

Actually, this cycle characterizes most of life in the material world. Think about the experience of taking up a new hobby, like playing a musical instrument. At first, it's exciting. You have a guitar in your hands, and it turns out it's nowhere near as hard to play as you thought. But after a while, it starts to feel like drudgery. The notes sound flat, you start to notice all of your mistakes, you just can't bring yourself to play that one song again. But if you persevere through this time, you find that everything gets better. Your playing improves, you can do things you never used to be able to.

And then, as long as we remain here in the material world, the cycle begins again.

The Mysteries of the rosary

The joyful Mysteries

1. The Annunciation

The Archangel Gabriel is sent to the virgin Mary, who is espoused to Joseph but as yet unwed. Gabriel announces to Mary that she will bear a child by the Holy Spirit, and that child will be the savior of the world. Mary does not flinch from her duty but utters the words, "Behold the handmaiden of the Lord. Be it done unto me according to thy word."

Inner meaning: In the first Creation of mankind, the male is created first, and the female from him. Eve follows the temptation of the serpent, and Adam follows her into sin. The soul descends into matter.

In the second Creation, the female is first: This is Mary, the New Eve. She is "female" because she is receptive to the influence and power of God, able to receive his grace and, mixing it with her own substance, bring forth the New Adam, who is Christ. This is an image of the purified human soul.

Spiritual fruit: Humility

2. The visitation

Mary learns that her cousin Elizabeth is pregnant, despite her advanced age, with a baby who will later become John the Baptist. Mary, now pregnant herself, visits Elizabeth, and upon her arrival the baby leaps in Elizabeth's womb. Elizabeth exclaims, "Blessed art thou among women, and blessed is the fruit of thy womb." Mary responds with the prayer which will later be called the Magnificat (full text in appendix):

My soul doth magnify the Lord,
And my spirit hath rejoiced in God my Savior.
For he hath regarded the humility of his handmaiden:
Behold, henceforth all generations shall call me blessed.

Inner meaning: The nature of the divinized human being is presented in Mary, who sings the words, "My soul doth magnify the Lord." She is like a lamp in which the light of God shines with unsurpassing brightness, and this is the fruit of her "humility," which is her total receptivity to the power of God.

We see here, too, the relationship between Jesus and John the Baptist. John will begin his ministry first, and is called the Forerunner. For this reason John is associated with the summer solstice, when the light shines most brightly, but begins to decline, while Jesus is associated with the winter solstice, when the light is reborn in the darkness. As the last of the prophets, John represents all of the collected wisdom of the time before Christ, from every corner of the world. And we see here that he is born after Jesus, to show us that the wisdom which appears to have come before Christ, as John began his ministry before Christ, is in fact posterior to Christ in the order of things.

Spiritual fruit: Love of neighbor

3. The birth of Christ

Caesar Augustus orders a census of the entire world, and Joseph returns to his hometown of Galilee to be enrolled. Mary is near her term, but because there is no room at the inn in town, the couple is forced to spend the night in a cave which doubles as a stable for animals. At midnight, among the animals, amid the piercing cold, the savior is born.

Inner meaning: The census, in the ancient world, was a time in which the people of a city would gather to make atonement to their city's particular God. As Augustus orders a census of the whole world, we see that the God to whom atonement will be made is in fact the God of the whole world, hitherto unknown.

The stable itself represents the entire order of the material creation, into which the Creator himself now enters as a child.

Spiritual fruit: Spiritual poverty

4. Presentation of Jesus in the temple

Following His mother's traditional forty day period of withdrawal and purification, Jesus, as firstborn, is brought to the temple, and two doves are given in sacrifice. An old man named Simeon had been promised that he would not die until he had seen the savior. Seeing Jesus, he now says words which are known as the *Nunc dimittis* prayer:

> Lord, now lettest thou thy servant depart in peace according to thy word.
> For mine eyes have seen thy salvation,
> Which thou hast prepared before the face of all people;
> To be a light to lighten the Gentiles and to be the glory of thy people Israel.

To Mary, Simeon prophesies:

> Behold, this child is set for the fall and rising again of many in Israel;
> and for a sign which shall be spoken against;
> (Yea, a sword shall pierce through thy own soul also)
> that the thoughts of many hearts may be revealed.

Inner meaning: The presentation functions on a number of different levels. Mary and Joseph fulfill the commandments of the divine law.

In this and the previous Mystery we see a version in miniature of the entire journey of the human soul. Christ is born in the cave amid the animals, which represents the material world into which we are born. He then returns to the temple of God, which represents the spiritual world, and animals are given in sacrifice, representing the way in which we must shed our animal nature to rise to the higher levels of being. In an ancient image, the soul is represented as a chariot pulled by two winged horses. One horse is obedient to the commands of the charioteer; the other disobedient. The doves can be seen to represent the two horses, and here we learn that both must ultimately be sacrificed together so that only the charioteer remains.

Spiritual fruit: Obedience to divine Law

5. The finding of Christ in the temple

When Jesus is a boy, Joseph and Mary take Him to Jerusalem for Passover, but find on their return journey that they have lost him. After three days of searching, they find him teaching in the temple. He says, "Did you not know that I would be in my Father's house?" After this he returns to them and obeys them in all things.

Inner meaning: It very often in life seems to us that Christ has abandoned us and is very far from us. Here He teaches us the truth of these things: "Did you not know that I would be in my Father's house?" It is not he who has been lost, but we who have departed from Him. If we would find him again, we have only to return to His temple. And if we make our own hearts a temple to Him, we will not have very far to look.

This Mystery, too, is a microcosm of the journey of the human soul. Here Joseph and Mary represent the soul who has departed from the Heavenly realm and now wanders in the desert of the material. The soul looks everywhere in the material world, but has only to return to its source in the eternal temple of God to find its salvation.

Spiritual fruit: Conversion of the soul

The sorrowful Mysteries

1. The Agony in the Garden

While awaiting the arrival of the authorities, Jesus retires to the Garden of Gethsemene, asking his disciples to keep watch. Knowing what must come, he prays, "Father, I would that this cup might pass from me, but thy will, not mine, be done."

Inner meaning: The Garden of Gethsemene is an image of the Garden of Eden. Christ, the New Adam, now returns to the beginning. Where the First Adam disobeyed God at the suggestion of the serpent, seeking power and eternal life, the New Adam now obeys God, though it means humiliation and death.

Spiritual fruit: Union with the will of God

2. The scourging at the pillar

Jesus is taken before Pontius Pilate, the Roman governor of Judaea, and questioned. Jesus tells Pilate,

> Thou sayest that I am a king. To this end was I born, and for this cause came I into the world, that I should bear witness unto the truth. Every one that is of the truth heareth my voice.

Pilate replies, "What is truth?" He then orders Jesus to be scourged at the pillar, though he says he finds no fault in him. The scourge, please remember, is no mere whip, which would be painful enough. It is a weapon with many whips, which end in balls of metal or hooks. At the end of his scourging, Jesus's flesh is torn, and he is left broken and bleeding.

Inner meaning: Having accepted His Father's will, Jesus now dies to the flesh, as his flesh is torn by the scourge. This is what is called "mortification of the flesh," and it is a painful but inevitable part of the journey of return. We must, like Christ, die to the flesh, which is our attachment to our material bodies, to their passions, and to the things of this world. Jesus tells Pilate that his kingdom is not of this world; Pilate, a ruler in this world, has Jesus scourged although he is innocent. The kingdom of this world means both the age and culture in which we are born and our condition, bound to matter and the flesh. It is a kingdom in which tyrants rule by force and scourge the innocent. As we continue our work in liberating ourselves, we must give up attachment to this world and we must not be surprised when its rulers turn on us.

Spiritual fruit: Mortification of the flesh

3. The crown of thorns

The Roman soldiers, after scourging Jesus, weave a crown of thorns and stick it on his head, and place a purple robe on his shoulders. Then they mock him, saying, "Hail the king of the Jews!"

Inner meaning: The soldiers believe they are mocking Jesus, and yet it is they who honor him as king of the Jews. The crown of thorns is the first crown that he wears. It is a sign of his rejection of and his rejection by the powers of this world, and of his dominion in the spiritual world.

This is the fate of all who look upon the light of the eternal world, which is the world of real being: to be mocked and rejected by those bound to the powers of this world. And yet in their very rejection of him, they crown him.

Spiritual fruit: Self-mastery

4. The carrying of the cross

Jesus carries his cross to Golgotha, the Place of the Skull, where he will be crucified. On the way he falls three times, and each time he rises and continues on.

Inner meaning: Jesus taught (Matthew 16): "If you would follow after me, abandon yourselves, take up your cross and follow me." In the Way of the Cross, which is depicted in the Catholic devotion called the Stations of the Cross, we see, once again, a microcosm of the entire spiritual journey. It is a journey on which we gradually abandon our attachments to our passions and to the material world. On the way we will fall, but every time, we must rise and continue on. We will receive help, and we will follow in the footsteps of the Eternal Man, who went before us and walks with us.

Spiritual fruit: Perseverance in the spiritual life

5. The death of Christ on the cross

At Golgotha, Jesus is crucified between two criminals. One mocks him much as Pilate and the Roman soldiers had, saying, "If you are the King of the Jews, save yourself!"

But the other says only, "Jesus, remember me when you come in your kingdom."

And Jesus tells him, "This day you will be with me in Paradise."

And Jesus dies on the cross. Matthew and Mark give his last words as "Eli, Eli, lamma sabachtani?" which means, "My God, my God, why hast thou forsaken me?" Luke gives his last words as "It is accomplished." And John, as "Father, into your hands I commend my spirit."

The Sun is darkened at noon, and the veil in the temple is torn in half. Jesus is taken from his cross and laid in a tomb.

Inner meaning: A full description of the inner meaning of this Mystery would fill an entire book, and, indeed, entire libraries of books have been written on it. It is more important for you to enter into this great Mystery and experience it for yourself than for me to tell you what I think about it. And so I will highlight a few things.

Golgotha is "the place of the skull." Traditionally, this was understood to be the skull of Adam. The skull or head center is the seat of the intellect or nous, which is that faculty within us which is capable of perceiving higher realities directly. Jesus, as the archetypal man, thus represents in his death the total sacrifice of all of the lower faculties and the awakening to the higher life of the intellect. Adam's journey is complete.

The cave always represents the material world as a whole. As he dies, he enters into the cave, and descends into Hell. Hell is the lowest and furthest reach of the material creation. Jesus's life and his providence thus extends to the last of things. This is a myth, and myths, as we know, always are: Jesus is always descending into the furthest reaches of material reality, and rising again.

Jesus's death on the cross is the image of the final sacrifice of the lower self, that allows us to awaken to the life of the higher self.

Spiritual fruit: Death to the lower self

The glorious Mysteries

1. The resurrection

On the third day after Jesus's death, Mary Magdalene and other women go to the tomb to anoint His body. But they find that the stone which blocked the entrance of the tomb has been rolled away, and the body is not there. They meet with angels robed in white, who tell them, "He is not here." Jesus appears to Mary Magdalene, and then to the disciples.

Inner meaning: Jesus dies, and is buried. It's important to remember that he isn't inactive during this time. He doesn't simply lie in the tomb waiting to wake up on Easter morning, but descends all the way down into Hell. There he breaks the gates of Hell, and releases the just who have been imprisoned there. In an ancient account, Satan and Death hear his coming and begin to bicker with one another, finally fleeing the scene when Jesus arrives and overthrows their kingdom. These are, of course, the powers of Sin and Death. These refer both to the dark and chaotic realm of the Lower Astral Plane, in which many souls abide in life and in death, and to our condition of imprisonment in the tomb of the body, the cave of the material world.

All these are broken by Christ. Remember that, whether or not these are historical events, they are primarily mythical events. As man's fall is outside of time, so too is his redemption.

Spiritual fruit: Faith

2. The ascension

Jesus breathes on his disciples, and gives to them the Holy Spirit, telling them, "Whose sins you forgive, they are forgiven; whose sins ye retain, they are retained." Then, giving them a final blessing, he promises them, "I am with you, even unto the ending of the Age." Then he ascends into Heaven. But John tells us,

And there are also many other things which Jesus did, the which, if they should be written every one, I suppose that even the world itself could not contain the books that should be written. Amen.

Inner meaning: As a man, Jesus has completed the cycle. As the "divine logos," Jesus is the complete cycle of all beings, which are created as ideas in the mind of God, descend unto the last of things, and rise and are restored to Heaven. As the nous of the Eternal Man, he is now ascended, and that of him which abides on Earth now lives with the whole of his true being fixed in the spiritual world; for this reason he makes disciples of all nations and pardons the sins of others. Christ is at once a man, the intellect of that man, and every man, and the intellect of every man, and every mind, and the Divine Mind, and one person of the Holy Trinity.

Spiritual fruit: Hope

3. The descent of the Holy Spirit

The disciples gather to pray in the upper room, together with Mary, the Mother of God, and others among the women. And the Holy Spirit descended upon them.

And suddenly there came a sound from heaven as of a rushing mighty wind, and it filled all the house where they were sitting.

And there appeared unto them cloven tongues like as of fire, and it sat upon each of them.

And they were all filled with the Holy Ghost, and began to speak with other tongues, as the Spirit gave them utterance.

Inner meaning: The Holy Spirit, as immovable divine principle, does not descend or go anywhere. Rather, we ascend to Him. As the spirit of life, He is the principle of the complete human being. The upper room is the summit of the material world, and here they transcend the material while embodied. The tongue of fire descends upon each of their heads, in the place called the crown chakra, signifying that the eye of their soul is now open to the vision of God. Each now speaks with "other tongues," for each has become a complete human being. In another sense, the Holy Spirit is the principle of return, and the disciples have now returned insofar as any can while still embodied.

We are told by the tradition that the disciples spent nine days in prayer, and on the tenth received the Holy Spirit. This is the first novena. I like to think that it is also the first rosary. The disciples, in this vision, spent each day in prayer, and at the end turned to Mary, recalling the words spoken of her many years earlier and asking for her intercession. Perhaps John began it, saying, "Hail Mary, full of grace, the Lord is with thee. Blessed art thou among women and blessed is the fruit of thy womb." Then Peter took it up. Then the others, until all as one prayed, "Holy Mary, Mother of God, pray for us sinners, now and at the hour of our death." Then the Holy Spirit came upon them, and all as one cried out, "Glory be to the Father, and the Son, and the Holy Ghost, as it was in the beginning, and is now, and forever shall be, world without end."

Spiritual fruit: The gifts of the Holy Ghost

4. The Assumption of Mary

Mary, who has gone to live with John, the "beloved disciple," at last reaches the fulfillment of her years on Earth. By a miracle, the Twelve, scattered far over the Earth by now, are transported to John's home and are with her at the last. She is laid in a tomb. But on the third day it is found to be empty, and flowers grow where she was laid. Like Her Son before her, she ascends bodily into Heaven.

Inner meaning: Mary is the New Eve, the soul of the complete human being; she now follows after her son, the nous of the complete human being. Mary is the first Christian and the model for all who follow after, and in her is the promise of that which awaits all who follow Christ.

I imagine the disciples, gathered about the place where she was laid. Again, John began it, saying, "Hail Mary, full of grace, the Lord is with thee." I imagine praying with the disciples beside her grave, and then glorifying God with them as it is discovered to be empty.

Spiritual fruit: The grace of a happy death

5. The crowning of Mary

Mary is assumed into Heaven, taken up in the body, and her son places the crown prepared for her on her head. She reigns now as Queen of Heaven and Earth, mediatrix of all graces, a source of help for all who turn to her.

Inner meaning: Neither Jesus nor Mary leave behind a body on the Earth, for they have transcended the body. It is said that Jesus "ascends" into Heaven, while Mary is "assumed" into Heaven. The nous ascends by its own nature; the soul is received by her participation in the nous.

I imagine her departing the material world. At first all is darkness. And then she hears the prayer, "Hail Mary, full of grace, the Lord is with thee …" These words are spoken by the angels, the lowest order of those beings who stand above and within the material world, shaping and governing it. They do not sin, but beyond them she hears the echo of the disciples, praying, "Pray for us sinners, now and at the hour of our death …" Then she hears the prayer of the archangels, exalted above the angels, and the principalities who stand above the archangels. Layer after layer of the world is peeled back, revealing within it a deeper world, more solid, more real. And in every one of those deeper worlds, the inhabitants, mighty powers who shape the world of our experience, bow to her, hail and praise her. She comes at last to the final place, the absolute reality, a sea of endless light. And again, she hears the prayer, "Hail Mary, full of grace, the Lord is with thee. Blessed art thou among women, and blessed is the fruit of thy womb."

And a crown is placed on her head. It seems that this crown is the source of the light, and she sees now clearly, and sees the hands that placed the crown upon her head. And she sees the hands of her son, which hold the crown. "Jesus," she says.

And as she sits upon the throne prepared for her, she hears the words that rise to her from across the universe: "Holy Mary, Mother of God, pray for us sinners, now and at the hour of our death."

Spiritual fruit: The crown of glory

You should be aware that there is another set of Mysteries, called the luminous Mysteries. This is a recent innovation, having been introduced in 2002. The luminous Mysteries are a fine devotion in their own right, but they aren't a part of the rosary as traditionally practiced, and including them disrupts the threefold rhythm of the rosary.

PART III

SACRAMENTAL THEURGY

Introduction

The word "theurgy" means "God working" in Greek. In magical terminology, it is understood to contrast with thaumaturgy, which means "wonder working." In practice, we can define theurgy as any magical ritual designed to elevate the soul of the magician to the presence of the angels and saints or to some aspect of God. Where thaumaturgy attempts to cause specific changes in the life of the magician, the purpose of theurgy is spiritual development. Through the rites of theurgy, we commune with the higher realms of being, and find ourselves transformed.

The part that follows consists of four lessons, all of them practical in nature. You should take time to work through each of them before proceeding onto the next one. This part is short, but it is foundational to the work that follows on it, and you should take your time with it.

We will begin by learning how to open a magical temple. This is a foundational magical practice, and key to everything that follows. Then we will learn a method of energy work to strengthen and purify our spirits for the work that follows. After this, we will begin to learn the work of theurgy properly so called.

In this book, we will divide theurgical rituals into two types: invocations and consecrations. Invocations are ways of making contact with a particular spiritual being, usually an angel or saint. The second type are consecrations. These are special rituals designed to unite the consciousness of the magician with a particular subject of devotion. Consecrations are designed to change the consciousness of the magician, elevating it toward some aspect of the higher realms of existence. Invocations, by themselves, also primarily work to change the consciousness of the magician, but they do so by bringing the magician into a relationship with another being. In this way, theurgical invocations lead directly to thaumaturgy, because once we have formed a relationship with an angel or saint, we can ask for their help in transforming our world.

LESSON 1

Opening a magical temple

Practical lesson

With the Asperges and Censing

In magical jargon, a "temple" simply refers to a space in which to do magical work, and "opening" refers to the methods of preparing that space with the appropriate practices. These practices, in turn, are meant to clear the space of unwanted energies and create a connection to the divine powers with which the magician is working.

Preparation

This ritual requires a few different pieces of equipment. First, you're going to need a space in which you can do your work. A private room of any kind with a door that can be shut is really the minimum requirement. Now, before you panic about lacking the needed space, don't worry: your own bedroom or home office will do. You can use your living room if no other option is available. In the past, some magical orders required members to have a room dedicated exclusively to magic.

This is great if you have access to it, but it isn't necessary. The truth is that this requirement was often nothing more than a way of weeding out anyone who wasn't part of the upper class. (This is especially true in Britain, where the average home is much smaller than in North America or Australia.) Especially since the only powers that we work with are the Holy Trinity and the saints, any room in your home will receive nothing but blessing from the work we're going to do.

In your temple space you will need a few things. The first is an altar. This can be a permanent structure. Many Catholics and other Christians create home altars, on which can be found a crucifix, images of saints, and other things like holy water. Keeping a home altar is a great practice and one that I'd encourage. That said, your magical altar doesn't need to be a permanent structure. It can be a dresser or end table which is used for magical work some of the time and then converted back to its usual use after the ritual is over. That's fine, and it's often a good option if your home altar is in your living room or kitchen and you'd prefer to do your magical work in your bedroom or garage.

Your altar can contain any type of sacred image that you want, provided it's appropriate to our work—no images of pagan deities or football jerseys. (Not even a terrible towel. I know Steelers fans were thinking of that so don't try to deny it.) For a magical working, it must contain all of the following:

1. A crucifix. This should stand upright. If necessary, it can be mounted on the wall above your altar, but a small standing crucifix can be purchased for a very reasonable price online or at most any Catholic supply store.
2. Holy water. Later we will learn how to make this ourselves. In the meantime, you can easily find holy water at any Catholic or Orthodox church and at many Anglican and Lutheran churches as well.
3. Incense. I'm aware that many people these days struggle with incense. In the appendices to this book you will find a guide to the use of incense; there are good options even for people who are sensitive to smoke. At a minimum, incense should be natural. The sort of stick incense that you can get at most shopping malls is usually a bad option, as these typically make use of artificial scents and adhesives, and contain a wooden core which smokes to excess. Good quality incense can be found online and at Catholic supply stores; some resources will be included in the appendix.

4. An image of Our Lady, and of any saints that you happen to be working with.
5. A candle. You should have a real candle with actual fire whenever this is possible. Beeswax is best, but soy or paraffin wax will do. A candle with an image of a saint or the Blessed Mother can do double-duty here, as both candle and icon.

The second requirement for your temple is simply somewhere to sit for meditation. What this looks like is up to you. Many people will find an ordinary kitchen chair will work just fine. If the side of your bed is all you can do, that will work too. Some people prefer to sit on the floor for meditation, using a *zafu* or meditation cushion of the sort popular in Eastern traditions. Others prefer to kneel, and a kneeler or the sort of meditation bench intended for kneeling meditation is a good option. Whatever you have been using in your meditation practice is fine.

The Opening ritual

Step 1. Stand before your altar, and say the following words, from Psalm 44:

I will go up to the altar of the Lord, unto God who giveth joy to my youth.

Step 2. Perform the Banishing Sign of the Cross.

Step 3. The Asperges. Take the container of holy water and hold it aloft. Say:

> Thou shalt cleans me with hyssop, O Lord, and I shall be clean; thou shalt wash me, and I shall be whiter than snow. Have mercy on me, O Lord, according to thy great mercy.

If you have an aspergillum, you can make use of it; otherwise, dip your fingers in the container of holy water, and flick it three times to each quarter of your space. First toward the East, then the South, then the West, then the North. While you do this, concentrate on the idea that the holy water is purifying the space and cleansing it of any remaining unbalanced energies.

Step 4. The Censing. Trace the sign of the cross over the incense, and say:

> Be thou blessed by him in whose honor thou shalt be burned.

Take the incense and hold it aloft. Say:

> May this incense, blessed by thee, O Lord, ascend to thee, and may thy mercy descend upon us.

Wave the incense to each quarter of the room, in the shape of a cross. While you do this, concentrate on the intention that the incense is blessing and consecrating everything with which it comes into contact.

Step 5. The Invocation. Stand before your altar with your hands stretched upward and away from your body, your palms turned upward toward Heaven. This is called the *orans* posture, and we will make more use of it as we continue. Say:

> Our help is in the Name of the Lord
> Who hath made the Heavens and the Earth.

As I open this temple I pray, O Lord, that thou wilt direct all my actions by thy holy inspirations and accompany them by thy grace. May the work which I will undertake herein have its origin in thee and reach its conclusion through thee, and may the fruit of its fulfillment be an offering unto thee. I ask this through Jesus Christ, Our Lord, Amen.

The temple is now open.

Closing the temple

After the work of an open temple has been accomplished, it needs to be closed again. Have you ever cleaned up your kitchen in order to have space in which to cook a meal, and then had to clean up all over again once the meal was cooked? If so—and who hasn't had this experience?—you understand the purpose of the Closing ritual.

Step 1. Offer a prayer of thanks. This will vary, depending upon the purpose of the open temple. The point is to give thanks to God for whatever it is that he's helped you accomplish—whether that's the invocation of a saint, a special devotion or consecration, or even just a period of meditation. In some of the rituals in this book, this prayer is provided. When it isn't, you can come up with your own prayer, using the following as a template:

Almighty God, Eternal Father, I thank you for your blessings this day, and especially for assisting me in [name the purpose of your temple].

I ask that you continue to direct and guide my actions and the effects of [name any particular working you have performed in the temple] by the power of your Holy Spirit. Amen.

Step 2. Repeat the Asperges with holy water.

Step 3. Repeat the Censing with the incense.

Step 4. Offer a closing prayer. Here again, you have your choice. This should be a general prayer, suitable to daily use, that fits whatever purpose you had in opening your temple. Good choices include the Fatima Prayer (this is especially suitable for confession and forgiveness rituals); the Holy Spirit Prayer (especially good for magical workings); the Hail Holy Queen (for Marian rituals); the Prayer of Saint Francis (especially suited for rituals of spiritual development); and the Prologue to the Gospel of John (a good all-purpose prayer).

This completes the Closing.

Notes for practice

Unlike the Banishing Ritual of the Cross or the practice of meditation, the Opening ritual isn't intended for daily practice. For now, you should learn and practice it until you can do it without looking at the book for reference. Within your temple, you can work with any of the practices given, including lectio divina, the Confiteor ritual, or the rosary.

LESSON 2

The kyrie energetic practice

Daily practice

This is a form of energy work, intended to charge your subtle body with the energy of the life force. As such, it bears a resemblance to related practices in traditions like qigong and yoga. The difference is that we will be working entirely within the Western tradition, using concepts and symbolism derived from the Catholic tradition and ultimately rooted in classical antiquity.

    Step 1. First, perform the complete Banishing Ritual of the Cross. After this you may either stand upright, with your feet shoulder-width apart, or else sit in a meditation posture, with your back straight, not leaning against a chair, and your body relaxed.

    Step 2. Now, return your attention to the source of the light. Imagine it as a single point of brilliant light, shining bright in infinite space. Imagine a current of light descending from the point, all the way down through the heavens, through the atmosphere of the Earth, arriving at last in the center of your head, where it forms another point of light, mirroring the first. Vibrate the words: KYRIE ELEISON. Try to feel the words in the center of your head. As you do so, imagine that the point of light expands into a sphere of light. The sphere fills your entire head, extending upward to your crown, out past your ears, and down to the base of your throat. Repeat the words, KYRIE ELEISON, KYRIE ELEISON twice more for a total of three times.

Step 3. From the point at the center of your head, which is now the center of a sphere, the column of light continues downward. Now, it forms a second star of light in the center of your heart. Chant the words CHRISTE ELEISON. As before, while you chant the words, imagine the point of light expanding and becoming a sphere. This sphere expands outward from your heart, as far upward as the base of your throat, down to your solar plexus, and outward to fill the sides of your chest. Repeat the words, CHRISTE ELEISON, CHRISTE ELEISON twice more for a total of three times.

Step 4. Now, the column of light continues downward to a point about two fingers below your navel, where it forms a third star of light in your body. Chant the words KYRIE ELEISON. See the point expand outward into a sphere which extends upward to your solar plexus, downward past your genitals, and outward to the sides of your abdomen. Repeat the words, KYRIE ELEISON, KYRIE ELEISON twice more for a total of three times.

Step 5. The column of light continues, rushing downward until it reaches the heart of the Earth itself. There, the white light of Heaven mingles with the red-golden light of the center of the Earth. This light now rushes back upward, through the central channel of your body, to a point about three feet above your head. There it radiates outward like a fountain, forming a sphere which surrounds your whole body, extending downward three feet below the soles of your feet. From there, it returns upward, pouring through your central channel and circulating around your aura a second time, and then a third time.

Step 6. After the third circulation, the column of light back upward, joining the star of light at the center of your heart.

Step 7. Chant or sing the words AGIOS ISCHYRIOS, AGIOS O THEOS, AGIOS ATHANATOS, ELEISON IMMAS. Imagine the words as light radiating outward from your heart and filling your entire aura.

Explanation and commentary

As we saw in Magical philosophy: macrocosm and microcosm, the soul is connected to the physical body through the medium of the energetic body. The energetic body is divided into two parts: the aura, or sphere of sensation, which surrounds the body, and the energetic body itself, which is organized along a central channel which extends from the crown of the head to the soles of the feet. Three major energy centers are connected by the central channel: The head is the center of the nous, the higher part of the soul, and of the animal spirit; the heart is the center of the thymos, the vital part of the soul, and of the vital spirit; the abdomen or "liver" is the center of the epithymia or appetite, and the natural spirits which govern digestion and procreation.

A properly ordered soul is, in the imagery given to us by Plato and adopted by the Middle Ages, like a well-governed kingdom. The nous is king, reigning with the authority of God, with whom he is always present. The thymos is like the knights or warrior class, who follow a code of honor and chivalry and serve the king in the interests of the kingdom as a whole. The epithymia is like the workers and the peasantry, who offer glad service to the king and the nobility in exchange for justice and protection.

We also saw above that each center also has its own particular virtue. Clarity is the virtue of the head center; charity is the virtue of the heart, and chastity is the virtue associated with the abdomen. Each of the energetic centers has its own peculiar vices or disorders. Opposing Clarity is Confusion; opposing Charity, Rage and Pride; opposing Chastity, every form of addiction.

Plato compared the nous to a human being, the thymos to a lion, and the epithymia to a many-headed dragon. If the dragon and the lion gang up on the human being, he doesn't have a chance. This is what happens in a disordered soul. The epithymia rules and the thymos cooperates with it. The thymos serves only itself and the appetites are given free reign, with the nous powerless to restrain them. The soul descends into sin and into the chaos of addiction, whether to food, sex, alcohol, screen time, or all of the above.

The words "Kyrie eleison, Christe eleison, Kyrie eleison" mean "Lord have mercy, Christ have mercy, Lord have mercy." Often the words "Have mercy" call to mind the idea of begging someone to stop hurting us. This isn't at all what we mean here. In the Gospels, whenever someone asks Jesus to "have mercy," it is always a plea for healing. And this is a critical point: the state of sin into which the disordered soul descends is, above all, a kind of sickness.

In the kyrie energetic practice, we invoke the healing power of Christ into each of our energetic centers, that he may transmute disordered thoughts into clarity of the nous, rage and pride into the charity of the heart, and addiction into the peace of chastity.

At the same time and by the same process, we gather energy that can also serve to heal the body, to enable us to heal others, and to carry out works of magic such as the consecration of sacramentals and the sacrament of the Eucharist.

Notes for practice

The kyrie energetic practice should be done on a daily basis. It is best done right after the Banishing Ritual of the Cross, before proceeding to your regular prayer and meditation.

LESSON 3

Working with the saints and angels

Practical lesson

Catholic and Orthodox as well as many Anglican and other Christians throughout the world call upon the saints and the angels on a daily basis. The number of saints with icons, feast days, and traditional prayers is very long, and a collection of such prayers could fill many books like this one. If you don't have such a book, I recommend that you get at least one; some recommendations will be included in the appendix.

    In magical terminology, the act of calling upon a spirit like an angel or saint is called *invocation*. There are many different forms of invocation in the magical traditions of the world. Sometimes, a distinction is made between invocation, in which a spirit is called into the mind or soul of the magician, and evocation, in which a spirit is summoned into a ritual space outside of the magician himself. This distinction is quite important in traditions that work with difficult, mischievous, or even evil spirits, of which there are many (quite unfortunately in the last case). In our work the distinction is less important as we will be working exclusively with divine spirits, and so we will use the term "invocation" throughout this book.

You may have already noticed that this kind of work straddles the border between theurgy and thaumaturgy. It would be simple to say that any time that we invoke a spirit in order to get to know them better, to ask their presence and blessing in our lives, we are practicing theurgy, while whenever we call upon a spirit to accomplish something in the world outside of ourselves we are practicing thaumaturgy. The truth is that this is an oversimplification. *Any* time we call upon a spirit of any kind which ranks higher than ourselves in the order of being, we are practicing theurgy. This is because of the following very simple magical principle:

You will become like any spirit you invoke.

The result is that, even if you only ever call upon, say, Saint Anthony to find your lost keys, or Saint Joseph to help you sell your house, you will become a tiny bit more saintly. The mere act of calling upon the saints draws you into their presence, with effects that will ripple through your life.

With that said, this part of this book is devoted to theurgy, and we are going to start our work by learning to work with the saints and angels in a theurgic fashion. Effectively, we're going to call up an angel or a saint and say Hi.

That might sound uninteresting compared to the work of summoning spirits down from the planets to accomplish great works upon the Earth, as is done by magicians in old stories and classic fantasy novels. This is an illusion. The act of making contact with a saint or angel will affect your life in positive ways. This is already magic. It will also greatly enhance your ability to bring about more directed sorts of changes in your life by working with the saints—that is, to work effective thaumaturgy. The saints want to help us; more than many other types of spirits, they are very forgiving of people who turn up out of nowhere asking for help. Despite that, it's still both more polite and more effective to get to know them before you start asking for favors. That's what the rituals of invocation that we are going to present here are for.

We are going to start by learning a general ritual of invocation, which will suffice for any angel or saint. Please note, this ritual *won't* suffice for working with a more difficult class of spirit, such as an elemental spirit or one of the planetary daimons. It's also, obviously, not suitable for the conjuring of evil spirits, which is a practice that you ought to avoid entirely in any case.

Ritual for the invocation of a saint

Preparation. Set up your temple in the usual way. On the altar, place an image, statue, or holy card for the saint or angel you are working with. These are very common, and often come with a prayer to the saint, which will be very helpful. Many grocery stores also carry candles dedicated to a range of saints, with images of the saint in question and prayers in good Spanish and bad English, and these can be very helpful.

You can also decorate the altar with the saint's colors and their attributes—a rose for Saint Therese of Lisieux, for example, or a lily for Saint Joseph.

1. Perform the complete Opening, including the Banishing Sign of the Cross, the Asperges and Censing, and the Confiteor.
2. Sit or kneel in front of your altar, and contemplate the image of the saint for a time.
3. If the holy card or statue came with a prayer to the saint, pray it now. You will usually come to a place which says, "Make your petition," or something else indicating that this is the part to ask the saint for what you want. At that point, skip to step 4:
4. Offer the following prayer:
   O Saint [Name], I greet you, and ask for your presence in my life. By the grace of God, be with me, teach me that which is given to you to teach, and help me to better understand you, your Mysteries, and your patronage.
5. Close your eyes, and enter into discursive meditation using rhythmic breathing. Imagine the saint standing in front of you, just as they appear on the image on your altar. Now, simply *talk to them*. Tell them why you want them in your life, in your own words.
6. Sit in silence for a time. You may hear a response from the saint, very clearly and immediately. You may receive a jumble of thoughts, some of which makes sense, others, less so. Anything you experience during this time should be written down. You may also perceive nothing directly at this time. That's okay; it doesn't mean that the ritual didn't work. Pay attention to sudden thoughts, inspirations, or "coincidences" over the next few days; these may also include a message.
7. Return to your breath for a few minutes. Then rise to your feet, and thank God for the gift of His saint and the saint for their presence

in your life. Then add a closing prayer such as the Prayer of Saint Francis, the Fatima Prayer, or the Prayer of the Holy Spirit.

This completes the ritual.

Example invocation: the guardian angel

Every one of us is assigned a guardian angel, who is a being chosen, usually from the order of the angels, to watch over and guide us in this life. Dom Prosper Gueranger, the well-known French priest and theologian, described the work of the guardian angels in the following way:

> To ward off dangers; to uphold man in his struggle against the demons; to awaken in him holy thoughts; to prevent him from sinning, and even, at times, to chastise him; to pray for him, and present his prayers to God; such is the office of the Guardian Angel. So special is his mission that one Angel does not undertake the guardianship of several persons simultaneously; so diligent is his care that he follows his ward from the first day to the last of his mortal existence, receiving the soul as it quits this life, and bearing it from the feet of the sovereign Judge to the place it has merited in heaven, or to its temporary sojourn in the place of expiation and purification.

We all have such a spirit, set over us, to accompany us in this life, watch us, guide us, and help us. It would be a very useful thing, I'm sure you'll agree, to get to know them better!

And so I recommend that your first work of invocation be an invocation of your guardian angel. Here is the procedure:

Preparation. Set up your altar in the usual way. In addition, make sure to have an image or a statue of a guardian angel; these can be purchased easily at Catholic or Orthodox supply stores. In a pinch you can print one out from the internet, or even create your own image if you have the artistic skills.

Step 1. Perform the complete Opening, including the Asperges and the Censing.

Step 2. Say: O God, I thank thee for the gift of the guardian angel which thou hast set over me, to care for and guide me in this life. I pray that by your grace I may enter into conversation with my angel this day, for the benefit of my soul and of the whole world.

Step 3. Recite St. Gertrude's guardian angel prayer:

> Most Holy Angel of God, appointed by God to be my guardian, I give thee thanks for all the benefits which thou hast ever bestowed on me in body and soul. I praise and glorify thee that thou condescended to assist me with such patient fidelity, and to defend me against all the assaults of my enemy. Blessed be the hour in which thou were assigned me for my guardian, my defender and my patron. In acknowledgment and return for all thy loving ministries to me, I offer thee the infinitely precious and noble Heart of Jesus, and firmly purpose to obey thee henceforward, and most faithfully to serve my God. Amen.

Say, I invoke my guardian angel. O Angel of God, appointed to me as my guard and guide, appear to me this day as I enter into meditation.

Step 4. Take your seat, close your eyes, and enter into meditation. Imagine a figure taking shape before you, an image of a guardian angel—whatever that looks like to you. When the figure appears, say:

In the name of Jesus Christ, I greet you. Do you confess the coming of Christ in the flesh?

If the being answers "Yes," you may proceed to step 5.

If the being answers "No," or if it is silent, then say,

"Then, in the Name of Jesus Christ, depart from this place, and do not return."

Immediately perform the Banishing Sign of the Cross and the complete Closing, including the Asperges and Censing. You may try again in three days' time.

Step 5. If the being answers in the affirmative, then you can welcome it into your presence and talk to it about anything you like. You may wish to ask it questions. This can look like anything you want. Ask it what it's like to be your guardian angel, if there is anything that you need to know at this time—anything you can think of. Sometimes you will not be able to perceive an answer; sometimes it will be very clear. Anything you hear should be written down in your practice journal as soon as possible.

Step 6. When you are ready to end the conversation, thank your guardian angel in your own words, making sure to add, "in the Name of Jesus Christ." Then simply come out of meditation in the usual way, returning to your breath and slowly opening your eyes.

Step 7. Close with the common guardian angel prayer:

> Angel of God, my guardian dear,
> To whom God's love commits me here,
> Ever this day be at my side,
> To light, and guard, and rule, and guide.

Then perform the complete Closing.

A note on guardian angels

Everything in the world of our experience has a guardian angel. This includes your home town, your country, the woods behind your house, and even your own family. You can follow the same procedure to invoke any of these beings, and this can be a helpful way to understand certain things, and accomplish certain effects. For example, if there is an issue in your family, you can invoke the angel set over your family, and ask him (or her: angels are genderless but may appear as men, women, or neuter spirits) for help understanding or resolving the problem.

You should also know that the guardian angels are as varied in their personalities as human beings; perhaps more so. I've found that my own guardian angel rolls his eyes at formal prayers, but is always willing to help in a pinch; the guardian angel of my family, on the other hand, is more like a stern but fair ruler or judge. What is your guardian angel like? What about the guardian angel of your family, or your town? This is as good a time as any to find out.

LESSON 4

Consecrations and the devotion to the Three Hearts

Practical lesson

We've already seen the term "consecration" used to refer to the magic of the sacramentals. We consecrate holy water, incense, and so on for specific magical purposes.

In this chapter, we're going to provide a special ritual of consecration to the three hearts of Joseph, Mary, and Jesus. This is both a self-consecration and an initiation into the Mysteries of Christian magic.

Before proceeding to the consecration to the Three Hearts, you should make sure that you know the Opening ritual well enough to perform it from memory. You should also have spent at least one month practicing the kyrie energetic practice on a daily basis, and have performed the invocation of your guardian angel.

Devotion to the Three Hearts: rising on the planes

This is a special theurgical ritual which is intended to elevate the consciousness to the highest realms of being. It should be practiced at least once while you work through this course, as a form of self-initiation.

After this, it can be practiced regularly, as part of your ongoing magical development.

Over many centuries, special devotions have grown to the hearts of all three members of the Holy Family. These devotions have been encouraged both by apparitions of saints, angels, and Our Lord and by the clergy.

Each of the three hearts has its own title, which conveys its special meaning. These are: The Sacred Heart of Jesus, the Immaculate Heart of Mary, and the Most Chaste Heart of Saint Joseph.

Now, we have already learned that each person of the Holy Trinity is linked to one of the three Higher Planes of Being. The Father is especially the person of the Divine Plane, the Son, the person of the Intellectual Plane, and the Holy Spirit, the person of the Astral Plane. Keep in mind that the Holy Trinity is never truly separate; the Son and the Spirit are operative on the Divine Plane, the Father and the Holy Spirit on the Intellectual Plane, and the Father and the Son on the Astral Plane.

In addition to this, each member of the Holy Family especially reveals to us one of the three higher planes of being, and teaches us how to properly interact with that plane. The Holy Family does this through their hearts. Heart, in this context, means the center of power, activity, and love. It's like what we mean when we talk about the "heart of the city" or the "heart of a forest," or even "getting to the heart of the matter."

The Most Chaste Heart of Saint Joseph reveals the Astral Plane, and through devotion to the Most Chaste Heart we can elevate our consciousness to the Higher Astral Plane. Remember that our consciousness is always astral, but we typically spend our time with the ordinary thoughts of the middle part of that plane, and we frequently descend into the obsessions and hatreds of the Lower Astral Plane. Devotion to the Most Chaste Heart elevates us above the storms of the Astral, to the stillness at its height.

The Heart of Joseph is called "most chaste." We have already learned that "chastity" means correct use of the forces of generation, which are above all energetic in nature and which bring forth physical forms. The heart of Joseph is called "chaste" because the Astral Plane enters into contact with the planes below. Joseph teaches us the proper way of life in physical incarnation. He is also called "Joseph the Worker," "Lover of Poverty," and "Guardian of the Holy Family." This is because he enters works in the material plane but is not seduced by it. Instead, he remains with his consciousness fixed in the Upper Astral Plane and his spiritual gaze turned toward the planes above, and so brings forth the Will of God on the Earth.

The Immaculate Heart of Mary reveals the Intellectual Plane. Mary is called "Queen of Angels," "More exalted by far than the Seraphim," "Mother of God," and "Star of the Sea." Now the angels are the powers which shape the world through the Intellectual Plane. Mary is set above all of these, and mediates between the Intellectual Plane and the Divine Plane. This is why she is called "mediatrix," and "Mother of God." We have already learned that the planes may be linked to the classical elements, with the five planes descending in sequence from the Divine Plane of Spirit to the Intellectual Plane of Fire, the Astral Plane of Air, the Energetic Plane of Water, and the Physical Plane of Earth. But there is another way to model the planes and the elements. In this way of looking at things, the Divine Plane is the Plane of Fire, the plane of primary activity. The Intellectual Plane is the Plane of Water, which receives the fire of the Divine Plane. Fire and water make steam, the air of the Astral Plane, which is the plane of active forms. The forms of the Astral Plane, finally, condense into the solid and semi-solid structures of the Physical and Energetic Planes, which together form the Plane of Earth. In this sense, Mary, abiding at the height of the Intellectual Plane and yet participating in the fire above, is the Star of the Sea.

The word immaculate means "unstained." The Heart of Mary is called "unstained" because she abides beyond contact with the material world. This is how she is also called "the immaculate conception," because she is free from the stain of sin that results from contact with matter.

The Sacred Heart of Jesus, finally, reveals the Divine Plane. The Sacred Heart is exalted beyond all forms that we can know. From it radiates light, which is the energy of God going forth from the Divine Plane.

Ritual of the Most Chaste Heart of Joseph

Preparation: Set up your temple in the usual way. On your altar, along with your crucifix and vessels for holy water and incense, you will need an image of the Most Chaste Heart of Joseph. These can be found at Catholic supply stores, or printed out from the internet.

1. Begin by performing the complete Opening ritual, including the Confiteor. If it seems appropriate, also perform the kyrie energetic practice.

2. Standing, say the following prayer:

Blessed Saint Joseph, spouse of the Holy Virgin, servant of God, who ever did the will of God upon the Earth, I thank you for your blessings and ask for your presence in my life. I pray that this day you will reveal to me the Mysteries of your Most Chaste Heart, that I may be united to you in love and through you to the Blessed Virgin Mary, your spouse, and to Jesus Christ, our Lord. Through the same Christ Our Lord, Amen.

3. Take your seat, in preparation for meditation. Take a few minutes to relax your muscles and to breathe rhythmically, in order to calm your energetic body. Then contemplate the Most Chaste Heart of Joseph.

First, you will simply look at the image on your altar. Focus on it, take it in, let it fill your consciousness. If your mind wanders, bring it back to the image, as many times as necessary.

The FIRST THREE TIMES you do this meditation, you will practice steps 4 and 5, and then skip directly to Step 11. On the fourth time and not before, skip steps 4 and 5 and go directly to Step 6.

4. Close your eyes, and enter into discursive meditation. Contemplate the meaning of the Most Chaste Heart. What does chastity mean? What do the figures in the image represent? How does the Most Chaste Heart relate to Saint Joseph's other titles, such as the Worker, the Lover of Poverty, the Guardian of the Holy Family, and so on?

After a while, release your thoughts and simply allow yourself to rest in the presence of the Most Chaste Heart.

5. Stand and offer a prayer to the Most Chaste Heart:

Most Chaste Heart of Saint Joseph, I pray that I may be united to you this day and every day. Be present in my life, teach me your Mysteries, and guide me to the Immaculate Heart of the Blessed Virgin Mary, your spouse, and the Sacred Heart of Our Lord Jesus Christ. Through the same Christ our Lord, Amen.

THE FOURTH TIME YOU PRACTICE THIS MEDITATION:

6. As before, spend a few minutes in relaxing your muscles and calming your energetic body through rhythmic breathing. Then spend a few minutes contemplating the image of the Most Chaste Heart.

7. Close your eyes, and visualize the Most Chaste Heart before you. Imagine the Most Chaste Heart of Joseph expanding, growing bigger

and bigger, until it fills your entire temple space. Then it continues to expand, until it fills the entire universe. Know and feel that you are in the presence of the Most Chaste Heart, set at the height of the Astral Plane. For a few moments, simply feel into the power and the presence of the Most Chaste Heart.

8. Silently, say the following prayer:

Most Chaste Heart of Saint Joseph, I consecrate myself to you this day. I pray that you will abide forever within me. Teach me your Mysteries, guide me in this life, and care for me at the hour of my death. Most Chaste Heart of Saint Joseph, I consecrate myself and my life to you this day and every day. Through Christ our Lord, Amen.

9. Now, imagine the Most Chaste Heart begins to shrink, gathering itself from the ends of the universe and rushing inward, with all of its power. At last, it gathers itself into the center of your body, in the space of your own heart. Imagine the Most Chaste Heart of Joseph in the middle of your chest, beating in time with your own heart and filling your life's blood with its holy and healing power. Know that the Most Chaste Heart is always within you.

10. Spend a few minutes in contemplation of the Most Chaste Heart within you. Then spend a few minutes breathing rhythmically. When you are ready, slowly open your eyes. Rise to your feet, and offer the following prayer:

Almighty God, Eternal Father, I thank you for the gift of your servant Saint Joseph and of his Most Chaste Heart. I pray that, through the heart of Saint Joseph to whom I consecrate myself this day I may be united to you and forever do your will upon the Earth. Through Christ our Lord, Amen.

11. Perform the Closing ritual.

Ritual of the Immaculate Heart of Mary

Preparation: Set up your temple in the usual way. On your altar, along with your crucifix and vessels for holy water and incense, you will need an image of the Immaculate Heart of Mary. These can be found at Catholic supply stores, or printed out from the internet.

1. Begin by performing the complete Opening ritual, including the Confiteor. If it seems appropriate, also perform the kyrie energetic practice.

2. Standing, say the following prayer:

Hail Holy Queen, Most Blessed Virgin Mary, Mother of God, Mediatrix of all Graces! I thank you for your blessings, and ask for your presence in my life. I pray that this day you will reveal to me the Mysteries of your Immaculate Heart, that I may be united to you in love and through you to Jesus Christ, our Lord. Through the same Christ Our Lord, Amen.

3. Take your seat, in preparation for meditation. Take a few minutes to relax your muscles and to breathe rhythmically, in order to calm your energetic body. Then contemplate the Immaculate Heart of Mary.

First, you will simply look at the image on your altar. Focus on it, take it in, let it fill your consciousness. If your mind wanders, bring it back to the image, as many times as necessary.

The FIRST THREE TIMES you do this meditation, you will practice steps 4 and 5, and then skip directly to Step 11. On the fourth time and not before, skip steps 4 and 5 and go directly to Step 6.

4. Close your eyes, and enter into discursive meditation. Contemplate the meaning of the Immaculate Heart. What does it mean to be "immaculate?" What do the figures in the image represent? How does the Immaculate Heart relate to Mary's other titles, such as Queen of Heaven and Earth, Mediatrix of All Graces, Mother of Sorrows, and so on?

After a while, release your thoughts and simply allow yourself to rest in the presence of the Immaculate Heart.

5. Stand and offer a prayer to the Immaculate Heart:

O Immaculate Heart of Our Lady, Mary the Mother of God, I pray that I may be united to you this day and every day. Be present in my life, teach me your Mysteries, and guide me to the Sacred Heart of your son, our Lord Jesus Christ. Through the same Christ our Lord, Amen.

THE FOURTH TIME YOU PRACTICE THIS MEDITATION:

6. As before, spend a few minutes in relaxing your muscles and calming your energetic body through rhythmic breathing. Then spend a few minutes contemplating the image of the Immaculate Heart.

7. Close your eyes, and visualize the Immaculate Heart before you. Imagine the Immaculate Heart of Mary expanding, growing bigger and bigger, until it fills your entire temple space. Then it continues to

expand, until it fills the entire universe. Know and feel that you are in the presence of the Immaculate Heart of Mary, set at the height of the Intellectual Plane. For a few moments, simply feel into the power and the presence of the Immaculate Heart.

8. Silently, say the following prayer:

O Immaculate Heart of Mary, I consecrate myself to you this day. With confidence do I come before you, O Throne of Grace and Mother of the Word Incarnate. Inflame in me the same Divine Fire which has inflamed your own Sorrowful and Immaculate Heart. Make my heart and my home your shrine, and through me, make the Divine Fire of the Sacred Heart of Jesus triumph in every heart and home. O Immaculate Heart of Mary, I consecrate myself and my life to you this day and every day. Through Jesus Christ our Lord, Amen.

9. Now, imagine the Immaculate Heart begins to shrink, gathering itself from the ends of the universe and rushing inward, with all of its power. At last, it gathers itself into the center of your body, in the space of your own heart. Imagine the Immaculate Heart of Mary in the middle of your chest, beating in time with your own heart and filling your life's blood with its holy and healing power. Know that the Immaculate Heart is always within you.

10. Spend a few minutes in contemplation of the Immaculate Heart within you. Then spend a few minutes breathing rhythmically. When you are ready, slowly open your eyes. Rise to your feet, and offer the following prayer:

Almighty God, Eternal Father, I thank you for the gift of Our Lady, the Most Blessed Virgin Mary. I pray that, through the heart of Mary to whom I consecrate myself this day I may be united to you and forever do your will upon the Earth. Through Christ our Lord, Amen.

11. Perform the Closing ritual.

Ritual of the Sacred Heart of Jesus

Preparation: Set up your temple in the usual way. On your altar, along with your crucifix and vessels for holy water and incense, you will need an image of the Most Chaste Heart of Joseph. These can be found at Catholic supply stores, or printed out from the internet.

1. Begin by performing the complete Opening ritual, including the Confiteor. If it seems appropriate, also perform the kyrie energetic practice.

2. Standing, say the following prayer:

Lord Jesus Christ, Son of God, unto thee I give thanks this day for every blessing thou hast given me, and for all things whatsoever that thou hast ordained that I face in this life. Thou who art Divine Mind, thou who art Word of God, thou who art true man and true God, I ask this day that you receive me into thy presence and reveal to me the Mysteries of your Most Sacred Heart, that I may be united to you forever in this life, and in this life to come. Amen.

3. Take your seat, in preparation for meditation. Take a few minutes to relax your muscles and to breathe rhythmically, in order to calm your energetic body. Then contemplate the Sacred Heart.

First, you will simply look at the image on your altar. Focus on it, take it in, let it fill your consciousness. If your mind wanders, bring it back to the image, as many times as necessary.

The FIRST THREE TIMES you do this meditation, you will practice steps 4 and 5, and then skip directly to Step 11. On the fourth time and not before, skip steps 4 and 4 and go directly to Step 6.

4. Close your eyes, and enter into discursive meditation. Contemplate the meaning of the Sacred Heart. What does it mean, that word, "sacred"? What do the other images represent? What does it truly mean to be the heart of the Son of God, the heart of the Divine Mind?

After a time, release your thoughts and simply allow yourself to rest in the presence of the Sacred Heart.

5. Stand and offer a prayer to the Sacred Heart:

Lord Jesus Christ, Son of God, I pray that I may be united this day to your Sacred Heart. Be present in my life, teach me your Mysteries, that I may be united with you always in this life and in the life to come.

THE FOURTH TIME YOU PRACTICE THIS MEDITATION:

6. As before, spend a few minutes in relaxing your muscles and calming your energetic body through rhythmic breathing. Then spend a few minutes contemplating the image of the Sacred Heart.

7. Close your eyes, and visualize the Sacred Heart before you. Imagine the Sacred Heart of Jesus expanding, growing bigger and bigger, until it

fills your entire temple space. Then it continues to expand, until it fills the entire universe. Know and feel that you are in the presence of the Sacred Heart, the clearest image of the Divine Plane that it is possible for the human mind to grasp at this stage of our development. For a few moments, simply feel into the power and the presence of the Sacred Heart.

8. Silently, say the following prayer:

O Sacred Heart of Jesus, to Thee I consecrate and offer up my person and my life, my actions, trials, and sufferings, that my entire being may henceforth only be employed in loving, honoring, and glorifying Thee. This is my irrevocable will, to belong entirely to Thee, and to do all for Thy love, renouncing with my whole heart all that can displease Thee.

I take Thee, O Sacred Heart, for the sole object of my love, the protection of my life, the pledge of my salvation, the remedy of my frailty and inconstancy, the reparation for all the defects of my life, and my secure refuge at the hour of my death. Be Thou, O Most Merciful Heart, my justification before God Thy Father, and screen me from His anger which I have so justly merited. I fear all from my own weakness and malice, but placing my entire confidence in Thee, O Heart of Love, I hope all from Thine infinite Goodness. Annihilate in me all that can displease or resist Thee. Imprint Thy pure love so deeply in my heart that I may never forget Thee or be separated from Thee.

I beseech Thee, through Thine infinite Goodness, grant that my name be engraved upon Thy Heart, for in this I place all my happiness and all my glory, to live and to die as one of Thy devoted servants.

9. Now, imagine the Sacred Heart begins to shrink, gathering itself from the ends of the universe and rushing inward, with all of its power. At last, it gathers itself into the center of your body, in the space of your own heart. Imagine the Sacred Heart of Jesus in the middle of your chest, beating in time with your own heart and filling your life's blood with its holy and healing power. Know that the Sacred Heart is always within you.

10. Spend a few minutes in contemplation of the Sacred Heart within you. Then spend a few minutes breathing rhythmically. When you are ready, slowly open your eyes. Rise to your feet, and offer the following prayer:

Almighty God, Eternal Father, I thank you for the gift of your son, Our Lord Jesus Christ, and of his most Sacred Heart. I pray that, as I consecrate myself this day to the Sacred Heart of Jesus, I may be united to you and forever do your will upon the Earth. Through the same Jesus Christ our Lord, Amen.

11. Perform the Closing ritual.

PART IV

SACRAMENTAL THAUMATURGY

Introduction

As previously discussed, thaumaturgy means "wonder working." While a theurgical rite elevates the consciousness of the magician, a work of thaumaturgy seeks to cause some change outside of the magician's own consciousness. This is why theurgy always has to come before thaumaturgy. Before we start changing things in our world, we need to make sure that we are the kinds of people who ought to be causing those changes. And as we've said many times in this book, we do so by uniting our own will to the eternal will of God.

In practice, rites of thaumaturgy look much the same as rites of theurgy. We will begin with the Opening in most cases, but rather than simply invoking a saint or performing a devotion, we will then proceed to a series of prayers designed to bring about the effect that we want.

Thaumaturgy is actually very common in Church tradition. The best-known forms of Christian thaumaturgy are the consecration of sacramentals and the praying of special prayers to saints and angels. At one time it was also very common to pray the Psalms in order to bring about specific magical effects. This has fallen out of practice in recent years in Britain and North America, but this is still done in many parts of the Christian world. In the chapters to follow we will look at all of these methods of thaumaturgy, and a few others as well.

LESSON 1

The principles of effective magic

Knowledge lecture

Magic is a practical art, and it is an experiential art. As with any art, it relies on certain principles in order to achieve its effects. Many people think that we don't know how magic works, or that the rules of magic were given once, perhaps by ancient gods or angels, in some previous epoch now forgotten. Still other people think that magic can simply be whatever you want it to be. Finally, many people simply think that magic doesn't work at all, because they expect it to work "like magic," which is to say, like magic works in TV and movies.

None of this is true. While it is certainly the case that much of the magic of the Western world has been lost in the various catastrophes of the past 2,000-odd years, it is also the case that magic as it is now practiced relies on a set of fairly straightforward principles to achieve its results. When these principles are practiced carefully, magic usually works; when they are not, it usually fails. The following knowledge lecture presents the principles of effective magic in the form of six laws. Read these carefully before you move on to the chapters that follow.

The law of the planes: know the landscape

As discussed above, everything on the material plane corresponds to forces on the planes above it: energetic, astral, intellectual, and divine. This is a major part of how magic works: On the material level, we can make use of natural objects or human artifacts which are attuned to specific influences on higher levels. For example, gold, sunflowers, frankincense, and the colors yellow and white are physical substances which are said to correspond to the Sun on the Astral Plane. The energy of the Sun and solar objects raises the vital spirits and restores health and enthusiasm. On the Intellectual Plane, the Sun is said to be governed by the Archangel Michael. On the Divine Plane, it is sometimes assigned to a certain name of God, usually Yahweh Elo'ah Ve'Da'ath, which is Hebrew for "God of Knowledge." (Note that we don't mean a separate divine being named "the God of Knowledge," but rather God Himself as the God of Knowledge.) In order to bring solar influences into our life, we can combine all these things, including solar stones and frankincense, images of Saint Michael the Archangel, and calling upon God under the appropriate name.

It is important to note, however, that the structure of the planes (see below) isn't limited to astrology and applies whether or not you wish to make use of astrology. Every saint has their particular patronage, as we have seen. They also have their special attributes, which are special objects, natural substances, and colors associated with them. And, as we have seen, each also relates to a particular activity of God. Saint Therese of Lisieux, for example, is associated with roses. If you wish to form a relationship with her, you might set up a small shrine with an image of the saint and a rose flower, and burn some incense with rose in it, then say a special prayer associated with her. Remember that all prayer is ultimately directed to God, and when we close the prayer with "Pray for us" (Ora pro nobis), we call on that special divine current of which the saint is a conduit.

The law of intention: what is your goal?

Intention is central to all magical practice.

It is critical to understand this. In order to accomplish any work of magic, you need to be clear as to exactly what you are trying to accomplish.

This may seem obvious, and sometimes it is. You may have a specific health condition that you want to overcome, or you may want to sell your house or to buy a new house. Frequently, though, our desires are not this straightforward. Often when we examine our desires, we discover that what we want isn't really what we want—and we just as frequently discover that we don't actually know what we want!

Consider a very simple magical intention. Suppose that you want a better job. Okay, that's a great start. But what do you mean by "better"? Do you mean a job that you will enjoy more, or a job where you will be more respected? A job with better benefits? Perhaps a job with coworkers who you will like—or at least, a job without the coworkers that you currently dislike. Maybe you want a job that's closer to home, so you don't have to commute. Or maybe you just want a job that pays more. Also, what do you mean by "job"? Are you looking to advance in your current career, to shift gears to a different area, or to change careers entirely? Perhaps you're looking to turn a current hobby into a full-time job, or perhaps you simply don't know what you want to do, and you'd like to find out.

Let's suppose you're struggling with a job that pays poorly, and where you are not respected. Let's suppose, further, that you have a family to support. You'd like to see your children able to afford extracurricular activities at school, and to be able to take them on a nice vacation once or twice a year. That's all perfectly reasonable. Furthermore, you've decided that you're happy with your current career, but not with the company you are working for or your current position. You'd like more money for the reasons specified, and you'd like the sense of dignity and self-respect that you'd derive from a better position.

These are the things to focus on when formulating your magical working. "I would like to find a job which gives me both more authority and responsibility, and in which I will make enough money to afford to pay for my children's extracurricular activities and take them on vacation twice a year."

It is critical, when formulating an intention, to focus on what you want to accomplish, not what you want to avoid. Intention should always be positive, not negative. "I want a job," not, "I want to stop being poor." "I want to be healthy," not, "I want to stop being sick." "I want a satisfying romantic relationship," not, "I want to stop being lonely." "I want to heal my marriage," not, "I want us to stop fighting."

This is even true when your focus actually is on something that you want to stop. Many people, especially in recent years, have wasted enormous amounts of magical energy by flinging curses, bindings, and similarly destructive forms of magic at their enemies. Both as a matter of ethics and as a matter of simple strategy it is far better to build what you want than to destroy what you hate.

The law of correspondences: choosing the right source of power

This one is fairly simple. Once you have your intention worked out, you need to figure out who you are going to turn to for help. It's important to pick the right source of power for a job. You can't turn the lights on with water or make coffee out of electricity. You don't hire a plumber to watch your cat or a cat-sitter to fix your drains.

The things on Earth are governed by the things in Heaven. Different traditions have different means of invoking the heavenly powers which rule and give form to the things on Earth. In the Christian tradition, we turn to the angels and saints. And so it's important to pick the right saint for the job.

In this case, your very best bet is to turn to Saint Joseph. He is both the patron of workers and the guardian of the Holy Family, and an excellent source of help for working parents, particularly fathers. There are many forms of devotion to Saint Joseph, and simply taking up the act of regularly praying to him and getting to know him will help. But in this case, your best bet is to pray a novena to him.

The novena to Saint Joseph consists of nine days of prayer to the saint. Many different traditional novenas to Saint Joseph exist, and you can find them by searching online or by looking in a novena book. In a pinch, you can simply say Saint Joseph's traditional prayer for nine days. Every time, you will mention your specific intention, as in the following example:

The traditional prayer of Saint Joseph:

> O Saint Joseph, whose protection is so great, so strong, so prompt before the Throne of God, I place in you all my interests and desires.
> O Saint Joseph, do assist me by your powerful intercession and obtain for me from your Divine Son, all spiritual blessings through Jesus Christ, Our Lord, so that having engaged here below your

heavenly power, I may offer my thanksgiving and homage to the most loving of fathers.

O Saint Joseph, I never weary of contemplating you and Jesus asleep in your arms. I dare not approach while He reposes near your heart. Press Him in my name and kiss His fine head for me, and ask Him to return the kiss when I draw my dying breath.

Add your intention:

Saint Joseph, please help me to find a job which gives me both more authority and responsibility, and in which I will make enough money to afford to pay for my children's extracurricular activities and take them on vacation twice a year.

The traditional prayer of Saint Joseph ends with the following words:
Saint Joseph, patron of the departing souls, pray for us. Amen.
In this case, you might modify this a bit, and say:

Saint Joseph, Patron of the departing souls, of working men, and of fathers, pray for us. Amen.

The law of Heaven and Earth: pick the time and place

The term "Heaven and Earth" is derived from *The Art of War*, the ancient Chinese text by Sun Tzu. *The Art of War* is a book of military strategy, but its lessons are applicable to nearly any area of life—magic very much included.

In Sun Tzu's terms, "Heaven" means weather conditions, the season of the year, and other outside influences such as astrological factors. "Earth" means terrain—where a battle will be fought, the kinds of landforms through which an army will have to march, and so on. In the context of magical work, we can think of Heaven and Earth simply as time and place.

To return to our example, if you are looking for another job in your field, are there particular seasons of the year in which new hiring takes place? Some companies employ workers on a seasonal basis only. Farms hire extra hands during the harvest season; resorts hire for the summer time. I once knew a guy who had a pool cleaning business.

His crews began work in the spring, continued through summer, put in sixty hours a week during the fall, and then took off December through February. If it's November and you need a new job this week, you're going to be out of luck with a company like that. Be willing to put in a little legwork and find out details like these. If you're looking to work for a specific company, is there a time of year they like to bring in new hires? Or does it look like a position is going to open up in three months, when someone retires? Knowledge like this will always help you.

Furthermore, you need to think about your own time frame. If you say a novena to Saint Joseph asking for a better job, it's best to give the saint a time frame in which to work. If you keep it vague, you won't be able to judge success. If, on the other hand, you demand your desire be accomplished in an unreasonable amount of time, you're less likely to succeed or to obtain the specific results you want. At the same time, sometimes a narrow time frame is necessary. You may need a new job by next Monday in order to pay the mortgage, and, if so, you need to say so.

All other things being equal, it's best to allow one year for your desires to manifest. And so we would modify the prayer above in the following way:

> Saint Joseph, please help me to find a job *in the next year* which gives me both more authority and responsibility, and in which I will make enough money to afford to pay for my children's extracurricular activities and take them on vacation twice a year.

In *The Art of War*, "Earth" refers to terrain—will the army need to cross a river, will the chariots be able to make it through a mountain pass, and so on. For our purposes, many of the same details apply. Consider the terrain. Is there a specific company you want to work for? If so, you need to learn as much about them as you can. Is there a specific place in which you wish to work? Are you only willing to consider jobs within thirty minutes of your home, are you willing to accept a longer commute, or are you looking to relocate? If so, where to?

If you decide you don't care which specific company you work for as long as it meets your specifications, but you're okay with a commute, you might modify the prayer to say:

> Saint Joseph, please help me to find a job in the next year, *within an hour of my home*, which gives me both more authority and

responsibility, and in which I will make enough money to afford to pay for my children's extracurricular activities and take them on vacation twice a year.

The law of form: create an appropriate form

One of the misconceptions that non-practitioners have about magic is that we just don't know how it works. Maybe in a certain, final sense this is true—the sense in which we can't *really* know anything. For all practical purposes, we have a very simple and straightforward model of how magic works, which shows us what we need to do in order to successfully accomplish a magical operation.

We've seen that we need to start by keeping our model of the universe in mind, formulating an intention, and connecting with an appropriate source of power. The next step is to create a form in which that power can manifest.

How do we do this?

That's where imagination comes in.

Remember that imagination is the substance of the Astral Plane. The Astral Plane will provide the form for our magical workings. This form will then be "charged" with the force that we've called upon from those higher realms, the Divine and Intellectual Planes. Whenever we want to accomplish something through magic, we need to create a suitable form on the Astral Plane, and we do that by visualizing exactly what we want, in as much detail as possible. We do this as part of the process of the magical working itself. Every prayer or novena should include a period of meditation during which you will visualize exactly what you are trying to accomplish. The astral image is the form; the higher planes provide the force. It will then descend downward into the Physical and Energetic Planes. We will discuss this more as we proceed.

In the example given above, after saying the prayer to Saint Joseph, the next thing to do is to sit down, enter into meditation, and imagine the results of your working as though they were happening right now. Picture yourself looking at your bank statement and seeing enough money that you feel yourself relax. Imagine buying your children new equipment for sports or other activities and relaxing with them on the beach in the Outer Banks or Ocean City.

Of course, the form that we create will in many cases also include a material base. In some cases, our goal is specifically to charge a material form with some sort of magical intention. Often the intention is a general blessing, healing, or protective power: This is the case with sacramentals such as holy water or incense. Sometimes the intention is more specific, as when a sachet of roses is consecrated in order to bring love, or cinquefoil is consecrated to bring wealth. In this case, the material form is provided by an image of the saint, the use of incense, and the actions and posture of your body as you pray and enter into meditation. If you need to, you can pray a novena by connecting to the saint and reciting the suitable prayers while sitting on a bus or driving your car, but you should never totally neglect the Material Plane.

A note of warning

The following is critical:

When you create a form on the Astral Plane, you must *not* interfere with your own magic by setting up contrary forms. If you're trying to get a job, you need to have confidence that your intention is accomplished, and *not* spend your time worrying about it. On the Astral Plane, feelings are things, and all of that worry is itself an astral form. If you draw down energy in order to charge a form of "getting a job," but the form you create is one of "not having a job and fretting about it," you will set up a massive current of interference which can block you from achieving your goals. This is a mistake that a great many people make in magic.

It's also a very easy mistake to make. After all, you wouldn't be asking a saint for help if you didn't need something. And so it's very easy to spend your time worrying about the thing that you don't have and thinking about just how much you don't have it—and that's precisely what's going to keep you from getting it. Fortunately, there are a few ways to work around it.

The first workaround is a very important spiritual practice under any circumstances. It's a simple yet powerful form of magic, which in English we call *gratitude*. Gratitude has a healing power which is easy to underestimate. The simple act of making a list of all the things in our lives that we're grateful for and giving thanks to God has a transformative effect on the soul as potent as any complex magical ritual. This is a great way to short-circuit your worries, and create an astral form based on *having*, not *wanting*.

Of course, it can sometimes be hard to be grateful for what you have, especially when you've deliberately turned to magic in order to get something that you lack. But it's still possible and still important. In the case above, you would be advised to think, regularly, about everything that your current job has given you. You would remember how much you needed that job back when you got it a few years ago, and how grateful you were to have it. You would think on how grateful you are to have a job at all, given the state of the economy. And you would think on all of the things that your current job gives you—money, even if you'd like more; colleagues you know and like; a chance to gain skills which will help you in the future.

Gratitude is possible even under the darkest circumstances. It is a hard thing to experience a health crisis, but if we allow it, very often we find that underlying our ill health is our body rebelling against our own bad habits. If we can listen now and change our lifestyles, we often find that our health clears up on its own—and we feel much better.

Even in cases of great personal tragedy gratitude is possible. When someone we love dies, we can be grateful for having them in our lives and for the time we were able to share with them. We can be grateful that they are released from pain and suffering, and from bondage to the material world. We can be grateful for the love and support that we receive from others in our hour of need. Indeed, it's often the case that death and loss bring people together who were otherwise at odds or not even speaking to one another. To persevere in gratitude in the face of loss is a hard thing, but it will heal our souls if we allow it to.

The second method for overcoming the currents of interference that our negative thoughts can produce is simply to create a workaround. This will vary from circumstance to circumstance, but it basically consists of "hedging your bets." If you want a specific thing, you should focus on that, but you should consider alternatives which would be *good enough* to relieve the pressure you feel around it. Once my wife and I were in urgent need of a new place to live, for the simple reason that she'd found a new job in another state—starting in a week! We sent out applications to as many different rental agencies as possible, but heard nothing back. As the days wore on and we grew more desperate, we decided that we would rent a house on Airbnb for the week. This was more expensive than simply having a house to live in, and certainly a temporary solution. But once we had set up the rental, we were able to relax. We knew that, if nothing else, we would at least have somewhere to sleep at night, and we could return to the state we lived in on the weekend. Once we had done this, we promptly got calls from three different rental agencies, telling us that our application had been accepted. We went with the best offer, and within a couple of years were able to buy the place outright from the landlord.

The same principle can be applied to most circumstances. If you're a writer trying to publish a book, you can commit to yourself that if you don't find a publisher by a certain date, you'll simply publish the book yourself. Research self-publishing platforms and marketing methods, and prepare your manuscript for publication. To return to our example, there are a few different things you could do. First, you can take another close look at what expenses you can cut to save money. And second, you can come up with a list of possible second jobs, perhaps offering either temporary employment or work from home, in order to come up with the extra funds you need. This might be something like a department store which needs extra help during Christmas or a farm hiring extra hands for the fall. It isn't ideal, but something where you can work one or two days a week might be enough to cover you for right now.

The law of action: take the first step

Once you've formulated your intention and created your magical working, the next step is to take action.

It is critical, immediately after any magical working, to take at least one small step to bring it into manifestation. In the example above, the very next thing to do after your first prayer to Saint Joseph is to look for jobs and send out at least one resume. That is, unless your resume isn't up to date. Then you need to start with that. If you simply pray for a job and hope one will fall into your lap—well, sometimes this actually will work, but most of the time, you're going to need to do the legwork yourself.

This step then needs to be continued daily. One resume sent out once won't do it—unless you hear back right away. You need to take daily action, until your intention is completed.

One very effective way to enhance your magical work is through giving. This may seem difficult, especially when you're feeling desperate. It is always worth it. By giving, we do several different things at once. First, we remind ourselves that we have more than we think. No matter how poorly off you think you are, there is always someone you can help. In addition to simply being the right thing to do, this will also reinforce your sense of gratitude in what you have and your own sense of self-worth.

Giving can also be used strategically, in order to connect with the specific energies you want to bring into manifestation. If you're looking for housing, you can donate to a charity which provides homes to those in need. If you're a musician releasing an album or an artist hoping to sell a painting, you can make a donation to a charity which helps people learn how to perform music or paint, or which provides instruments or art supplies to people in need.

In our example, you might make a $100 donation to a job-training organization, especially in the field you work in. You might also make a donation directly to any church or charity which has Saint Joseph for its patron.

When you make donations of this kind, it's important to do so without expectation of reward. Think of it, instead, as giving back. God and the saints have already helped you, and so you're taking the opportunity to help someone else—and to become closer to the saints and to God in this way.

As a final note on this subject, never assume that "giving" is limited to either monetary donations or to formal charities. Often this isn't the best form of giving. Leaving a $100 tip at a restaurant can often make a bigger difference in someone's life than donating that $100 to a large charity which will pay most of it out to its staff. Mowing your neighbor's lawn in addition to your own, calling someone you know who might be lonely, or picking up trash all by yourself and without a group or permit at a local park are all great ways to give. Giving in this way should be part of your regular spiritual practice. When you're trying to accomplish some specific magical intention, well, that's not time to *start* giving. It's time to give something more.

LESSON 2

Sacred things: the sacramentals of the Church

An introduction to sacramentals

We come now to what are probably the best known sacramentals, the sacramental objects. This includes a wide range of material substances traditionally blessed and consecrated in order to confer certain virtues. Holy water is probably the best known, as even most Novus Ordo Catholic churches still make it available. We will refer to these objects as "sacramentals" generally, and you should understand that, in this chapter, it is these sacred substances that we are referring to.

Sacramentals can be divided into two broad categories. We will call these traditional sacramentals and natural sacramentals. Traditional sacramentals include all those sacred objects which have historically been blessed for various purposes by the Catholic Church and other sacramental Churches. Among these are holy water and consecrated salt, olive oil and incense, the palms used on Palm Sunday, crucifixes, images of saints, bells, and images.

There are traditional blessings for a far wider range of things than many people are now aware of. The old Roman Ritual includes blessings for animals of every variety, crop and pasture lands, even the cornerstones of buildings. This is because the traditional worldview, which is also the magical worldview, sees the spiritual and the material as continuous with one another, not as totally separate realms. Every work of Nature or of human hands is a fit receptacle for the grace of God.

We'll define "natural sacramentals" as those sacramentals which you can create for yourself, using natural substances. We've seen that everything in the world of Nature may be assigned to the seven classical planets and to the four traditional elements. In addition to these categories, many plants, stones, and even animals have their own traditional magical properties. In order to create a sacramental which will confer whatever power we instruct it in, we can make use of these natural objects and enhance their natural properties through a ritual of consecration.

Whether you are using a traditional or a natural sacramental, it is critical that you be very specific in your intention, both in your own mind and when you instruct the sacramental in its purpose. It will take on exactly the properties which you give it. To give an example of how this looks, to anyone with their faculties of inner vision developed even modestly can see and feel that the holy water used in modern Catholic churches is extremely weak. It isn't useless—it just doesn't do that much. In my experience, it has a thin, milk-like quality, and is certainly nothing I'd rely on for spiritual protection. Holy water blessed in the traditional rite, on the other hand, is far more robust.

You can understand the reason if you compare the two blessings. Traditional holy water is actually a combination of two substances, water and salt. These two have their own properties—water purifies, and salt absorbs negativity. Each is exorcised, so that any evil power or negative energy residing in the substance is driven out. They are then blessed and given the power to protect any person or place which they touch from evil spirits and harmful magic, and to bring health to both body and soul. Modern "holy water," by contrast, is not exorcised, rarely mixed with salt, and instructed only to be a reminder of Jesus and to "refresh" those who make use of it. Each of these works precisely as advertised.

Blessing sacramentals

The Church has its own standard formulae for blessing sacramentals. In our work, we can make use of these as they are, and we can modify them based on the principles of magical philosophy. This allows us to make use of the built-up energy of the traditional modes of blessing, while also using the techniques of ceremonial magic to enhance their power using tried and tested means.

In the following part, we will present a general formula for blessing sacramentals, which you can use for either traditional or natural sacramentals. This will be followed by two separate lists, one for traditional and one for natural sacramentals. The traditional sacramentals can be blessed by following the general formula, and then blessing the sacramental by use of the traditional prayers. The natural sacramentals will require a slightly different approach. We will provide a short list of natural objects, and a few examples, but in terms of their function, you are on your own.

The Universal Ritual of Blessing

The setup and the structure of the ritual for sacramentals of both types is the same. We will call this the Universal Ritual of Blessing.

Preparation. Set up your temple space in the usual way. You will need your altar, with holy water and incense, and whatever sacramental you plan to bless.

If you are consecrating a traditional sacramental, you should do your best to memorize the prayers of blessing *before* the ritual. Meditation can be a great help to this process. If the prayers are lengthy, as those for holy water, take one or two lines each day as a theme for meditation. This will both enable you to understand the hidden depths of the prayer and the sacramental, and to commit the prayer to memory. This is helpful even if you already know the prayer. Especially the first time you consecrate a particular sacramental, you should devote at least one session of serious meditation on the sacramental and its associated prayers, before the ritual itself.

If you are consecrating a natural sacramental, you should make sure to prepare ahead of time in the same way. Spend some time meditating on your intention for the sacramental and its purpose.

Step 1. Perform the complete Opening Ritual, including the Asperges, the Censing, and the Invocation.

Step 2. Declaration of purpose. Say:

I proclaim this temple open for the purpose of [name the purpose: consecration of holy oil, consecration of oil, etc.]. Direct, O Lord, I beseech thee, the completion of this work by thy holy inspirations, and carry it on by thy gracious assistance, that every prayer and work of ours may begin always from thee, and by thee be happily ended. Through Christ our Lord. Amen.

Step 3. *At this point and not before*, proceed to the steps given for the specific sacramental. When you reach the end of the consecration given, proceed to the next step.

Step 4. You may now enter into meditation, taking the sacramental itself and your purposes for it as your theme. Imagine it as a kind of living being, as it has become a channel of divine grace. It might be that certain ideas regarding its use may come to you, and you should pay special attention to these.

Step 5. Close the temple in the usual way. Your sacramental is now ready for use.

Notes for practice

The Ritual of Blessing should be memorized before you proceed. Once you can practice it from memory, you should proceed to the following lesson, which gives specific formulae of blessing for many different sacramentals of the Church. Of these, you should be prepared to at least bless holy water and incense. If you plan to proceed on to the *next* part of the book, you should take the time to consecrate *all* of the traditional sacramentals.

LESSON 3

Traditional sacramentals

You should be prepared to consecrate each of the following sacramentals. You will find some more useful than others, but all have a role to play both on their own and in our work as we progress in magic.

Remember: In each case, we will begin by performing the complete Opening ritual, including the Banishing Ritual of the Cross, the Asperges with holy water, the Censing with incense, and the Invocation. The first sacramental we are going to consecrate is holy water itself, so you will need to begin by acquiring holy water from another source, such as a local Catholic or Orthodox church.

After performing the Opening, proceed to the steps listed under each sacramental.

A note: Remember, any time you come across a plus sign (+), draw a cross with your fingers over the sacramental. Visualize it in bright white light, and imagine the power of the cross descends into the sacramental.

Holy water

Preparation. The creation of holy water is actually a multi-step process. You will need not only water but salt. Both of these should be as pure as possible. For the salt, do not use ordinary table salt. This is usually adulterated with additional chemicals such as anti-caking agents. Any salt which is labeled "Kosher salt" will be free of additives, and you can also use sea salt or a mineral salt such as Himalayan pink salt.

Water can be ordinary tap water, but it's better to use water from a natural source such as a river. If you have a healing spring of some kind nearby, especially if there is a shrine there, this is a very good option. Rainwater is also a nice option, especially in the spring.

Step 1. The exorcism of salt

Turn your attention to the salt and say the following words:

> I exorcise thee, creature of salt, by the + living God, by the true + God, by God, who, commanded thee to be cast by the Prophet Eliseus into the water to heal it of its sterility: so that thou mayest be a purified salt, a means of health for the faithful; and a means of health for the soul and body of all who make use of thee. May all fantasies, all evil, and all cunning of the devil be driven far from the place in which thou art cast, and may every evil spirit be driven forth by He who is coming to judge the living and the dead and the world by fire. Amen.

Step 3: The blessing of salt

> Almighty and Eternal God, we humbly implore thy great mercy, that you may deign to + bless and + sanctify that this creature of salt, which is given by thee for the use of mankind, so that all who make use of it may find in it a remedy for mind and body. And may whatsoever is touched or sprinkled by it be freed from every uncleanness and evil influence of the evil spirit. Through Christ our Lord, Amen.

Step 4: The exorcism of water

> I exorcise thee, creature of water, in the name of almighty God the Father, and in the name of Jesus Christ, his son, our lord, and in

the power of the Holy Spirit: so that thou may be a purified water, empowered to drive out all power of the Enemy, and to uproot and drive forth the Enemy himself, with his fallen angels, through the power of Jesus Christ our Lord, who is coming to judge the living and the dead and the world by fire. Amen.

Step 5: The blessing of water

Let us pray. God, who for the health of mankind established the Mysteries of the substance of water: Hear our prayer and pour forth the power of thy + blessing on this element prepared by the various rites of purification. So that thy creature, in service of thy Mysteries, may serve to drive forth demons and banish disease by the power of thy grace. May whatsoever is sprinkled by this water in the homes or in the places of the faithful be delivered from all that is unclean and harmful. Let no breath of contagion hover there, no taint of corruption; let all the deception of the hidden enemy come to nothing. By the sprinkling of this water may everything opposed to the peace and safety of those who dwell in these homes be banished, so that by the invocation of thy holy name they may know the well-being they seek, and be protected from every danger. Through Jesus Christ thine only Son our Lord, who lives and reigns with you in the unity of the Holy Spirit, God for ever unto the ages of ages.

Pour the salt into the water, and say:

Let this salt and this water be mixed together, in the name of the + Father, and of the + Son, and of the + Holy Spirit. Amen.

Step 6: The final blessing
Hold your hands in the orans posture, and say:

Let us pray.
God, author of power unconquered, king of an unsurpassable realm, ever glorious conqueror: who restrains the forces of the adversary, silencing the uproar of his rage and subduing his wickedness. Thee O Lord, in fear and trembling, we ask, that you look with favor upon this creature of salt and water. Let the

light of thy goodness shine upon it and sanctify it with the dew
of thy mercy; so that wherever it is sprinkled and thy holy name
invoked, every assault of the unclean spirit may be baffled, and
all dread for the serpent's venom be cast out. Through Jesus
Christ thine only Son Our Lord: Who livest and reignest with
thee in the unity of the Holy Spirit, God forever and unto the ages
of ages. Amen.

Step 7. Close your temple in the usual way. The holy water may now be used for whatever purpose you desire.

Incense

Preparation. Incense can be stick incense, loose resin, or dried plant material. It should always be 100% natural. If you have any doubts about this, don't use it. Natural incense can be purchased cheaply online, and it's much more pleasant than the sort of incense sticks that you can find at the mall.

Frankincense or a mix of frankincense and myrrh are good choices, as are sandalwood and benzoin. Smudges made from sage, cedar, juniper, or sweetgrass are easy to find and are also very good, though you should note that sage produces a very great deal of smoke. Some notes on incenses will be included in the appendix.

You should also have an image of St. Michael the Archangel on your altar.

Step 1. Hold your hands in the orans posture, and say:

> By the intercession of Blessed Michael the Archangel, who stands
> at the right hand of the altar of incense, and all of his elect, may
> the Lord design to bless + this incense, and to receive it as a sweet
> fragrance. Through Christ our Lord, amen.

Hold the incense aloft, and say:

May this incense blessed by thee ascend unto thee, O Lord, and may thy mercy descend upon us.

You may burn the incense immediately, or reserve all or some of it for future use.

Step 3. Close the temple in the usual way.

Candles and fire

Fire is a powerful source of spiritual nourishment. In very ancient times, the hearth fire of every family was the family's god and protective spirit. This idea is not at all foreign to our tradition—we simply see that the protective spirit of the fire is gathered under St. Michael the Archangel, who governs the element of fire, and that even the highest of the angels are but servants of God.

Candles are regularly used in many kinds of Christian traditional magic. They play a role in the mass itself. Candles are blessed on Candlemas, February 2nd, and blessed candles are used to confer a protective blessing on the throats of parishioners on St. Blaise's Day, February 3rd. They are also used in prayers to the saints and to the Trinity directed toward specific intentions. Some of this traditional candle magic was lost in modern America, but with mass immigration from countries in which the tradition was preserved, this situation has been reversed. Now, across the United States, one can find candles for use in magic, with images of the saints and prayers in good Spanish and bad English. Don't be afraid to make use of these; they are quite powerful.

The blessing of candles presented here is a general purpose blessing, derived from the blessing of candles on Candlemas. Candles so blessed will prove to be a source of spiritual nourishment and protection, and may be put to any purpose you like. It can easily be modified to bless hearth fires, bonfires, or candles used for more specific ends.

The blessing of candles

Preparation. For this you will need an altar with a crucifix and whatever other holy images you like, as well as a cup or bowl of holy water and a censor or bowl for incense. You will also need a candle. Candles made from natural waxes such as soy or tallow are best. Beeswax candles are best of all. But the ritual will suffice to bless a common paraffin wax candle as well. You can even bless scented candles such as those which people often use at Christmas or in the fall. Scents derived from natural material are more magically effective, but as a general rule they are not very strong. So use your own judgment.

Step 1. Hold your hands over the candle and say the following prayer:

O Lord Jesus Christ, the true light, who enlightenest every man coming into this world, pour forth Thy blessing + upon these candles, and sanctify + them with the light of Thy grace; and mercifully grant, that as these lights enkindled with visible fire dispel the darkness of night, so our hearts illumined by invisible fire, that is, the light of thy Holy Spirit, may be free from the blindness of every sin; that the eye of our minds being purified, we may be able to discern what is pleasing to Thee and conducive to our salvation; so that after the perilous darkness of this life we may merit to arrive in the light that never fails. Through Thee, Christ Jesus, Saviour of the world, who in perfect Trinity livest and reignest God, world without end.

Sprinkle the candle three times with holy water.

Step 3. You may enter into meditation for a time, considering the words of the prayer and your intention for the candle so blessed.

Step 4. Perform the complete Closing. This completes the ritual.

You may now use your blessed candle for any purpose you desire. If it is at all possible—if you have a wall sconce in a safe location—you should keep it burning. Especially in homes with children and animals, this is often inadvisable. When you have to snuff your candle, make the sign of the cross over it and say a prayer such as, "Though the light of this candle is extinguished for a time, let it continue to shine hiddenly within this home and the hearts of all who dwell herein, and may its blessing endure until such time as it be lit again."

Holy oil

Consecrated olive oil has a long history of use in traditional Christian magic. In fact, it is necessary to several of the sacraments.

In Catholicism there are three forms of blessed oil. The first is called the Oil of the Catechumens. The second is the Holy Chrism. And the third is the Oil of the Sick. The Oil of the Catechumens is used to anoint the body of those about to be baptized, and the baptismal font itself and to anoint the hands of the priest. It is also used to anoint a monarch at their coronation. The Oil of the Sick is used to anoint the body of a person on the brink of death, during the sacrament of Extreme Unction or Anointing of the Sick. The Holy Chrism is the most powerful of the oils. It is used at a confirmation and at the consecration of a bishop, and also to consecrate a few of the most important of sacred objects, especially altars, churches, and church bells.

For our purposes, it will suffice to create two oils. We will call the first the Oil of Healing, and the second the Oil of Empowerment.

The purpose of the Oil of Healing is similar to that of the Oil of the Sick. The difference is that it will not be used only in the case of the sacrament of Extreme Unction, but as a general purpose healing oil. This is also done to an extent with the Oil of the Sick, as it is also used to anoint church bells, but we will take it further. In practice it will be found to be a helpful remedy, especially for afflictions of the spirit and the energetic body. In the place of the Holy Chrism we will use the Oil of Empowerment. This will also serve a similar purpose, but will have a broader range of applications.

The Oil of Healing

Preparation. For this ritual, you will need your altar, set up in the usual way. You will also need a container of oil. Please make sure that it is 100% olive oil, organic if at all possible, from a container which has not previously been opened. Olive oil is sometimes sold adulterated with canola or sunflower oil. Avoid this. Canola oil by itself, "vegetable" oil, coconut oil, or some other oil is not suitable for our purposes. (At least at first. Down the road a ways, once you get a good feel for the results of magical workings like this, you may experiment with other oils if you wish.)

Please note that this is a general purpose oil, which is why it uses pure olive oil alone, and its consecration refers to its intention as kind of all-purpose oil. But oils for more specific purposes can be made and consecrated, by infusing olive oil with particular plants or by adding the essential oils of those plants. We will discuss this in greater detail in the next chapter. For now, we're going to consecrate pure olive oil, all by itself.

Step 1. Say:

> Almighty God, I pray that you will + bless this oil of healing, that it may wipe out every weakness and infirmity of body or soul of whosoever is anointed by it, and that it may act as a remedy against every work of the evil spirit and every act of evil magic; that it may lead whosoever is anointed by it to repentance, and guide them

to salvation and eternal life; and that it may be a source of perfect well-being. Let it be blessed in the Name of the + Father and of the + Son and of the + Holy Spirit. Amen.

The oil may now be used for whatever purpose you desire.

The Oil of Empowerment

Preparation. See the instructions for preparing the Oil of Healing. Use 100% olive oil, from a container which has not previously been opened.

In the traditional rites, the oil of the Holy Chrism is scented with resin, unlike the Oil of the Sick. We will follow this custom in the preparation of the Oil of Empowerment. Here you have two options. You may either add one to three drops of a pure essential oil to your Oil of Empowerment, or you may infuse the oil with whole plant material. If you use essential oils, make sure to buy them from a reputable source. They should be labeled "therapeutic grade." Beware of suspiciously cheap essential oils for sale on the internet, often produced in China; these are usually fraudulent. Resources for purchasing herbs and essential oils will be found in the appendix.

In order to make an herbal infusion, you simply need to take a small amount of fresh or dried plant material and soak it in your oil for six weeks. After that time, remove the plant material and consecrate the oil. One very good option is to take cuttings from Christmas trees, which are usually firs or spruces, in December, when these are widely available. Even if you don't use a live Christmas tree in your home, it's easy to find garlands or to ask a friend or neighbor for some cuttings from their tree; they'll almost certainly have them as trees usually need to be trimmed before they'll fit in a tree stand. You may use essential oils of fir, spruce, or cedar. Frankincense is also a nice option.

Step 1. Say:

> Lord God almighty, before whom the hosts of angels stand in awe, and whose heavenly service we acknowledge; may it please you to regard favorably and to bless + and hallow + this creature, oil, which by your power has been pressed from the juice of olives.
>
> Let the power of the Holy Spirit descend into it, that the divine gifts may descend upon all those who are anointed by it.

Step 2. The invocation of the Holy Spirit.
Say the Holy Spirit prayer:

> Come, Holy Spirit, fill the hearts of thy faithful, and enkindle in them the fire of thy love. Thou shalt send forth thy spirit, and they shall be created, and thou shalt renew the face of the Earth.

Visualize a column of brilliant white light descending from Heaven and pouring into the oil, filling it until it seems to glow like fire.

Step 3: With hands in the orans posture, say:

> O God, who didst instruct the hearts of the apostles in the Holy Spirit, grant now that this sacred oil may be infused with the power of the Holy Spirit, and that his gifts may be imparted to all upon whom this oil is anointed. Amen.

The oil may now be used for any purpose you like, some of which will be detailed as we continue.

Bells

Bells are used in nearly every traditional Christian congregation, Catholic, Orthodox, and Protestant. There are various types of church bells, which serve different functions in different traditions. Bells are rung at the beginning of mass or worship services, and at morning, noon, and night as a signal to prayer. Bells are used in exorcisms to drive out evil spirits, and small altar bells are rung during the elevation of the host at the Eucharist to call the attention of the faithful.

For our purposes, it will be enough to have a single bell, which can serve multiple functions. The tradition of using bells or other musical instruments to purify the energy of a space is found in many traditions, as is the use of sound in healing. We will incorporate these ideas along with the traditional Christian functions of church bells in order to consecrate a single, multipurpose bell.

The traditional consecration of a church bell is a beautiful and complicated ritual, sometimes called the Baptism of the Bell. During this ceremony, the bell is washed with holy water, blessed with incense, and anointed with both the oil of healing and the oil of chrismation. Then it is given a name, just as an infant receives a name at his or her baptism.

A church bell is not merely blessed, but empowered to drive away evil spirits and even to avert storms!

The use of sound and music for magical purposes is a very rich topic, and we will not be able to adequately explore it here. A future volume in this series will consider it in more detail. In the meantime, the following ritual is intended to provide you with a bell that can be used in your magical and spiritual practice. Properly consecrated, a bell can clear and calm the energy of an entire room or even an entire house. This is very useful when, for various reasons, you don't have the ability to perform an entire banishing ritual.

The blessing of a bell

Preparation. In addition to your altar, set up with the usual crucifix and containers for water and incense, you will, of course, need a bell. A bell should be made of metal, rather than other materials such as glass or ceramic. In my experience, a "singing bowl" of the sort common in Asia, which is similar to an ordinary Western bell turned upside down, works just as well. A chime does not, but anything will do in a pinch.

You will also need both the Oil of Healing and the Oil of Empowerment. Lacking these, you can still produce a blessed bell, but not one with the same degree of power. Plan ahead.

Step 1. With hands in the orans posture, say the 29th Psalm:

> Give unto the Lord, O ye mighty, give unto the Lord glory and strength.
>
> Give unto the Lord the glory due unto his name; worship the Lord in the beauty of holiness.
>
> The voice of the Lord is upon the waters: the God of glory thundereth: the Lord is upon many waters.
>
> The voice of the Lord is powerful; the voice of the Lord is full of majesty.
>
> The voice of the Lord breaketh the cedars; yea, the Lord breaketh the cedars of Lebanon.
>
> He maketh them also to skip like a calf; Lebanon and Sirion like a young unicorn.
>
> The voice of the Lord divideth the flames of fire.
>
> The voice of the Lord shaketh the wilderness; the Lord shaketh the wilderness of Kadesh.

> The voice of the Lord maketh the hinds to calve, and discovereth the forests: and in his temple doth every one speak of his glory.
>
> The Lord sitteth upon the flood; yea, the Lord sitteth King for ever.
>
> The Lord will give strength unto his people; the Lord will bless his people with peace.

Step 4. Walk three times around the bell in a clockwise fashion (counterclockwise in the Southern Hemisphere). While you do so, sprinkle the bell on every side with holy water, and say the words of the Asperges, just as in the Opening.

Step 5. Again walk three times around the bell in a clockwise fashion (counterclockwise in the Southern Hemisphere). This time you will cense the bell on every side with incense, and pray the words of the Censing, just as in the Opening.

Step 6. Dip the thumb of your right hand in the oil of the Oil of Healing, and draw seven crosses around the outside of the bell. Wipe your thumb on a cloth or piece of bread, and then draw four crosses on the inside of the bell in the same way, this time using the Oil of Empowerment.

Step 7. Either place the bell over your burning incense, or, if you're using a singing bowl, hold it over the incense. Keep it there for a time, and imagine the power of the blessed incense permeating the bell.

Step 8. Say the following prayer:

> O God, who decreed through blessed Moses, your servant and lawgiver, that silver trumpets should be made and be sounded at the time of sacrifice: Grant, I pray, that this bell may be blessed and hallowed + by the Holy Spirit. Let the people's faith and piety wax stronger whenever they hear its melodious peals. At its sound let all evil spirits and works of destructive magic be driven afar; let thunder and lightning, hail and storm be banished; let the power of your hand put down the evil powers of the air, causing them to tremble at the sound of this bell, and to flee at the sight of the holy cross engraved thereon. May our Lord Himself grant this, who overcame death upon the cross, and who reigns now in the glory of God the Father, in the unity of the Father and the Holy Spirit, forever and ever. Amen.

Crosses

The cross, particularly when it is set with a corpus (the image of the body of Christ), has a great deal of spiritual power all on its own. That said, a cross or crucifix used in ritual or worship ought to be blessed in order to enhance its power and effectiveness.

Preparation. If you are blessing a crucifix for regular use, it will be the only cross on the altar. If you are blessing a second cross or crucifix for other uses, set it on the altar before your usual crucifix.

Step 1. Say:

> Holy Lord, almighty Father, everlasting God, be pleased to bless + this cross, that it may be a saving help to mankind. Let it be the support of faith, an encouragement to good works, the redemption of souls; and let it be consolation, protection, and a shield against the cruel darts of the enemy; through Jesus Christ our Lord. Amen.
>
> Lord Jesus Christ, bless + this cross by which you snatched the world from Satan's grasp, and on which you overcame by your suffering the tempter to sin, who rejoiced in the first man's fall in eating of the forbidden tree.

Step 2. Sprinkle the cross three times with holy water, and say:

> May this cross be hallowed in the name of the + Father, and of the + Son, and of the + Holy Spirit; and may all who kneel and pray before this cross in honor of our Lord find health in body and soul; through Christ our Lord.

Step 3. Cense the cross three times with incense.

Step 4. It is appropriate now to kneel and kiss the cross before entering into meditation.

Sacred images

"Sacred images" is a very broad category covering a wide variety of sacred images, including holy cards, icons such as are common in the Orthodox Church, as well as statues and saints' medals. This blessing will also work for rosaries and similar chaplets, such as the Saint Michael Chaplet or the Seven Sorrows chaplet. The number of items in this category is, of course, far too broad to provide individual blessings for each one. We will, instead, provide a general blessing, and a few examples.

Some medals worth mentioning specifically include the Saint Benedict Medal, the Saint Christopher Medal, and the Miraculous Medal.

General blessing for sacred images

Preparation. You will, of course, need an image to be blessed. Place it in the center of your altar. The best day to bless an image of a particular saint is on their feast day, but you can bless an image at any time. Traditionally, Tuesdays are dedicated to the angels, Wednesdays to Saint Joseph, and Saturdays to the Blessed Mother, and these are appropriate days to bless any of their images.

Step 1. With hands in the orans posture, say:

> Almighty and everlasting God, who hath not forbade us to carve or paint likenesses of your saints, in order that whenever we look at them with our bodily eyes we may call to mind their holy lives, and resolve to follow in their footsteps; may it please thee to bless + and to hallow + this image (statue, saint's medal, etc.), which has been made in memory and honor of (thine only begotten son, Jesus Christ; the Blessed Virgin Mary; blessed N., thy servant; etc.). And grant that all who in its presence pay devout homage to (thine only-begotten Son; the blessed Virgin; the blessed saint N., etc.) may by his (her) merits (and intercession, if an image of a saint) obtain your grace in this life and everlasting glory in the life to come; through Christ our Lord. Amen.

Step 2. Sprinkle the image three times with holy water.

LESSON 4

Natural sacramentals

Practical lesson

Natural sacramentals consist of natural substances which are consecrated in order to achieve a specific purpose. Because of their nature, natural sacramentals have a kind of double action. The natural material has an energy of its own, and we can then enhance and modify that through the use of prayer.

Before using a natural sacramental, it's important to understand its energy, and not to instruct it in a purpose contrary to that. Roses can be used for love magic of many different kinds; you shouldn't try to use them to induce celibacy. Frankincense is used to connect with divine energies and enhance prayer and meditation in this way, and it also has a natural protective effect. So don't try to use it in a working intended to bring wealth.

As in the case of the traditional sacramentals, this list is meant to get you started. There is an enormous literature on the subject of natural magic from every part of the world which can take you further. Some resources are mentioned in the appendixes. As a magician, you should be prepared to do your own research and read as widely as possible.

It's important to note that the use of natural sacramentals does not put us outside of the tradition of the mainstream Church. Herbs, stones, and other natural substances have been used for centuries in Christian magic. This includes practices such as passing cattle through the smoke of Saint John's wort on his Feast Day to protect them from witchcraft, the use of blessed roses on the Feast of Saint Therese, and the blessing of herbs for various purposes on the Feast of the Assumption of the Blessed Virgin Mary. In the following notes I'm going to include the astrological correspondences of various herbs. In traditional astrology and traditional magic, everything on Earth is said to be governed by things in the heavens, and many people make use of these astrological correspondences in their practice. You're welcome to make whatever use of them you like, or to ignore them if you prefer.

A list of natural sacramentals

Rose. Ruled by Venus, rose is the flower of love first and foremost. Note that this can mean romantic love, but it can also mean the higher love which unites the individual soul with the Divine.

Frankincense. Ruled by the Sun, frankincense is the incense especially suited for worship.

Patchouli. Patchouli is ruled by Venus, and it is associated with the Earth. It is earthy and musky, associated with sexuality and generation.

Cedar and juniper. These are ruled by Mars, and are powerful plants of protective magic. In cultures across the world cedar and juniper are burned in order to clear the air of negative energies, harmful magic, and sickness.

Five-finger grass. Ruled by Mercury, this herb is associated with wealth and with eloquence.

Lemon balm. Ruled by Jupiter, lemon balm is a sweet leaf in the mint family, best taken fresh in tea. It brightens the mood, brings love and happiness, and has protective properties.

Hyssop. This is a potent herb of protective magic. Take it in tea in small doses in order to bring on spiritual healing and protection.

Ginger. Ruled by Mars, ginger has protective properties but is best known as an aphrodisiac. It will restore the vital energies generally.

Chamomile. Ruled by the Sun, chamomile is known for its relaxing properties, but it is also a potent herb of blessing and protection, as are all solar herbs.

Myrrh. Ruled by Saturn, myrrh was the resin used to anoint the bodies of the dead in ancient times. It will banish ghosts and provide protection and even magical invisibility.

Fir, spruce, and pine. The most common Christmas trees, these are less commonly found in older books of natural magic. In my experience, they can be burned as incense, especially at Christmas time, both in worship and for magical protection.

Palo santo. This is a South American wood related to frankincense, and shares its properties; use it for worship and magical protection.

Lavender. This is an herb of relaxation. Its power is to calm the vital spirits. As such it is useful for meditation, and also for cultivating celibacy.

Rosemary. Rosemary strengthens the mind and grants intelligence, and it is also excellent for magical protection. Living rosemary plants will brighten the energy in and around the home. A sprig of it can be traced along the outside of the body like a kind of energetic lint roller, clearing the aura of stagnant or harmful energies.

Gemstones. Many of these have magical properties. Of the best known, the emerald is related to elemental earth; the sapphire, to water; the garnet, to air, and the ruby, to fire. Garnets are also used to strengthen the will, and sapphires to bring peace. Rubies confer strength, and emeralds bring peace. Diamonds are also worth mentioning: they are ruled by Mars, and provide magical protection, but can also, thanks to the presence of Mars, provoke conflict.

General blessing for natural sacramentals

Preparation. Set up your altar in the usual way, with the sacramental in the middle.

Step 1. Perform the complete Opening, including the Asperges, Censing, and Invocation.

Step 2. Declaration of purpose. Be specific in this. Say:

> I proclaim this temple open for the purpose of [consecrating this living rosemary plant, that it may serve to repel evil and hostile energies from this place; this chamomile, that it may become a

tea of blessing; this palo santo, that it may become an incense of protection; etc.].

Direct, O Lord, I beseech thee, the completion of this work by thy holy inspirations, and carry it on by thy gracious assistance, that every prayer and work of ours may begin always from thee, and by thee be happily ended. Through Christ our Lord. Amen.

Step 3. The exorcism. Say: O [name the substance], creature of God, I exorcise thee by God the Father + almighty, who made heaven and earth and sea, and all that they contain. Let the adversary's power, the devil's legions, and all of Satan's attacks and machinations be dispelled and driven far from this creature, [name]. Let it bring [health in body and mind to all who use it, freedom from the work of evil spirits, tranquility of mind for the sake of meditation, etc.] in the name of God + the Father Almighty, and of our Lord Jesus + Christ, His Son, and of the Holy + Spirit. Through the power the same Jesus Christ our Lord, who is coming to judge both the living and the dead and the world by fire.

Step 4. The blessing. Say,

> Almighty and everlasting God, who commanded that the Earth may be made to bring forth grass, the herb yielding seed, and the fruit tree yielding fruit, each after its kind, may it please thee to bless + and to hallow + this, thy creature of [name the substance], that it may serve to [name the intention of the working.] Through the merits of our savior Jesus Christ, who is coming to judge both the living and the dead and the world by fire. Amen.

Step 5. Enter into meditation on the consecrated sacramental, visualizing its purpose as though it were already accomplished.

Step 6. Close the temple in the usual way.

Blessing of sacramentals, short form

Sometimes you don't have time for a lengthy consecration. You may need holy water or blessed incense on the fly, or you may simply wish to give the natural virtues of a stone, an incense stick, or an herbal tea a little boost. In this case, it's perfectly acceptable to do a shortened form of the blessing. What this looks like may vary depending on circumstances. The very simplest way to bless something is to simply trace the sign of the cross over it and say an extemporaneous prayer, asking Our Lord and any appropriate saint or angel to bless the object. You might, for example, trace the sign of the cross, and say words like, "In the Name of the Father, and of the Son, and of the Holy Spirit, may you be blessed, creature of ____, and may your natural powers of ____ be brought forth by the grace of God. Through Jesus Christ, our Lord, Amen." You can do this surreptitiously in a public place, if you'd like to turn, say, an ordinary cup of herbal tea, purchased at a café, into a minor work of magic.

LESSON 5

Novenas, psalms, and other prayers

Practical lesson

A novena is a nine-day prayer, usually directed at a particular saint, asking for a blessing such as healing for yourself or a loved one, finding a job, or achieving some other goal such as selling or buying a house. Novenas are one of the most potent forms of traditional Christian magic, and done properly, they are very effective indeed.

One of the things that adds to the potency of novena is magical timing. Now, there is nothing really to stop you from praying any novena at any time. But the tradition is—in most cases—to begin the novena ten days before the Feast Day associated with the saint or other devotional subject. The prayer is repeated for nine days. On the tenth, you should attend church services if possible—especially if you have access to a sacramental church which honors the saints—and make a suitable offering in the saint's name.

Now, there are hundreds, possibly thousands of traditional novenas, guides to novenas, and books of popular novenas. Rather than trying to reproduce all of those here, I'm going to give you a general guide to the use of novenas, and a few examples to get you started. You will be able to use the format given to modify any traditional novena in order to increase its potency. Books of novenas can be easily obtained at Catholic supply stores, and you can find a great many for free online.

You can also create your own novenas, and these don't have to be directed toward canonized saints in any particular Church. Until the Council of Trent, most saints began their careers through the ordinary devotion of men and women who experienced their miraculous powers either in life or after death. Later, Rome would investigate the situation and provide a formal canonization as a "stamp of approval." This is still how things work in the Orthodox Church today. If obedience to Rome is important to you, you may wish to avoid this practice, but otherwise you are perfectly free to direct your devotions toward any saint you want, canonized or not. In many parts of the Catholic world, unapproved "folk saints" like Saint Expedite or Santa Muerte are venerated. In my own practice I regularly invoke non-canonical saints like the Renaissance magicians Pico della Mira and Marsilio Ficino, the traditional archangels of the seven planets, and the Greek philosopher Plato under the title "Prophet to the Gentiles." Basically, any dead person whom you admire can be invoked as a saint, with whatever their role was in life as their patronage. If there is someone from the past you admire, try invoking their help and see what results you get.

Finally, it's important to note that, while we often make use of novenas as a form of thaumaturgy, this isn't the only way to work with them. If you want to form a stronger connection to a particular saint or to an aspect of the Holy Trinity, a novena is a great way to do it.

The novena prayer

Preparation. The first time you say a novena prayer, you should set up your magical working space with altar, incense, and holy water. You should also have an image of the particular saint you are working with, if applicable.

You should also take some time to review the chapter entitled Principles of Effective Magic, especially if you haven't worked with a novena before. This will keep you focused on your work, and keep you from making the mistakes that many people make with novenas. Above all, you should keep in mind that the saints are not vending machines; you are working with powerful spiritual beings and with God Himself. Treat a novena as a way of participating in the grace of God with the help of his saints. That said, you should approach novenas with humility and confidence—not with desperation. As was discussed in the Principles, if you spend your time fretting about not having something, even something very important, you will create a current of interference that can keep you from getting what you desire.

Step 1. Perform the complete Opening ritual.

Step 2. Say the novena prayer.

Step 3. Enter into meditation. During this time you should visualize the outcome you hope to achieve through the novena. If you aren't trying to achieve a particular outcome, simply spend time contemplating the saint or other subject of devotion.

Step 4. When you are ready, rise, and say a suitable closing prayer. Ask, if appropriate, that your desires be accomplished if it be the will of God, through Jesus Christ, our Lord, and thank the saint (if applicable) for their presence in your life.

Step 5. Close the temple in the usual way.

Step 6. Repeat the prayer and visualization eight more times, for a total of nine prayers performed over consecutive days. You do not need to repeat the temple working on the succeeding days. Instead, you can incorporate the prayer and meditation into your daily practice, or as an additional practice whenever you find the time.

Example novena: Our Lady of Lourdes

"Our Lady of Lourdes" is one of Mary's titles, derived from her appearance in 1858 to Saint Bernadette at Lourdes, France. Following Our Lady's appearance, a healing spring began to flow at Lourdes, which has been the cause of many miraculous cures. As you'd imagine, Our Lady of Lourdes is a patron of healing, and can be invoked for healing any illness.

The following novena to Our Lady of Lourdes is taken from *A Book of Novenas for the Principal Feasts of the Year*, published in 1878.

Timing: This novena begins on February 2nd and ends on February 10th.

Step 1. Perform the complete Opening and Invocation.

Step 2. Say the following prayers:

> Blessed be the holy and immaculate conception of the blessed Virgin Mary!

> O immaculate Virgin,
>> Mother of Mercy,
>> Health of the weak, Refuge of sinners,
>> Comfortress of the afflicted,
>> Thou knowest our needs and our sufferings:
>
> Deign to look on us pityingly, and to help us bountifully.
>
> By appearing in the grotto of Lourdes, thou hast shown that thou didst wish it to be a privileged spot, whence thou shouldst dispense thy favors with especial abundance. Already very many have found there the cure both of their souls and of their bodies. Though we are so far distant from that holy place, yet even from afar we call to thee, O dear Lady of Lourdes, and ask that we may be sharers in those blessings. Here our humble prayer, O loving and beloved Mother, and obtain for us [HERE NAME YOUR DESIRE.] Help us in our bodily needs and spiritual infirmities; may our gratitude for thy favors make us still more careful to imitate thy virtues during all our life, so that we may one day come to share with thee in the glory of heaven. Our Lady of Lourdes, pray for us. Amen.

Step 3. Enter into meditation using rhythmic breathing, and then, in your mind, speak directly to Our Lady, and explain to her what you are asking of her. Let go of your discursive thoughts, and visualize your desired outcome.

Don't concentrate on *how* you will attain your desires. Leave that to God and the saints. In this case, instead of imagining a miracle cure for an illness or the sudden appearance of a new doctor, just imagine yourself or your loved one free from illness and healthy.

Step 4. When you are ready, let go of the visualization, and spend a few more minutes in rhythmic breathing. Then rise to your feet. Thank Our Lady for her intercession, and offer a suitable closing prayer, such as the Prayer of the Holy Spirit or the Fatima Prayer.

Step 5. Perform the complete Closing ritual.

Step 6. Repeat at least the prayer and meditation for the next eight days, for a total of nine days.

Step 7. The next day should be February 11th, the Feast Day of Our Lady of Lourdes. On this day, attend mass or other church services if you can. Then make a suitable offering in the name of Our Lady of Lourdes.

This can be a monetary donation to a church or shrine devoted to Our Lady of Lourdes, of which there are many around the world. You can also say a prayer to Our Lady of Lourdes and do some charitable work on her behalf. A few hours of work associated with whatever illness you are seeking to cure would be especially appropriate.

Notes for practice

Remember that you can pray a novena any time you like, to any saint you like. There are, as noted above, many thousands of actual or potential novenas. You should get ahold of one or two good collections of novenas, which can be easily found online. If you are willing, you should also experiment with creating your own novenas. Any dead person whom you admire can be invoked as a saint, with whatever their role was in life as their patronage. If there is someone from the past you admire, try invoking their help and see what results you get.

LESSON 6

The magic of the psalms

Practical lesson

The use of the psalms for magical purposes is very ancient, and probably predates Christianity as do the psalms themselves.

If you have been following the book to this point, you already know nearly everything you need to know. Everything, that is, except the uses of the particular psalms!

Like other forms of magic, the psalms are especially potent when used in a magical temple, but you can use them at other times, too. To consider a few examples: The 34th psalm is traditionally used for protection from evil spirits. If you have a situation in which someone you live with (or you yourself!) may be under attack by demonic spirits, you could open a magical temple and pray this psalm. The 27th psalm has a history of use in protecting the common people from the depredations of an enemy army. If you are particularly concerned with one of the conflicts taking place globally, you could offer this psalm along with prayers for protection for the civilian population as part of your morning practice. Finally, the 65th psalm is used for prosperity for merchants. If you are setting up a stand at a farmer's market or craft fair, you could repeat this psalm silently to yourself at times throughout the day, in order that you may sell your wares and prosper.

When working with the psalms, you may want to use the King James Bible, as this has the longest tradition of use in psalm magic in English. On the other hand, if your Latin is good or if you simply enjoy working with the language, you can use Saint Jerome's Latin Vulgate.

Sixteen psalms for magic and blessing

The following is a list of sixteen psalms commonly used in magic. These are derived from two somewhat different sources. The first is the Book of Gold, a sixteenth-century grimoire of psalm magic. The second is the Blessing Psalter of St. Arsenios of Cappadocia. If you find this work appealing, you may find through exploration and research that there are other variations on the use of the psalms as well.

Be aware that the systems for numbering the psalms are slightly different in different Bibles, including the two I suggested above, the King James Version and the Latin Vulgate. In the list to follow, the first number represents the King James Version, the second number in (parentheses) represents the Vulgate.

Psalm 1. This psalm is prayed to bring fertility when planting a tree or a garden.
Psalm 6. This psalm is prayed to reverse the effects of witchcraft and evil magic.
Psalm 17. This psalm is prayed three times daily in cases of false accusations and slander.
Psalm 18. This psalm is prayed to avert natural disasters.
Psalm 23. This psalm is an apotropaic, meaning a protection against every sort of evil.
Psalm 27. This psalm is prayed to protect civilians in wartime.
Psalm 31. This is a prayer for fertility for crops and fields, and against conditions of drought.
Psalm 44. This psalm is prayed for peace and reconciliation between husband and wife.
Psalm 47. This psalm is prayed for help finding work, especially after a difficult separation from a previous employer.
Psalm 68 (67). This psalm is prayed to help women recover from miscarriage.

Psalm 76 (75). This psalm is prayed to help mothers in childbirth.
Psalm 91 (90). This psalm is prayed to drive off evil spirits.
Psalm 105. This psalm is prayed to bring about the repentance of an entire group of people.
Psalm 122 (121). This psalm is prayed to cure the "evil eye," which is any form of psychic attack, especially those accidental and rooted in jealousy or envy.
Psalm 132. This psalm is prayed to bring about peace and an end to war.
Psalm 148. This psalm is prayed to bring about good weather.

Other works of magic

Christian magic is as old as Christianity itself. An enormous variety of practices and prayers, blessings and devotions exist which may be strengthened and enhanced by the application of magical principles. This includes both practices and devotions approved by the various Church hierarchies, and those which have developed as folk practices among the people. Ask the Holy Spirit to guide you, and then apply your will and imagination, your intuition and your understanding of magical principles, and you will find success.

PART V

THE SACRAMENTS

Introduction

Beyond the sacramentals are the sacraments. Even more than the sacramentals, I suspect, in the minds of most people the sacraments can only be performed by an ordained priest. The truth is actually somewhat more complicated than that. In the sacramental Churches, *some* sacraments can only be performed by priests. Others must be performed not by a priest but by a bishop, and two can be performed by the laity.

The perspective of this book is that the sacraments are magical acts, and magical acts can be performed by anybody. It is an open question, however, whether a sacrament performed by a layperson can have the same effect as a sacrament performed by a priest. I will leave this open, but offer the following thoughts.

Consider the Eurcharist. This is the fundamental magical rite of the Christian Church, and it is a work of high magic of the greatest possible power.

Now, the formula of the Eucharist is similar to that of consecrating a talisman or amulet in other traditions of magic. To consecrate a talisman, you invoke a particular name of God—or, in pagan traditions, a particular god—associated with the effect you want the talisman to achieve. Then you ask God—or the particular god—to direct divine energy into the talisman, so that it may achieve its effects. Every talisman needs a suitable material base, and these are typically natural materials appropriate to the working. A talisman of Jupiter might take the form of an inscription on a disk of tin, for example, as tin is the metal of Jupiter. But other material bases are possible—for example, a wine made from a Jovian herb such as dandelion would also do quite nicely as the material basis for a talisman of Jupiter.

And so we can see that if one has the skills to open a magic temple and call upon divine energy, it should be a simple matter to create a talisman of any kind using a material base. If one opens a temple in the Christian tradition, calls upon Christ, and consecrates a talisman in the form of bread and wine, what do we have?

Well, this is where it gets complicated.

According to the Roman Catholic Church, during the Eucharist the bread and wine are literally transformed into the body and blood of Christ, through the process of transubstantiation. This, furthermore, is only possible when the sacrament is confected by a properly ordained priest.

On the other hand, other traditions reject the Catholic Church's hierarchy and its rules, and believe that bread and wine can simply be shared by everyone as a communion meal.

Which is correct? Ultimately, we can't know, because we have many different Churches which are all making equally reasonable claims. What we can know from experience is that it is, ultimately, a very simple thing to consecrate a talisman if you know what you are doing, and that everyone can do it. Does that mean that everyone can bring about transubstantiation?

Maybe, and maybe not. This is another area where I prefer not to tell the readers of this book what to think. What I say instead is that *at minimum* it is possible to consecrate bread and wine as a "talisman of the eucharist," and that it *may* also be possible to achieve everything that an ordained priest achieves.

And so in the pages that follow I will present the seven sacraments of the Church as magical rituals. We will begin with a home mass, which centers on a magical eucharist. This can be used by anyone, but will be especially suitable for those who don't have access to a church community in which to receive the sacrament. We will then discuss the seven sacraments of the church from an esoteric perspective, and go through the remaining sacraments one at a time.

In some cases, of course, there will be very little to say. In the case of baptism, for example, everyone agrees that all that is really required for baptism is for any person to sprinkle water onto the head of another person and, with sincerity, say the words "I baptize you in the Name of the Father and of the Son and of the Holy Spirit." In other cases, we will be able to take the sacraments as we have them and modify them using our magical principles, as we will see.

As always, you may find that the preceding parts are as much as you need for yourself and your practice. If so, that's all right—if you've worked your way to this point, you have enough material for a lifetime of spiritual growth.

A rite of self-dedication

The following part of this book gives instructions on performing many of the traditional seven sacraments, centering on a version of the mass which can be performed at home. Many of these sacraments, and especially the mass, are reserved for ordained priests. You cannot ordain yourself as such, but you can perform a ritual of self-initiation which will open you more fully to divine energies, so that the versions of the sacraments that you do perform can be as powerful and effective as possible.

Hence this ritual of self-dedication. You should only perform this under two conditions:

1. You have read and worked through all of the rituals given in this book up to this point.
2. You intend to work with the home mass and other sacraments given in the following part. If you haven't already done so, you should pause and read through the next part of the book now. If this seems like work that you're interested in taking upon yourself, proceed with the following ritual. If not, that's okay—you've already gotten what you need from this book, and I wish you well on your journey.

Preparation. You should set up an altar with a crucifix, holy water, and incense, and an image of Our Lady. You will also need a container of the Oil of Empowerment.

You are going to need a stole, which is a vestment worn by Roman Catholic priests, consisting of a long strip of cloth worn about the shoulders. At the beginning of the ritual, this will be placed on the altar, folded so it takes up as little space as possible. The stole can be one of those worn by priests, which can be easily purchased online, or you can make your own out of any fabric you like.

Finally, you should read through the home mass in the following chapter and understand its contents. You are going to be performing part of it during this ritual.

Step 1. Perform the complete Opening ritual and the Confiteor.

Step 2. With hands in the orans posture, say:

> Almighty God, I give thee thanks for all things. This day I present myself as one who wishes to serve you in the role of a priest.

(Make the sign of the cross over yourself at every +)

> May I be blessed +, and sanctified +, and consecrated + by thee to thy holy service, O God.

Step 3. Take your seat, and enter into meditation, reflecting upon the vows which you have just made and the service to which you are committing yourself.

After a time, release your discursive thoughts, and sit in silence. Then kneel, and close your eyes. Continue to breathe rhythmically, and slowly come to imagine an angel or saint—you will know which one—standing before you and laying their invisible hands upon your head. Feel warmth and power flowing into you. Rest for a time in this sensation.

Step 4. Self-investiture

Still kneeling, take the stole from the altar. Drape it over your neck, and say the following words:

> The yoke of the Lord is sweet and his burden is light. I take upon myself the yoke of the Lord. O God, source of all holiness, I pray that thou wilt pour out upon me the gift of thy blessing. May my life be an example to others. May I meditate day and night upon

the way of holiness, so that I may understand thy ways, teach them to others, and practice them in my life. May I act with wisdom and justice in thy service, this day and every day. I ask this through Jesus Christ our Lord, who lives and reigns with you in the unity of the Holy Spirit, God forever and ever. Amen.

Step 5. The anointing of the hands.

With the Oil of Empowerment, draw a cross on each of your palms using the index and middle fingers of the opposite hands. Say,

> I ask that my hands may be consecrated by thee, O Lord, to thy holy service. Whatsoever I bless, may it be blessed; whatsoever I consecrate, may it be consecrated. In the Name + of the Father, and of the Son, and of the Holy Spirit.

Step 6. Trace the sign of the cross over the bread and the wine on the altar, and say,

> May I be given the power to offer sacrifice to thee, O Lord.

Step 7. Standing, raise your hands in the orans posture, and say the following prayer:

> O Lord, you said, "No longer do I call you servants, but my friends, for you have known all the things I have wrought among you." May I receive the Holy Spirit within me this day.

Visualize a column of brilliant white light descending from Heaven, filling first the central column of your energetic body and then spreading outward to fill your entire body, flowing out from you to fill the entire space.
Say:

> Glory be to the Father, and to the Son, and to the Holy Spirit. As it was in the beginning and is now and forever, unto the ages of ages. Amen.

Step 8. The home mass

Proceed from here to consecration given in the home mass (see below). After you have communicated (that is, eaten the bread and drunk the wine):

Step 9. Close with the following words:

> As I take upon myself the work of the Lord, I offer the following vows:
>
> As I enter thy service, I vow to faithfully offer the mass on my own behalf and on behalf of all those who ask it of me.
>
> I vow to hold the teachings, stories, rituals, and traditions of the Christian faith in reverence, as methods for the uplifting and enlightenment of myself and of others.
>
> Not being sacramentally ordained, I vow not to claim ordination in any particular Church or the right to offer ordination to others, but to claim only to be one who wishes to serve God to the greatest extent that I am able. Not being, in this particular service, under the jurisdiction of any particular bishop, I furthermore vow not to claim any authority derived from any particular Church, neither to demand the submission of others to any particular Christian authority or to participate in attacks upon any such authority.
>
> O Lord, keep me in thy steadfast ways and hold me always to my word. Amen.

Step 10. The final blessing
Say:

> May the blessing of Almighty God, + Father, Son, and Holy Spirit, be upon me this day and always. May I conduct my work in the service of the Lord faithfully and truly, and may the sacrifices that I offer be pleasing to Almighty God, to whom be honor and glory forever and ever. Amen.

A home mass

Introduction

The mass has three major parts. We are going to call these the **Opening**, the **Propers**, and the **Consecration**. Please note that this is slightly different from the way the structure of the mass is divided in the Roman Catholic and other sacramental Churches. We will go through these parts and their various subdivisions one at a time, and then present the mass as a whole.

A Catholic mass is divided into two major parts, called the Mass of the Catechumens and the Mass of the Faithful. Now, the word "catechumens" refers to people who have not yet been baptized. In ancient times, the mass of the catechumens included the beginning of the mass and the readings from Scripture. After that, the catechumens were asked to leave, and only those who had been initiated into the Christian Mysteries through baptism remained for the Mass of the Faithful, which was centered around the Eucharist.

Now, obviously a division like that isn't going to be suited for home use. The point of this mass is that you can make use of it as a private ceremony for yourself, yourself and one other person (this is very helpful), or for a small group. Unless you're a stickler for these things, you're not going to want to ask your family or friends to leave if they aren't baptized. It's also very necessary, in a small group context and especially in a personal context, to keep things simple. A mass that goes on for more than an hour is perfectly fine when you have a large group gathered in a church and a whole team of priests, deacons, altar servers, readers, porters, and so on. On a personal scale, thirty minutes is usually more than enough. You want to be able to keep your focus through the whole mass, and after a long while our attention tends to waver. We're effectively performing the mass as a sacramental, rather than a sacrament, and at this point you should know the rule about sacramentals: you will get as much out of it as you are able to put into it. If it goes on so long that you find yourself getting bored and rushing through very long readings, you aren't going to get as much out of it.

Outline of the home mass

1. The Opening
   A. The Banishing
   B. The Asperges
   C. The Censing
   D. The Invocation of the Guardian Angel
   E. The Confiteor
   F. The Kyrie
   G. The Gloria
2. The Propers
   A. The Collect
   B. The Lesson
   C. The Gospel
   D. The Meditation
   E. The Creed
3. Before the Eucharist
   A. The Offertory
   B. The Censing and Lavabo
   C. Orate Fratres
4. The Canon
   A. The Sign of Peace
   B. The Offertory
   C. The Great Thanksgiving
   D. The Preface

E. The Angelic Prayer (Sanctus)
F. The Prayer of Consecration
G. The Lord's Prayer
H. The Fraction of the Host
I. The Agnus Dei
J. Communion
K. Postcommunion

As you can see, the home mass is largely composed of rituals and practices which you have already learned. We prepare our space by a powerful combination of the Opening, the Confiteor, and the Kyrie energetic practice. This is then aided by the invocation of an angel. We then proceed to the Propers of the mass, which are a set of readings and prayers that provide a theme for meditation. After this comes the Eucharist, which is a powerful magical ritual of consecration, a fitting end to a magical ritual of this kind.

The home mass: instructions

Part 1. Opening

The Opening prepares the space for worship through banishing, purifying the energetic bodies of all those present, and charging the energetic body of the celebrant with magical energies.

Introductory rite

Begin with the Banishing Sign of the Cross. Then follow this with the Asperges with holy water and the Censing with incense, exactly as in the Opening ritual.

The Invocation of the guardian angel

Say the words:

> Almighty God, hear our prayer, and send to us thy holy angel from Heaven, to watch over, bless, protect, defend, and comfort all we who come here before you in worship. Through Christ our Lord, Amen.

Visualize a light filling your worship space. A figure takes shape in the light, in the form of a guardian angel. This angel will watch over the home mass as you perform it, and may be called upon at any time by you or anyone else attending the mass with you.

The Confiteor

Having prepared a space on the Astral Plane, purified it energetically, we must now purify the vessel of our own astral bodies. We do this by confessing our sins, and invoking the healing power of divine mercy.

Perform the complete Confiteor ritual. If you are performing the mass with a group of people, every person can read the Confiteor, or the celebrant can simply read it in the plural: that is, saying "We confess" instead of "I confess."

Close with the words:

> May almighty God have mercy on us, forgive us our sins, and lead us to life everlasting. Amen.

Charging the energetic body of the celebrant

Having purified our space and ourselves and invoked the presence of the divine power, we now charge our energetic body with divine power, so that we may use that power in our celebration.

At this point, the celebrant performs the complete Kyrie energetic practice. If there are other participants, they may either sing or chant the words along with the celebrant or sit in silent meditation.

The Gloria

Afterwards, recite or sing the following words.

> Glory to God in the highest, and peace to his people on earth.
>
> Lord God, heavenly King, almighty God and Father. We praise Thee, we bless Thee, we adore Thee, we glorify Thee. We give Thee thanks for Thy Glory. Lord God, Heavenly King, almighty God and Father.
>
> Lord Jesus Christ, only begotten Son. Lord God, Lamb of God, only Son of the Father. Thou who takest away the sins of the world,

have mercy on us. Thou who takest away the sins of the world, receive our prayer. Thou who art seated at the right hand of the Father, have mercy on us. For Thou alone art the Holy One, thou alone art the Lord, thou alone art the most high, Jesus Christ.

With the Holy Spirit, in the Glory of God the Father. Amen.

If you have a group, say:

C: May the Lord be with you.
R: And with thy spirit.

For individuals, simply say:

May the Lord be with my spirit as I prepare to celebrate this mass.

Part 2: The Propers

The Propers

The Propers are the part of the mass that changes from day to day. The Propers both readings from Scripture, as well as other prayers dedicated to whatever saint or feast of the Church is being celebrated that particular day.

This is going to be the part of the home mass that is most individual, as you will need to tailor it to meet your needs and the needs of whatever congregation may have joined you in celebration. Every Church has its own Propers, and you are free to use the form from whatever tradition you like. To do this you'll need to get ahold of the Propers of the mass. These are easily available in books or on the internet. Choose whatever set of Propers is appropriate for your practice and for whatever group that may be worshiping with you.

Of course, you can also invent your own Propers. While modern Christian Churches have a standard set of readings that come from whichever version of the Bible their Church approves as "canonical," the same standard didn't exist in the early centuries after Christ's resurrection and it needn't exist today. You may find you want to incorporate non-canonical saints and readings from Gnostic or other sources. You may wish to include readings from technically extra-Christian sources like the *Corpus Hermeticum* or the *Dialogues of Plato*. Feel free to experiment and see what works for you and any who may be celebrating with you.

The Collect

The Collect is a short opening prayer which follows the introductory part of the mass. It usually includes an invocation of the saint being commemorated on that day or an introduction to the feast being celebrated. At one time, the Collect was a single prayer, said at every mass, by everyone. Today the Collect changes from day to day, and so you will need to refer to the book of Propers of which you are making use. (If you don't have a book of Propers yet, a general-purpose Collectwill be provided below). Here are a few examples of Collects for different occasions:

The Collect for the Feast of the Holy Name of Mary

O Almighty God, Thy faithful people rejoice in the protection of the Most Holy Virgin Mary and delight in her name. Deliver them from all evil here on Earth and make them worthy of everlasting happiness in Heaven through her loving intercession. Through Christ our Lord. Amen.

The collect for Christmas

O Almighty God, free us from the old bondage and yoke of sin by Thy only-begotten Son's new birth as man. Through the same Jesus Christ, Our Lord. Amen.

Collect for Saint Marsilio Ficino

Almighty God, Thou hast revealed to Thy servant Saint Marsilio Ficino the hidden things of the orders of Nature and the orders above Nature. Grant that we may rightly understand and make right use of the wisdom that Thy servant has revealed, for the glory of Thy ineffable Name. Through Christ our Lord. Amen.

If you don't have a collection of the Collects available, you can use a simple universal Collect, such as the following from the Liberal Catholic tradition:

Almighty God, unto whom all hearts be open, all desires known, and from whom no secrets are hid: Cleanse the thoughts of our hearts by the inspiration of Thy Holy Spirit, that we may perfectly love Thee, and worthily magnify Thy Holy Name. Through Christ, our Lord. Amen.

The readings

Following the Collect, various passages from Scripture are read. In some Churches, this includes a passage from the Old Testament, a "Lesson" derived from one of the Epistles, and a reading from the Gospel. Other Churches simply use the Lesson and the Gospel. In this home mass, I've decided to include the Lesson and Gospel only, but that shouldn't stop you from using the Old Testament if you like.

Of course, you're going to need a source for your readings, and these vary quite widely from one tradition to another. It's very easy to find the readings for any Sunday or feast day online.

And this is another area in which you can also make this your own. If you prefer a different set of readings from any of those available, you can come up with your own cycle of readings. If you'd like to read a passage from one of the Gnostic Gospels, an esoteric text like the *Corpus Hermeticum*, or to choose extra-Christian sources like the *Dialogues of Plato* or the *Daodejing*, no one is going to stop you because no one is going to know. The most important thing is to choose your readings ahead of time—you don't want to be scrambling to find something when you're halfway through your mass!

Lesson

A short selection from Scripture, usually from one of the Epistles, is read.
   This should be prefaced with the following words:
   "A reading from the Book of …"
   After the reading, close with the following:

C: The word of the Lord.
R: Thanks be to God.

Gospel

A selection from one of the Gospels is read.
   Before reading, say:
   "A reading from the holy Gospel according to Saint …"
   The celebrant and any others present say:
   "Glory to you, O Lord."

This is then followed by drawing a small cross with the thumb, the rest of the fingers folded against the palm over the forehead, heart, and lips. As always, you may visualize the cross in white fire, and imagine that the cross is activating the third eye, heart, and throat chakras.

Meditation

In an ordinary mass, this is when the priest would offer a sermon or homily, discussing the lessons to be drawn from the readings and whatever feast day it may be. If you are practicing the home mass on your own, this is a good time to enter into discursive meditation, contemplating this same set of themes. Consider the lesson, the Gospel, the saint or feast of the day, the time of year.

If you have a group, you may present your own homily or sermon at this time. That isn't necessary, however. Discursive meditation can be practiced with a group, and it can be a very good experience to meditate together for a set period of time. Afterward, invite everyone to share their experience in meditation if they choose, and then move on to the next section.

The Creed

We conclude this section with the Creed or Statement of Faith. You may use any of the following, or one of your own:

Nicene Creed

> We believe in one God,
> the Father, the Almighty,
> maker of heaven and earth,
> of all that is, seen and unseen.
>
> We believe in one Lord, Jesus Christ,
> the only Son of God,
> eternally begotten of the Father,
> God from God, Light from Light,
> true God from true God,
> begotten, not made,
> of one Being with the Father.
> Through him all things were made.

For us and for our salvation
he came down from heaven:
by the power of the Holy Spirit
he became incarnate from the Virgin Mary,
and was made man.

For our sake he was crucified under Pontius Pilate;
he suffered death and was buried.
On the third day he rose again
in accordance with the Scriptures;
he ascended into heaven
and is seated at the right hand of the Father.

He will come again in glory to judge the living and the dead,
and his kingdom will have no end.

We believe in the Holy Spirit, the Lord, the giver of life,
who proceeds from the Father and the Son.
With the Father and the Son he is worshiped and glorified.
He has spoken through the Prophets.
We believe in one holy catholic and apostolic Church.
We acknowledge one baptism for the forgiveness of sins.
We look for the resurrection of the dead,
and the life of the world to come.

Amen.

Statement of faith of the Liberal Catholic Church

We believe that God is Love, and Power, and Truth, and Light;
That perfect justice rules the world;
That all His children shall one day reach His feet, however far they stray.

We hold the Fatherhood of God, the kinship of all people;
We know that we do serve Him best when best we serve our fellow human being.

So shall His blessing rest on us, and peace for evermore.

Amen.

An esoteric christian statement of faith

I believe in the one transcendent cause of all things, the First Father, unknowable and unnamable, abiding beyond all that can be known and all that can be named.

I believe in the Divine Mind, the living Word of God, eternally united with God in substance, in power proceeding forth from the Father as Light from the Sun, constituting by his very nature all things knowable and namable, rightly called the only Son of God.

I believe in the Soul of the Universe, the source of all life and action, proceeding in his activity from the Father and from the Son, united in his essence with the Father and the Son, returning in his activity to the Father, rightly called the Holy Spirit of God.

I believe that the nature of the Divine Mind is revealed to mankind in the person of Jesus Christ. I believe, therefore, in his descent from Heaven, his birth of the Virgin Mary and the Holy Spirit; his crucifixion under Pontius Pilate; his death, and resurrection, and that he abides eternally with God the Father. I believe that he comes again to all men as they return to him. I believe in the union in time and in eternity of men in the Divine Mind, which is Christ, and that grace everlasting will unite all of Creation to Him, their eternal Source. Amen.

Part 3: The Eucharist

This is the center of the mass, the ritual of consecration by which bread and wine are transformed into the body and blood of Jesus. This should be treated with absolute reverence.

The sign of peace

Before we begin, we take a moment to invoke the peace of Christ into our worship space and offer it to others. If you have a group, say:

C: May the peace of the Lord be with you always.
R: And with thy spirit.
C: Let us offer to one another a sign of Christ's peace.

Everyone in the room now has a chance to offer the same sign of peace to one another.

If you are practicing by yourself, simply say:

May the peace of the Lord be with my spirit this day, and with the whole world.

The Offertory

Place before you on the altar the bread and wine which you have prepared.

Say the words,

Unto thee, Almighty God, we offer these gifts of bread and wine, fruits of the living Earth and of the labor of men and women, that they may become the body and blood of our savior, Jesus Christ.

May the Lord accept this sacrifice at my hands (or thy hands), for the praise and glory of his name, for our good, and the good of all of his holy church.

The Great Thanksgiving

For a group:

C: The Lord be with you.
R: And with thy spirit.
C: Lift up your hearts.
R: We lift them up to the Lord.
C: Let us give thanks to the Lord our God.
R: It is right and just.

For an individual:

> May the Lord be with my spirit as I celebrate this home mass. I lift up my heart to the Lord, for it is right and just to give him thanks and praise.

Continue to say:

> It is truly right and just, our duty and our salvation, always and everywhere to give thee thanks, O Lord, Holy Father, Almighty and Eternal God, through Christ our Lord.

By His birth we are reborn. In His suffering we are freed from sin. By His rising from the dead we rise to everlasting life. In His return to Thee in glory we enter into Thy heavenly kingdom.

And so, raising our voice together as one with the saints, the angels, archangels, and principalities; powers, dominations, and virtues; thrones, cherubim, and seraphim we pray:

Holy, holy, holy Lord God of Hosts. Heaven and Earth are full of thy glory. Hosannah in the highest. Blessed is he who cometh in the name of the Lord. Hosannah in the highest. Hosannah in the highest.

The prayers of consecration

Wherefore, O Most Merciful Father, we humbly pray and beseech thee, through Jesus Christ, Thine Only Son, Our Lord, that thou wouldst receive +, purify +, and hallow + these holy and unblemished sacrifices which we offer unto thee on behalf of all thy church and of the whole world.

This, our offering, do thou, O God, vouchsafe to bless +, perfect +, and consecrate +, so that it may become for us the + Body and + Blood of thy most beloved Son, Jesus Christ.

Who, the night before he suffered, took bread into his holy and venerable hands, and, with his eyes lifted up to Heaven and to thee His Father, giving thanks to thee, + blessed and broke the bread, giving it to his disciples and saying Take this, all of you, and eat of it, for this is my body. (Elevation: Raise the paten with the bread over your head.)

In like manner, after he had supped, taking the chalice into his holy and venerable hands and again giving thanks unto thee, he blessed + and gave it to his disciples, saying: Take this, all of you, and drink of it, for this is the chalice of my blood, the blood of the new and eternal covenant, the Mystery of faith, which shall be shed for you and for many for the forgiveness of sins. (Elevation: Raise the chalice in the same way.)

As often as ye shall do these things, ye shall do them in memory of me.

Wherefore, Lord, in memory of the blessed passion of the same Christ, your Son, our Lord, of his resurrection from the dead and of his ascension to heavenly glory, we thy servants and with all thy holy people offer to thy sovereign majesty, from among thy gifts bestowed upon us, a victim + perfect, + holy and + spotless, the holy + bread of everlasting life and the + chalice of everlasting salvation.

Be pleased to look upon these offerings with a favorable and gracious countenance; accept them as thou wert pleased to accept the offerings of thy servant Abel the righteous, the sacrifice of our father Abraham, and that of Melchisedech, thy high priest, a holy sacrifice, a spotless victim.

We humbly implore thee, almighty God, that these offerings be carried by the hands of thy holy angel to your altar on high, in the sight of thy divine majesty, that all who are partakers at the altar of the precious + Body and + Blood of Thy Son may be filled with all heavenly grace and + blessing.

Prayers of intercession

During this section, we can offer prayers for those who are not present with us, who have either died or are suffering from illness or some other difficulty.

Remember also, Lord, thy servants [Name any departed person for whom you wish to pray] who are gone hence before us, marked with the sign of faith, and sleep the sleep of peace. To them, Lord, and to all that rest in Christ grant, we implore thee, a place of happiness, light, and peace. Be mindful, too, O Lord, of all those who suffer from disease, hardship, or any of the many troubles that afflict us in this life, especially [Name any other person for whom you wish to pray, and the reason]. To us also, thy servants, who hope in the multitude of your mercies, be pleased to grant some place and fellowship with thy holy saints. Through Christ our Lord.

Through him, O Lord, thou ever createst these good things. Be pleased now to + hallow, + quicken, and bless + them as gifts for us. By + Him and with + Him and in + Him are ever given to thee, God the + Father Almighty, in the unity of the + Holy Spirit all honor and glory for ever and ever. Amen.

The Lord's prayer

As our savior taught us, we pray:

> Our Father, Who art in Heaven, hallowed be Thy Name,
> Thy kingdom come; Thy will be done;
> On Earth as it is in Heaven.
> Give us this day our daily bread,

And forgive us our trespasses, as we forgive those who trespass against us.
And lead us not into temptation, but deliver us from evil.

For thine is the kingdom, the power, and the glory, now and forever. Amen.

The fraction of the host

During the fraction, a piece of the host is broken off and placed in the chalice. This is accompanied by the following prayer:

O Lord, we believe that in this (break a piece of the bread or host) breaking of thy body and pouring out of thy blood we become thy redeemed people; We confess that in taking the gifts of this pledge here, we lay hold in hope of enjoying its true fruits in the heavenly places. (+++ Place the particle in the chalice.)

The Agnus Dei (Lamb of God)

Say (or sing) the following words:

Lamb of God, who takest away the sins of the world, have mercy on us.
Lamb of God, who takest away the sins of the world, have mercy on us.
Lamb of God, who takest away the sins of the world, grant us peace.
C: Jesus is the Lamb of God who takes away the sins of the world. Happy are those who are called to the supper of the lamb.
R: Lord, I am not worthy to receive you, but only say the word and my soul shall be healed.

The Celebrant receives Holy Communion and says:

He gives heavenly bread to the hungry, and to the thirsty water from the living spring. Christ the Lord himself comes, who is Alpha and Omega. He shall come again to judge us all.

If there are others present, pray:

> Come all of you and receive the body of Christ, drinking the holy blood by which you were redeemed

The sacrament is administered with the words, "The Body of Christ," "The Blood of Christ."

Postcommunion

A postcommunion prayer is said, such as:

> Father of all we give thee thanks and praise that while we were still far off thou hast found us in thy Son and brought us home. Dying and living he declared thy love, gave us grace and opened the gate of glory. May we who share Christ's body, live his risen life; we who drink his cup bring life to others; we whom the Spirit lights, give light to the world. Keep us firm in the hope thou hast set before us, so that we and all thy children may be free, and the whole earth live to praise thy name; through Christ our Lord. Amen.

If there are others present, the celebrant should bless them, saying,

> May the Lord bless us in the name of the Father and of the Son and of the Holy Spirit. The mass is ended. Let us go in peace to love and serve the Lord.

Baking bread for the home mass

Not many of us will be able to make our own wine, although this is also increasingly becoming an option. If you're interested in learning to brew wine, there are now homebrew supply stores selling starter kits, and it might be easier than you think. But you're going to have to wait at least six months from the arrival of your supplies to the first day you're able to crack open a bottle. In the meantime, you can start a loaf of bread right now, and it will be ready as soon as this evening.

In Catholic churches these days, the bread used for communion is called a "host"; it's a small, tasteless wafer made by one or two specialized factories. Hosts can be purchased online as well if you like. But if you're serious about this practice, I really recommend learning to bake your own bread. In earlier times, the bread used in communion would have been baked by a member of the community, and this is still the practice throughout the Orthodox and Eastern Rite Churches. A loaf of bread is specially baked by a parishioner, and is referred to as a prosphora, a word which means "offering." We will simply refer to it as our communion bread.

Preparation

In order to bake your own prosphora bread, the only thing you really need is a kitchen and a few ingredients.

I would say that this is different from ordinary cooking, because it is a type of magic, but the truth is that every act of cooking is an act of magic. As you progress on your magical journey, you will find yourself becoming more sensitive to the energies of things that you encounter in everyday life. This can have unpleasant side effects: Sometime you may find yourself handed a plate of food at a restaurant that is totally fine to all outward appearance but simply feels *wrong*. What's happening in these situations is that the cooks, and very likely the whole staff of the restaurant, are feeling stressed out, tired, bored, and angry; some of them may even, after a long day, have started to hate the restaurant's customers and to wish that they would all just go home. Remember that everything that we think and feel exists as a reality on the Astral Plane. When we transmute raw ingredients into food, some of our energy, including our thoughts and feelings, enters into our work and transforms the product that results.

For this reason, spiritual preparation is very important when baking communion bread.

First, it's traditional to fast for a time beforehand. Some sources recommend at least six hours. During this time, you should abstain from food and drink. You should also avoid technological distractions. Finally, it's important to avoid sexual activity during this time, and also for women to avoid making communion bread during menstruation. The reason for this has nothing to do with any puritanical fear around the body, sexuality, or women in particular. It's simply that both sex and menstruation involve fluids in which the life force is very concentrated, and this has strong effects both on the aura and on the environment. Sex also has a very strong effect on the energetic body, not altogether different from a magical ritual. And so we abstain. If this bothers you, don't worry; you can always get down to it later.

You should begin your work, first, by cleaning and blessing your working space and the tools and ingredients you will be using. It will be much more effective if you can use natural materials to clean your kitchen and your tools. Industrial chemicals have peculiar and, in my experience, quite harmful effects on the energetic environment. (If you don't believe me, open up a bottle of Lysol, sit next to it, and try to meditate. See how it goes.) Moreover, if you make use of natural materials, you can also turn cleaning into a magical act. In order to both cleanse and bless a space, you can infuse white vinegar with magically potent plant materials. This takes some time; the plants will need several weeks for the preparation to complete. You can speed up the process by simply using essential oils. In fact, essential oils in hot water with baking soda make a fine cleaner all on their own. Try a mix of lemongrass, frankincense, and fir or cedar.

Next, bless your space by first performing the Banishing Sign of the Cross. Then say the following prayer:

Almighty and eternal God, fountain of being and life and wisdom, to you I give thanks for all things. And I ask this day that thou wilt aid me in the preparation of this communion bread, according to thy holy will, that it may be an aid to the salvation of my soul and the souls of all who will partake of it. Through Christ our Lord. Amen.

Make the sign of the cross over your ingredients and cooking implements. Imagine the cross taking shape in the form of white light, descending from Heaven, blessing your work.

The recipe

This is the simplest method of baking bread. If you already know what you're doing, you use the recipe that you prefer, but make sure not to use any other ingredients besides bread and yeast, salt and water. No butter, oil, sugar, herbs, or what have you.

Three cups all purpose flour
One teaspoon Fleischman's bread yeast or other dry yeast.
One teaspoon salt.
Twelve ounces warm (not hot!) water

Pour the yeast into the water and let it sit for a minute or so, then add yeast water and salt to the flour, mix it until it is smooth, then cover it with a towel and leave it to rise overnight.

In the morning, you will find that the dough has risen. Wet your hands thoroughly. You are going to reach into the bowl and pull all of the dough out as a single, stretchy mass. Pull it up, sliding your fingers under the sticky dough as necessary. Now, fold it in half. Turn the bowl, and fold it in half again. Do this five or six times, and cover the dough again.

In an hour, repeat the process another time, lifting and folding the dough five or six times. In thirty minutes, repeat the process a third time.

Now, preheat your oven to 450 degrees, and thoroughly grease a baking dish. When the oven is ready, take the dough out of the bowl and transfer it onto your baking dish. It may keep the shape of a flattened ball, or you can form it into a loaf. It doesn't matter.

Put the pan in the oven and bake for twenty-five minutes.

At the end of this time, remove the loaf from the oven. Allow it to cool for an hour. After this, you can cover it in a towel and put it in a bread box.

If you plan on using the bread on Sunday morning, you will want to start the loaf on Friday, bake it on Saturday, and use it on Sunday.

The remaining sacraments

The Eucharist is the central sacrament of the Christian faith; there are, of course, six others. Some of these require at least a priest; others require at least one other participant. In the following section, we will go through the sacraments, one by one, except for the Eucharist, which we have already covered. All of these may, like the Eucharist, be modified for home use. We will present the orthodox perspective on the sacraments where appropriate, but our primary focus is on how you can make the sacraments your own, should you either not have access to an official church, or not desire one.

If continuing to learn and practice the sacraments, as opposed to the sacramentals, is of interest to you, then you should get a copy of the *Rituale Romanum* and study. The *Rituale Romanum* is the Roman Catholic Church's book of rites, which details the form of each of the sacraments. (Try to find a copy from 1964 or earlier, as the new rites introduced after Vatican II have far less power.) You should also study the sacraments as practiced in other traditions. *The Science of the Sacraments*, by C. W. Leadbeater, is the best existing guide to an esoteric perspective on the sacraments, and details the sacraments as performed in the Liberal Catholic Church. It deserves a place on your book shelf next to the *Rituale*. *The Book of Common Prayer* is to the Anglican Church as the *Rituale Romanum* is to the Catholic, and you should find a copy of this as well—here again, older editions will be found to be more helpful.

Baptism

In many ways this is the simplest of the sacraments. There are three requirements: one person to baptize; a second, to be baptized; and water, with which to baptize.

In its very simplest form, all that is required for baptism is for the baptizer to sprinkle water over the catechumen three times, and say the words, "I baptize you in the name of the Father, and of the Son, and of the Holy Spirit."

Even according to the strict rules of the Roman Catholic Church, that is all that is necessary. In theory, a lay person should only baptize someone when a priest is unavailable or when the other person is in danger of death, but in your own practice you can baptize anyone you like, provided they agree to it.

The exact method is also up to you. According to the Catechism of the Catholic Church, "Baptism is performed in the most expressive way by triple immersion in the baptismal water. However, from ancient times it has also been able to be conferred by pouring the water three times over the candidate's head." The very best way is to perform the baptism by full immersion into a natural body of water. A moving river or stream is best, since it carries negative energies away, but you will want to be careful of the current. Lacking this, water from a lake or the ocean will do just as well. You can also use holy water, rain water, or a specially prepared baptismal font. The *Rituale Romanum* provides instructions for preparing a baptismal font, and if you've followed this book up to this point, you have the resources that you need to prepare one for your own practice.

Confession

In the earlier part of this book, we gave an entire ritual of private confession, designed to purify the soul of the initiate of his sins. Practiced regularly, this will prove to be very effective on its own.

The tradition of the Church, however, emphasizes confessing our sins to another person, called our confessor. When our confessor is a priest, he is said to be able to fully confer the sacrament of Confession.

In my own experience, the presence of an ordained priest is a great help to confession but it isn't necessary. Other traditions besides Catholicism have their own version of confession. One of the best known comes from the Twelve Step tradition. In Twelve Step groups, the Fourth and Fifth Steps consist in making a searching and fearless moral inventory of ourselves, and sharing the exact nature of our wrongs with God, ourselves, and one other person. In practice, the Fifth Step has a healing and purifying effect that is on a par with sacramental Confession. Even the experience of psychotherapy can work as well, provided both patient and therapist are honest. Indeed, Carl Jung himself is said to have claimed that he had many Protestant and Jewish patients, but very few Catholics, because the Catholics already had what he was offering in therapy in the form of Confession.

What all of this points to is the power of confessing our sins out loud, to another person. It isn't that the rite of private confession that we've provided here isn't effective—if you've made it this far, you've already found that it is. But there is something which can be gained with another person's help that we can't find all on our own.

Consider what happens when we speak out loud the words of our confession. We begin by asking God, in prayer, to guide our thoughts as we examine our conscience. The guidance and inspiration of the Holy Spirit then directs our thoughts, which form themselves into words. The words, having begun life in our thoughts, descend from there into our soul. From the soul they are spoken out loud by the voice, and thus take on a physical body in the form of sound waves. The sound waves are received by the senses of our confessor, and journey from there into his soul, and into his mind. From there, through his prayers and ours, they return to God.

The act of confessing to another thus imitates the entire process of descent into matter and return to God. There is much that this whole process has to teach about magic in general, by the way.

The Anamchara

Anamchara is a term from the Celtic Christian tradition. In Gaelic the word means "soul friend." In the Celtic tradition an anamchara was a wider, usually older mentor that can help us on our spiritual journey. An anamchara can be a priest, but this isn't strictly necessary. What is necessary is that your anamchara be someone that you can trust absolutely, who you admire, and whose own spiritual life is in order.

If you have someone who is willing to act as an anamchara to you at least for the purpose of the rite of Confession, then you may find the following very useful.

A rite of confession

Preparation. As with the Confiteor, the best preparation for confession is to make a list. This process is called "examination of conscience" in the Catholic Church, and its tools are a pen, paper, and your own memory.

Take a moment to sit by yourself and clear your mind. A banishing ritual will help, and you should pray to the Holy Spirit for inspiration and to your guardian angel for guidance.

After that, begin making your list. Again we will find the Seven Deadly Sins a very useful guide, and you should refer to the chapter where the Confiteor ritual is given for an understanding of these. List each sin one by one, and write out all those occasions when you have committed it.

Of course, if it's been many years or a lifetime since you've last confessed your sins, this will take a very long time. Perhaps too long. For now, you should focus on two things. The first is habitual sin: if you always find yourself treating others with arrogance or rudeness, for example, or if you have a bad temper or a drinking problem. The second is major incidents that jump out at you—maybe you're usually good at keeping your temper, but screamed at your husband last week; maybe you're usually good at controlling yourself, but got drunk at a work function.

When you are ready, sit together with your anamchara, somewhere you can have privacy.

Step 1: Opening prayer. Begin by offering a prayer. Now, the precise prayer is up to you. Your anamchara may come from a different spiritual background from you—they may or may not be comfortable with Christian formulae like the sign of the cross. Either way, you should pray together, and ask for the guidance of God.

Step 2: Confession. Go through your list. Your anamchara should sit, listen, and not judge. They aren't there to condemn you, but to listen to you. Questions should be directed at the following:

Why do you do this? How often do you do this? How did you hurt another person by doing this? How did your hurt yourself?

Step 3: Penance and amendment. Together with your anamchara, come up with a plan for addressing your sins. Yes, all of them.

In some cases this will be simple. If you've stolen something, you can give it back or arrange to make a payment to the business or person in question. If you've lost your temper with someone, you should apologize, and you should also come up with strategies for controlling yourself when you become angry.

In other cases, it may be more complicated. You should not make a direct amends or apology to someone if it would hurt them. If you had a relationship in the past where you were unfaithful or abusive, that person may not want to hear from you, period. Contacting them to apologize may only reopen old wounds for them while allowing you to feel better about yourself. In other cases, the nature that the penance or amends takes may be indirect. If you're the sort of person who often loses your temper and apologizes, then chances are good no one wants to hear your apologies anymore. They know you don't mean it. Instead, look into ways to address your underlying anger issues, and let them notice that you've changed.

You may also find that there are certain "sins" that don't actually require any sort of action on your part, because you didn't actually do anything! This is one of the purposes of the anamchara—to help you recognize where you've actually gone wrong, and where you're beating yourself up inappropriately.

Step 4: Absolution. Your anamchara should say a prayer for God's forgiveness. If they are working within the Christian tradition, that might be a variation on the prayer priests use in the confessional:

"May almighty God grant you absolution from all of your sins."

Together you might then say:

Anamchara: Give thanks to the Lord, for He is good.
Response: His mercy endures forever.

Matrimony

According to the official teaching of both the Catholic and Orthodox Churches, the only participants in the sacrament of matrimony are the two people to be married. The priest is there as a witness, to confirm and bless the ceremony. This is why these Churches honor the marriages of people from other Christian traditions and other religious backgrounds;

they recognize that two people are fully capable of uniting themselves together in holy matrimony.

In our time, traditional marriage rites have often given way to homemade marriages, with a ceremony and vows written by the participants and an ordained friend or relative instead of a full-time priest or minister to officiate. There is nothing wrong with this, and such rituals of marriage work as well as any other—that is, they work as well as the two participants are willing to make them work.

If you wish to perform weddings, then you will need to do two things. The first is to study the form of the sacrament of marriage. This can be found in the books recommended above—the Roman Catholic in the *Rituale Romanum*, the Anglican in *The Book of Common Prayer*, the Liberal Catholic in *The Science of the Sacraments*. Based on the knowledge you already have, you will be able to come up with a version of the rite that you feel comfortable with. Of course, you will need to make sure that the people who want to get married also feel comfortable with it! Then you can proceed to the second thing you need to do, which is simply to become licensed to perform marriages in your jurisdiction.

Sacraments of initiation: Confirmation and Holy Orders

Together with Baptism, Confirmation and Holy Orders are described as "sacraments of initiation." These are said to place "an indelible mark on the soul." What this means in practice is that the astral body of the person who receives these sacraments is altered in a way to make it more receptive to particular divine energies.

Like Baptism, both of these sacraments must be conferred by another person. In this case, only a bishop will do.

But the experience of occult orders is that many initiations which are ordinarily performed by another can, in fact, be performed by a solo individual. These are called *self-initiations*. Self-initiations differ from ordinary initiations in two ways.

The first, obviously, is that the person performing the initiation is also the person being initiated.

The second is that they require more work. An initiation performed by another person transfers the power being initiated, all at once, to the extent that that other person's own level of initiation will allow. A self-initiation, on the other hand, is more difficult. Usually, self-initiations take the form of rituals which are preceded by a long course of study—sometimes up to several years in length. The initiate then performs the ritual, and, after that, returns to the course of study for a time.

It's hard to explain how self-initiations work to people who haven't done them, but when they work, you know it. It isn't anything abstract or vague either, a situation where you can fool yourself. Remember that *magic is the art and science of causing changes in consciousness in accordance with will*. When your consciousness has changed, you know it, because you become different in ways that are obvious and measurable.

And so we can't confirm ourselves and we can't ordain ourselves, but we can perform self-initiations which will allow us to have at least a part of what these rituals confer when performed by a bishop.

A rite of Self-Confirmation

Preparation. You will need to have an altar set up with at least a crucifix, an image of Our Lady, holy water and incense, and a container of the Oil of Empowerment.

Finally, it is customary to choose a Confirmation Name, which is the name of a particular saint whom you admire and who you will now take on as a guide and patron.

Step 1. Perform the complete Opening and the Confiteor.

Step 2. Say the following words:

> Our help is in the Name of the Lord
> Who hath made the Heavens and the Earth

Let us pray:

Almighty everlasting God, who once gave life to me by water and the Holy Spirit, forgiving me my sins, I ask now that you will send forth upon me from heaven your Holy Spirit, the Advocate, along with His sevenfold gifts.

Amen.
The Spirit of wisdom and understanding.
Amen.
The Spirit of counsel and fortitude.
Amen.
The Spirit of knowledge and piety.
Amen.

May I be filled with the Holy Spirit and sealed with the sign + of the cross of Christ, in token of everlasting life. Through our Lord Jesus Christ, your Son, who lives and reigns with you, in the unity of the Holy Spirit, One God, forever and ever. Amen.

Step 3. Say:

I take upon myself the name of Saint N. (name your confirmation saint), and ask that he (or she) may guide me in this life and lead me into life everlasting.

During the following section, use your thumb to draw a cross on your forehead with the Oil of Empowerment when you come to the first +:

May I be sealed + with the sign of the cross, and may I be confirmed with the chrism that sanctifies in the name of the + the Father, and of the Son, and of the Holy Spirit. Amen.

Step 4. Take your seat, and enter into meditation for a time. When you are ready, rise and say:

Confirm, O God, the work you have begun in us from your heavenly sanctuary, the new Jerusalem. Glory be to the Father, and to the Son, and to the Holy Spirit. As it was in the beginning, is now, and ever shall be, world without end. Amen.

Then say:

Lord show us your mercy

And grant us your salvation.

May the Lord be with me this day and always.

God, who gave to your apostles the Holy Spirit, ordaining that they and their successors should hand down that gift to the rest of the faithful; look with favor on our lowly service, and grant that the same Holy Spirit may come upon me. May my heart be consecrated as a worthy dwelling for His glory. I ask this through Christ our Lord, who lives and reigns with the Father and the Holy Spirit, God, forever and ever. Amen.

Step 5. Perform the Closing of the temple.

Ordination

We have already given a ritual of self-dedication which will serve in lieu of ordination at the hands of a bishop, and I'm not going to repeat that here. Some of those reading will wish to seek out true ordination at the hands of a bishop, and that's what I want to talk about now.

If you're reading this book, then it's likely that ordination in one of the mainstream Churches is closed to you. At least, that's probably the case—if you are, say, a Catholic seminarian reading this book out of curiosity, I wish you every blessing on your journey!

For the rest of us, however, ordination may seem out of reach.

As is so often the case, however, this is an illusion.

The power to ordain a priest in sacramental form is given to every bishop, and not every bishop is in communion with either the Roman or any other of the large Churches. Beyond the boundaries of orthodoxy, there are many bishops involved with something called the Independent Sacramental Movement.

The Independent Sacramental Movement, or ISM for short, is a broad collection of independent churches and lone priests and bishops. The congregations are small, sometimes consisting of only two or three people, or of a few hundred connected through the internet. In terms of their beliefs, the ISM communities range very widely. Some groups are faithful Catholics or Orthodox Christians who believe their own Churches strayed from their missions at some point in the past. Others may be largely similar to mainstream sacramental Christians in their beliefs, but hold to officially heretical doctrines like the ordination of women or gay marriage. Still others are Gnostics or other esoteric Christians who hold to very different beliefs from the mainstream Churches but prefer to worship in a sacramental form.

What most of these groups have in common is *apostolic succession*. This is the power conferred by Jesus to the apostles, and passed from the apostles to their successors, the first bishops. Apostolic succession is the power whereby a bishop is given the ability to ordain a person to the priesthood—among other things.

And so if you wish to seek out ordination but don't wish to participate in any of the larger Christian communions, the road is not closed to you by any means. You are going to need to do a fair bit of research, as well as discernment. The ISM is geographically dispersed and extremely diverse. Some groups are well-organized, others not so much. Some groups reject Roman or Orthodox or Anglican dogma, but adhere to other dogmas just as rigid. In particular, many demand adherence to political ideologies associated with the extreme Left or the far Right which you may find unpalatable. And still others are simply "ordination mills," granting the rights of the priesthood to anyone who is willing to pay a few bucks. (Those who have experience in martial arts may be familiar with "McDojos" which hand out black belts to anyone who can pay. Some parts of the ISM are similar.)

With all of those caveats, the ISM can be a great resource for anyone who wishes to pursue a sacramental Christian life in fellowship with others but independent of any of the larger Churches. Some groups which I know to be reputable will be included in the appendixes to this book.

The Sacrament of Unction: magical healing

Extreme Unction is typically offered to those in danger of death. Unless you are a chaplain or work in hospice care, you are unlikely to be in a position to offer that sacrament in any form, except in rare situations.

There is, however, an alternative form of extreme unction, which makes use of the Oil of Healing. This is a form of magical healing, and we will explore it presently.

Before we do that, it's important to discuss what magical healing can and can't do.

First, before you perform this service for another person, it's important that you don't make any medical claims. In many parts of the world you can be fined or even imprisoned for "practicing medicine without a license" if you do that. Claim only that, by the Oil of Healing, you will transmit the healing grace of God. What form that healing takes can vary. Sometimes results are stunning and immediate. More often, the recipient feels calmed and soothed, and their own body's healing powers are invigorated to take action to fight off infection or whatever other injury or ailment is troubling them.

Magical healing

Preparation. For this ritual, you will need to have consecrated the Oil of Healing. You can perform this ritual as part of a larger service within an open temple, or as a smaller healing ceremony, perhaps accompanied by massage or other forms of bodywork. The following section will include multiple methods of healing. We will begin with the most complex method of ritual healing, and then proceed to discuss simpler variations.

It might seem a bit back to front to work from the complex to the simple, but there is a reason for this. If you do not have much experience with magical healing or healing in general, the ritual forms function as a safeguard to protect your own aura when you are in contact with someone who is unwell.

The second thing you are going to need, of course, is a patient in need of healing. Before performing the healing ritual you should explain what you are going to do and how it will work. You will also need the person to be willing to participate actively, as this ritual requires them to participate in the prayers and some of the visualizations.

As always, whenever the participation of the patient is needed you will find the prayers labeled "C:" and "R:" You should read the part that begins with C; the patient reads the response, the part labeled R.

A ritual of magical healing

Step 1. Perform the complete Opening ritual, including the Asperges. If you are working with someone struggling from any kind of respiratory disease, you can skip the Censing or use only whatever level of light incense they can tolerate.

Step 2. Together with the patient say:

> C: Our Help is in the Name of the Lord
> R: Who hath made the Heavens and the Earth
> C: May the Lord be with you.
> R: And with thy spirit.
> Let us pray:
> C: Almighty God, your apostle James wrote,
>> Is any sick among you? Let him call for the elders of the church; and let them pray over him, anointing him with oil in the name of the Lord:
>> And the prayer of faith shall save the sick, and the Lord shall raise him up; and if he have committed sins, they shall be forgiven him.
>> Confess your faults one to another, and pray one for another, that ye may be healed. The effectual fervent prayer of a righteous man availeth much.
>
> As we gather together for this ceremony of healing, we pray for your guidance and your blessing. May the blessed archangel

Raphael be with us in this work and guide us. O Raphael, Divine Physician, be present with us this day, guide our healing work, and instruct us in the healing power of God.
R: Amen.

Step 2. Together with the patient, perform the Confiteor. Allow them to read the words of the prayer out loud, and then talk them through the visualization as a form of guided meditation, in the following manner:

Imagine a great column of healing golden light descending from the heavens. It pours down onto the crown of your head, healing, warming, and relaxing, and slowly descends through the centerline of your body, to your heart. Imagine your heart glowing with the light, which is the healing power of God. Slowly, the light expands outward, healing, warming, and relaxing the organs of your chest and your belly, expanding back upward through your head and downward through your legs. Feel it as it expands outward through the marrow, the bones, and the muscles of your body, your legs, your arms, your head. Feel it expand outward to heal and calm the surface of your skin, and then filling the field of energy that surrounds your body with healing light.

Imagine that many threads of light extend outward from your energetic field. These are the cords which connect you to every person in your life. Now, imagine the healing light which pours down from Heaven extending from you to light up all of these cords, sending healing to every person in your life, but especially those which you have harmed by sin. Feel and know that they too are healed.

After a time, pause, and say:

> May almighty God have mercy on you, forgive you your sins, and lead you to everlasting life.

Note: In order to do this correctly, it's important to be aware of your tone of voice, and it's important to have the ritual memorized if you haven't already. If you sound awkward or unsure of yourself, if you speak in a harsh or grating tone, or if you simply forget your lines, your patient isn't going to get what they could out of this. Try for a tone which is at once strong and soothing, and speak slowly.

If you don't know how to do this, listen to a few guided meditations online. These are easy enough to find. Take note of the way the person guiding the meditation speaks, and try to imitate them. Above all, have confidence in yourself and your work.

Step 4. Trace the sign of the cross over the Oil of Healing and say:

> May the blessed archangel Raphael guide my hands in this healing work. Through Christ our Lord. Amen.

Take the Oil of Healing, and with your thumb, draw a cross on the patient's forehead. Then proceed to draw crosses in the same way on the crown of the patient's head, the throat, and the base of their skull, under the hairline.

With every cross, say the words:

> Receive the healing grace of God.

As you do so, imagine the crosses glowing with healing light. Once you are done, imagine the whole head alive with healing fire. See that healing light sink into the patient's body, descend into their heart, and then radiate outward, filling their body and their entire aura with healing divine fire.

Step 5.

With the patient, say the Prayer of the Holy Spirit:

> Come, Holy Spirit, fill the hearts of thy faithful
> and kindle in them the fire of thy love.
>
> Send forth thy Spirit and they shall be created,
> and thou shalt renew the face of the earth.

As you say these words, imagine a final column of healing light descending from Heaven, filling the patient, you, and the room that you are in, until everything seems to glow with white light.

Say:

> O God, who hath instructed the hearts of the faithful
> by the light of the Holy Spirit,
> grant that in the same Spirit we may be truly wise
> and rejoice in his consolation always.
>
> Through Christ our Lord. Amen.

Step 5. Say:

> We thank thee, O Lord, for the gift of healing and for the assistance of thy blessed archangel, Raphael. O Raphael, we thank thee for guiding our hands and instructing us in the healing ways of God. Amen.

Step 5. Perform the complete Closing.
Step 6: With the patient, say:

> C: Unto God's love and protection we commit you. May the Lord bless you and keep you. May the Lord make his face to shine upon you and be gracious unto you. May the Lord lift up the light of His Countenance upon you and give you His peace, this day and always. Amen.
> R: Amen.
> C: Go in peace.

This concludes the healing service.

Simpler forms of healing

As you gain proficiency in magical healing, you can experiment with simpler forms of it. The Oil of Healing can be used to anoint injured parts of the body—though please use your common sense and don't apply it to open wounds or burns in lieu of first aid. It can also be used as a massage oil—or a few drops can be added to a pre-existing massage oil—and rubbed into sore muscles to promote healing. Chakras, energy centers, and acupuncture points can be anointed with the oil. And there are many other possibilities, which you will be able to discover through experiment.

Afterword

If you've made it this far, congratulations! Very few people who take up a book like this one complete even one part, let alone the entire course of study presented.

Now, you may be wondering what your next steps are. The practices given in this book are enough, on their own, for a lifetime of spiritual development—or perhaps for several lifetimes. And yet, Christianity is an ancient and very diverse religion, and the traditions of Christian magic equally diverse, equally ancient. There are entire branches of practice both exoteric and esoteric upon which we have barely touched, and others which we have not mentioned at all.

And so you have a choice before you. You may choose to specialize in one of the areas discussed in this book. It may be, for example, that you prefer to worship in one of the larger churches, but to keep a private practice in which you work with the forms of meditation given in this volume. You may, instead, prefer to use this book as part of a guide to developing your own ministry, with a small congregation. Or it may be that you wish to range further, and explore the esoteric traditions of the Rosicrucians, or Martinism, or Christian astrology or alchemy. Be quiet, go within yourself and listen to the voice of the Holy Spirit, and you will be guided along your proper path.

If you have found the work of this book especially helpful to your own practice and your spiritual growth, you should know that there will be further volumes in this series. We have not even touched on the magnificent cycle of the Church Year, the holy days, the fasts and the feasts. From Advent and Christmas, through the seasons of Lent and Easter, the summer feasts of Saint John's Day and the Assumption of Our Lady and the autumn feasts of Michaelmas and Hallowtide, the Christian Wheel of the Year is a magnificent icon to the work of God in creation. Every one of these seasons has customs, rituals, and secret works of magic, sometimes lost, sometimes still practiced but in a diminished form. Future volumes will cover each of these in detail, beginning with Advent. Other books will explore the magic of the elements, the stars, and planets, and the Tree of Life. If that is of interest, I will see you then.

May God bless you and keep you, in the meantime.

PART VI

APPENDIXES

APPENDIX 1

A prayer book

This is a short list of traditional prayers, all of which are suited to daily use.

Daily prayers

The Lord's prayer

Our Father, who art in Heaven, hallowed be thy name. Thy kingdom come, thy will be done, on Earth as it is in Heaven. Give us this day our daily bread, and forgive us our trespasses, as we forgive those who trespass against us. And lead us not into temptation, but deliver us from evil.

[For thine is the kingdom, the power, and the glory, now and forever.] Amen.

The last part is added by Protestants but not Catholics; you may use either version.

Latin: Pater Noster, qui es in caelis, sanctificetur nomen tuum. Adveniat regnum tuum. Fiat voluntas tua, sicut in caelo et in terra. Panem nostrum quotidianum da nobis hodie, et dimitte nobis debita nostra sicut et nos dimittimus debitoribus nostris. Et ne nos inducas in tentationem, sed libera nos a malo. Amen.

Hail Mary

English: Hail Mary, full of grace, the Lord is with thee; blessed art thou among women and blessed is the fruit of thy womb, Jesus.
   Holy Mary, Mother of God, pray for us sinners, now and at the hour of our death. Amen.

Latin: Ave Maria, gratia plena, Dominus tecum. Benedicta tu in mulieribus, et benedictus fructus ventris tui, Iesus.
   Sancta Maria, Mater Dei, ora pro nobis peccatoribus, nunc, et in hora mortis nostrae. Amen.

Glory Be

English: Glory be to the Father, the Son, and the Holy Spirit. As it was in the beginning, is now and forever, unto the ages of ages. Amen.

Latin: Gloria Patri, et Filio, et Spiritui Sancto. Sicut erat in principio, et nunc, et semper, et in saecula saeculorum. Amen.

Holy Spirit prayer

Come, Holy Spirit, fill the hearts of thy faithful and kindle in them the fire of thy love.
   Send forth thy Spirit and they shall be created, and thou shalt renew the face of the earth.
   Let us pray. O God, Who didst instruct the hearts of the faithful by the light of the Holy Spirit, grant us in the same Spirit to be truly wise, and ever to rejoice in His consolation. Through Christ our Lord.

Latin: Veni, Sancte Spiritus, reple tuorum corda fidelium, et tui amoris in eis ignem accende. Emitte Spiritum tuum et creabuntur; Et renovabis faciem terrae.

Oremus: Deus, qui corda fidelium Sancti Spiritus illustratione docuisti. Da nobis in eodem Spiritu recta sapere, et de eius semper consolatione gaudere. Per Christum Dominum nostrum. Amen.

Grace before meals

Bless us, O Lord, and these, thy gifts, which we are about to receive, from Thy bounty, through Christ, Our Lord. Amen.

Latin: Benedic, Domine, nos et haec tua dona, quae de tua largitate sumus sumpturi. Per Christum Dominum nostrum. Amen.

Creeds

Nicene Creed

> We believe in one God,
> the Father, the Almighty,
> maker of heaven and earth,
> of all that is, seen and unseen.
>
> We believe in one Lord, Jesus Christ,
> the only Son of God,
> eternally begotten of the Father,
> God from God, Light from Light,
> true God from true God,
> begotten, not made,
> of one Being with the Father.
> Through him all things were made.
>
> For us and for our salvation
> he came down from heaven:
> by the power of the Holy Spirit
> he became incarnate from the Virgin Mary,
> and was made man.
>
> For our sake he was crucified under Pontius Pilate;
> he suffered death and was buried.
> On the third day he rose again
> in accordance with the Scriptures;
> he ascended into heaven
> and is seated at the right hand of the Father.
>
> He will come again in glory to judge the living and the dead,
> and his kingdom will have no end.
>
> We believe in the Holy Spirit, the Lord, the giver of life,
> who proceeds from the Father and the Son.
> With the Father and the Son he is worshiped and glorified.
> He has spoken through the Prophets.
> We believe in one holy catholic and apostolic Church.

We acknowledge one baptism for the forgiveness of sins.
We look for the resurrection of the dead,
and the life of the world to come.

Amen.

Statement of faith of the Liberal Catholic Church

We believe that God is Love, and Power, and Truth, and Light;
That perfect justice rules the world;
That all His children shall one day reach His feet, however far they stray.

We hold the Fatherhood of God, the kinship of all people;
We know that we do serve Him best when best we serve our fellow human being.

So shall His blessing rest on us, and peace for evermore.

Amen.

An Esoteric Christian statement of faith

I believe in the one transcendent cause of all things, the First Father, unknowable and unnamable, abiding beyond all that can be known and all that can be named.

I believe in the Divine Mind, the living Word of God, eternally united with God in substance, in power proceeding forth from the Father as Light from the Sun, constituting by his very nature all things knowable and namable, rightly called the only Son of God.

I believe in the Soul of the Universe, the source of all life and action, proceeding in his activity from the Father and from the Son, united in his essence with the Father and the Son, returning in his activity to the Father, rightly called the Holy Spirit of God.

I believe that the nature of the Divine Mind is revealed to mankind in the person of Jesus Christ. I believe, therefore, in his descent from Heaven, his birth of the Virgin Mary and the Holy Spirit; his crucifixion under Pontius Pilate; his death, and resurrection, and that he abides eternally with God the Father. I believe that he comes again to all men as they return to him. I believe in the union in time and in eternity of men in the Divine Mind, which is Christ, and that grace everlasting will unite all of Creation to Him, their eternal Source. Amen.

Marian prayers

Magnificat

English:

> My soul doth magnify the Lord.
> And my spirit hath rejoiced in God my Savior.
> For he hath regarded: the lowliness of his handmaiden: For behold, from henceforth: all generations shall call me blessed.
> For he that is mighty hath magnified me: and holy is his Name.
> And his mercy is on them that fear him: throughout all generations.
> He hath shewed strength with his arm: he hath scattered the proud in the imagination of their hearts.
> He hath put down the mighty from their seat: and hath exalted the humble and meek.
> He hath filled the hungry with good things: and the rich he hath sent empty away.
> He remembering his mercy hath holpen his servant Israel:
> As he promised to our forefathers, Abraham and his seed for ever.

Latin:

> Magnificat anima mea Dominum;
> et exultavit spiritus meus in Deo salutari meo,
> quia respexit humilitatem ancillae suae;
> Ecce enim ex hoc beatam me dicent omnes generationes.
> quia fecit mihi magna, qui potens est, et sanctum nomen eius,
> Et misericordia eius a progenie in progenies timentibus eum.
> Fecit potentiam in brachio suo;
> dispersit superbos mente cordis sui;
> deposuit potentes de sede, et exaltavit humiles;
> esurientes implevit bonis
> et divites dimisit inanes.
> Suscepit Israel puerum suum, recordatus misericordiae suae,
> sicut locutus est ad patres nostros,
> Abraham et semini eius in saecula.

Memorare

Remember, O most gracious Virgin Mary, that never was it known that anyone who fled to thy protection, implored thy help, or sought thy intercession, was left unaided. Inspired by this confidence, I fly unto thee, O Virgin of virgins, my Mother. To thee do I come, before thee I stand, sinful and sorrowful. O Mother of the Word Incarnate, despise not my petitions, but in thy mercy hear and answer me. Amen

Hail, Holy Queen

> Hail, Holy Queen, Mother of Mercy,
> our life, our sweetness and our hope.
> To thee do we cry,
> poor banished children of Eve.
> To thee do we send up our sighs,
> mourning and weeping in this valley of tears.
> Turn then, most gracious advocate,
> thine eyes of mercy toward us,
> and after this our exile
> show unto us the blessed fruit of thy womb, Jesus.
> O clement, O loving,
> O sweet Virgin Mary.

The Angelus

Prayed three times daily, at 6 am or morning, 12 pm or midday, 6 pm or nightfall.

English:
The angel of the Lord declared unto Mary. And she conceived by the Holy Spirit.
Hail Mary, full of grace …
Behold the handmaiden of the Lord. Be it done unto me according to thy word.
Hail Mary, full of grace …
And the Word was made flesh. And dwelt among us.
Hail Mary, full of grace …
Pray for us, O Holy Mother of God, that we may be made worthy of the promises of Christ.

Pour forth, we beseech Thee, O Lord, Thy grace into our hearts, that we to whom the Incarnation of Christ, Thy Son, was made known by the message of an angel, may by His Passion and Cross be brought to the glory of His resurrection. Through the same Christ our Lord. Amen.

Latin: Angelus Domini nuntiavit Mariae. Et concepit de Spiritu Sancto.
Ave Maria, gratia plena …
Ecce ancilla Domini. Fiat mihi secundum verbum tuum.
Ave Maria, gratia plena …
Et Verbum caro factum est. Et habitavit in nobis.
Ave Maria, gratia plena …
Ora pro nobis, sancta Dei Genitrix. Ut digni efficiamur promissionibus Christi.
Gratiam tuam, quaesumus Domine, mentibus nostris infunde: ut qui, Angelo nuntiante, Christi Filii tui incarnationem cognovimus, per passionem ejus et crucem ad resurrectionis gloriam perducamur. Per eumdem Christum Dominum nostrum. Amen.

Additional prayers

Saint Michael prayer

English: Saint Michael the Archangel, defend us in battle. Be our protection against the malice and snares of the devil. May God rebuke him we humbly pray; and do thou, O Prince of the Heavenly host, by the power of God, thrust into hell Satan and all evil spirits who wander through the world for the ruin of souls. Amen.

Latin: Sáncte Míchael Archángele, defénde nos in proélio, cóntra nequítiam et insídias diáboli ésto præsídium. Ímperet ílli Déus, súpplices deprecámur: tuque, prínceps milítiæ cæléstis, Sátanam aliósque spíritus malígnos, qui ad perditiónem animárum pervagántur in múndo, divína virtúte, in inférnum detrúde. Ámen.

Guardian Angel prayer

> Angel of God, my guardian dear,
> To whom God's love commits me here,
> Ever this day (night) be at my side,
> To light and guard, to rule and guide. Amen.

Fatima prayer

O my Jesus, forgive us our sins, save us from the fires of hell, lead all souls to Heaven, especially those in most need of Thy mercy.

Prayer of Saint Francis

> Lord, make me a channel of thy peace.
> That where there is hatred,
> I may bring love.
> That where there is wrong,
> I may bring the spirit of forgiveness.
> That where there is discord,
> I may bring harmony.
> That where there is error,
> I may bring truth.
> That where there is doubt,
> I may bring faith.
> That where there is despair,
> I may bring hope.
> That where there are shadows,
> I may bring light.
> That where there is sadness,
> I may bring joy.
> Lord, grant that I may seek rather to comfort,
> than to be comforted.
> To understand,
> than to be understood.
> To love,
> than to be loved.
> For it is by self-forgetting that one finds.
> It is by forgiving that one is forgiven.
> It is by dying that one awakens to eternal life.

Prayer for the Souls in Purgatory

Eternal Father, I offer You the most Precious Blood of Your Divine Son, Jesus, in union with the Masses said throughout the world today, for all the Holy Souls in Purgatory, for sinners everywhere, for sinners in the Universal Church, those in my own home, and within my family. Amen.

APPENDIX 2

The saints

The following is a list of popular saints, with their attributes and their feast days. If you're new to working with the saints, this list is a good place to start. You should know, however, that there are thousands of canonized saints, and so even a list this long barely scratches the surface. I've listed the most common patronage for each saint. Some saints, however, are not the patrons of one or two things, but instead govern a very broad range of subjects in this material world. This is particularly the case for the older saints. Brigid of Kildare, for instance, is patroness of a range of subjects, while the power of the two Saints John extends so broadly that it's hard to say what they are the particular "saint of."

Aidan

Feast day: August 31st. Patronage: Northumbria, firefighters.

Andrew

Feast day: November 30th. Patronage: Scotland, Russia, fishermen.

Andrew's feast day is especially to be noted for the Saint Andrew novena, which is prayed from November 30th to December 24th. The reputation of this novena is well earned.

Anthony of Padua

Feast day: June 13th. Patronage: Lost items, lost people, and a great many other things.

Saint Anthony has a reputation for finding lost things, and my guess is that he finds thousands of lost keys every day. But his patronage goes well beyond this, and sometimes he finds things in very unexpected ways.

Bernadette of Lourdes

Feast day: February 16th. Patronage: Illnesses, the persecuted.

Bernadette was a young woman in France who experienced a series of apparitions of the Blessed Virgin Mary, leading to the establishment of the sanctuary at Lourdes.

Brigid

Feast day: February 2nd. Patronage: Fire, the hearth, handicrafts, poets, marriages, and many other things.

Brigid is one of those saints of whom not simply a book but an entire library could be devoted. Perhaps she was originally a Celtic fire goddess who became Christianized; perhaps that's a Protestant slander, and she was always a saint; and perhaps she was a Celtic goddess who converted to Christianity and altered her myths accordingly. In any case, she's a wonderful saint, and not just for people of Irish or Scottish heritage.

Catherine of Sienna

Feast day: Patronage: Nurses and the sick, mothers against miscarriage.

Catherine was an Italian mystic who is well known for a mystic treatise entitled *The Dialogue of Divine Providence*, dictated "while in a state of divine ecstasy" to her secretaries. A channeled work, in other words, as these things are now known. She is known as a patron of nurses, the sick, and pregnant mothers, but I suspect that you could call upon her for aid with any work of automatic writing as well.

Christopher

Feast day: July 25th. Patronage: Travel, dogs, werewolves.

Older icons of Saint Christopher portray him as a man with the head of a dog, and he is called either a werewolf or a "cyanocephalus." The latter means "dog headed man"; at one time, there was said to be a population of them living somewhere in the Caucasus. Now that we've decided that there are no dog headed people, these icons have been suppressed, but you can still find them easily enough online. In any case, Christopher watches over travelers, and you could do worse than to place an image of him in your car.

Cyprian

Feast day: September 26th (with Justina). Patronage: Christian magic.

Saint Cyprian was a wizard. It is said that he attempted to enchant a young woman named Justina, but that she banished his spells with the sign of the cross. Seeing a more effective source of magic than his old practices, he burned his books and became a priest. He is now a patron of Christian magicians, and you can invoke him for aid in this work.

David

Feast day: March 1st. Patronage: Wales and the Welsh, poets and poetry.

Saint David is the patron saint of Wales, and Saint David societies are common in the Welsh diaspora. Like many Celtic saints, he also lends his help to poets.

Francis of Assisi

Feast day: October 3rd. Patronage: Nature, animals, ecology.

Francis of Assisi is one of the best known and best loved saints of our age. Statues of him are often placed in gardens, and this is a very helpful practice. Whether he might aid a seeker of devout heart in working more directly with Nature spirits is a question as yet unexplored.

George

Feast day: April 23rd. Patronage: England, Georgia, and other countries; soldiers, especially in cavalry and armored units; dragon slayers.

In addition to being the patron saint of England and Georgia, Saint George is best known as a dragon slayer. The dragon also represents the devil and evil spirits and the reign of the passions in the human soul, and George's dragon-slaying skills can be called upon for help in these matters.

Gertrude the Great

Feast day: November 16th. Patronage: Saint Gertrude is a guide for anyone wishing to explore the devotion to the Sacred Heart or to work with the Holy Souls in Purgatory. She is also the patroness of the West Indies. Saint Gertrude was a German nun, a mystic, and a prolific writer. She is known for her devotion to the Sacred Heart, and can aid us in that aspect of this work. She is also known for her devotion to the souls in Purgatory, and wrote a well-known prayer for the souls in Purgatory. Our perspective is that Purgatory includes both an after-death state and the condition of continual return to incarnation on the Material Plane, and so we may call upon Gertrude for aid in escaping the cycle of reincarnation.

Hildegard of Bingen

Feast day: September 17th. Patronage: Musicians, writers, herbalists. Saint Hildegard was a mystic, a musician, a theologian, and a visionary. You can easily find recordings of her musical works, and they are excellent medicine for the soul. Her *Physica* is not, in my experience, the best guide to herbal medicine—but it's an excellent guide to the mind of a medieval thinker, for whom it made perfect sense to include an entry on the medicinal properties of dragon's blood and the proper method of harvesting mandrake.

Joan of Arc

Feast day: May 30th. Patronage: France, strength and courage for women.

Everyone knows Joan of Arc, the French girl who was inspired by St. Michael the Archangel to become a leader of armies. Absurdly, though Joan was cleared of charges of heresy in the years after her death, it took until 1894 for her visions to be declared authentic and until 1920 for her to be formally canonized.

John the Baptist

Feast days: June 24th, August 29th (beheading). Patronage: Extensive.

John the Baptist is called the Forerunner, and it's not an accident that his feast day is at the opposite pole of the year to Christmas. At the summer solstice, the light begins to wane; this is the light of the ancient world, which reached its climax and began to fade with the birth of Christ. I've sometimes wondered what it means that so much of Christianity is now centered in the global South, where the light begins to fade at Christmas, and to wax on Saint John's Day.

The Beheading of Saint John is its own Feast Day, and I believe that there are great secrets which can be found in this.

John the Evangelist

Feast day: December 27th. Patronage: Extensive

In addition to his role in the mainstream Churches, Saint John has a special role in many esoteric Christian traditions. The Johannite Gnostic tradition is centered upon secret revelations given (it is claimed) by Christ to John, and there are many small groups and churches dedicated to Johannite spirituality in our time.

Julian of Norwich

Feast day: May 8th. Patronage: Mystics, universalism.

Saint Julian was an English mystic, an anchorite who experienced visions of God in her cell. A central theme of her visions was that "All shall be well" and "Every manner of thing shall be well." She is commemorated in the Anglican and Lutheran Churches, but not the Catholic Church.

Martin of Tours

Feast day: November 11th. Patronage: Beggars, alcoholics, vintners, innkeepers, and many others.

Saint Martin of Tours was a Roman cavalryman who became a bishop. He is well known for having once cut his own cloak in two and giving one of the halves to a beggar. For this reason, he is a patron of beggars and the poor. He also helps recovering alcoholics, among many other groups—as usual, the rule is, "The older the saint, the broader the patronage."

Melangell

Feast day: May 27th. Patronage: Hares.

Saint Melangell is another saint who deserves to be better known. A Welsh saint, she saved the life of a hare in her lifetime, and became patron of hares afterward. I have reason to believe that she has become more active in America in recent years, and that here her patronage may extend beyond our native hares (jackrabbits) to ordinary rabbits as well. More interestingly, she can be called upon in order to invoke a hare- or rabbit-like spirit, when this is needed.

Patrick

Feast day: March 17th. Patronage: Ireland and the Irish.

Everyone knows that Saint Patrick is the patron saint of Ireland and of anyone around the world with so much as a drop of Irish blood in their veins. His feast day is typically a time of merriment and beer drinking, and that's as it should be, but there is more to Saint Patrick than that. Consider the old story that he drove the snakes from Ireland, and call upon him when the snakes of temptation and habitual thought patterns come slithering into your mind.

Paul

Feast day: June 29th. Patronage: Extensive.

Saint Paul was taken up to the Third Heaven and experienced a vision of Christ. We often suppose that this was a random event, but the evidence is that he was actually a Merkabah mystic and encountered Christ in a vision. Rather than a stodgy theologian, perhaps he could be better invoked as a patron of mystics, Kabbalists, and astral travel.

Peter

Feast day: June 29th. Patronage: Extensive.

Peter is called "the rock" and was given the "keys to Heaven." There is a deeper significance to these statements than they are often given, and time spent contemplating them will be time well spent.

Philomena

Feast day: August 10th (Coptic) or 11th (Catholic). Patronage: Mothers and children.

Philomena is an ancient saint of whom little is truly known, and so in our time those who despise myth and worship history have not wanted much to do with her. But for those who know better she has been found a patron of the poor, especially women, and especially single mothers.

Therese of Lisieux

Feast day: October 1st. Patronage: Missionaries, the homeless, alcoholics, orphans, florists.

Saint Therese is called the little flower, and it is said that a shower of rose petals fell from Heaven at her death. Her memoir, *The Story of a Soul*, is widely read by Catholics and others to this day.

APPENDIX 3

Sources and further reading

If you wish to continue to explore the tradition of sacramental magic, you may find the following resources helpful. I've relied on many of these for this book.

Sacraments and sacramentals

The Rituale Romanum

The *Rituale* is the Catholic Church's official book of rites for both the sacraments and sacramentals. If you can read Latin, you can find very old editions on websites like archive.org. St. Cyprian's Press has also released a complete translation in formal, Elizabethan English, rather than the pedestrian English of modern translations. You can find it online by going to lulu.com and searching for "Editors of Saint Cyprian Press."

The Daily Missal, with Vespers for Sundays and Feasts by Dom Gaspar Lefebvre

This is a 1925 English missal, including the propers of the mass for every Sunday of the year in both English and Latin. If you are working within a Roman Catholic tradition, this will provide you with the Propers for the home mass throughout the year. This is a big book, a century old now, and physical copies can be expensive. Fortunately, as it is a hundred years old, electronic copies can easily (and legally) be found online.

The Book of Common Prayer

The Book of Common Prayer includes the sacraments and the ordinary and propers of the mass in the Anglican tradition; if you are an Anglican or Episcopalian, or simply prefer their approach to the sacraments, this is the book you want. As in the case of the *Rituale Romanum and the various Roman missals*, there have been a number of revisions. Compare two or three different versions and pick the one that works for you.

The Science of the Sacraments by C. W. Leadbeater

Leadbeater was a well-known esotericist and member of the Theosophical Society, who later became a bishop in the Liberal Catholic Church. *TSoTS* is the only detailed exploration of the seven sacraments from the same sort of perspective that I've used in this book. It helpfully compares the texts of both the Tridentine and Liberal Catholic liturgies, and the differing effects of each.

A Book of Novenas for the Principal Feasts of the Year

Published in 1878, this is a nice traditional guide to novenas. The prayers are useful both for their own sake and as a guide to constructing novenas of your own.

Key of Heaven

The classic Catholic prayer book. Recent editions tend to be abridged and feature "updated" language. Fortunately, it was apparently required by law at one time for every Irish family in the United States to own at least three copies, so you can easily find older versions on the used book market.

Esoteric Christianity and Christian Magic

The Magic of Catholicism, by Brother A.D.A.

A must-have for any serious practitioner, in many ways, this book is the last word in magical Catholicism. Available along with many other books in the same vein at thauvmapub.com.

The Experience of the Inner Worlds, by Gareth Knight

Knight was at once a devout Anglican and an esotericist in the tradition of Dion Fortune, and this book provides a gentle and effective introduction to the traditions of Christian magic.

The Red Church, by Christopher Bilardi

This book explores the tradition of Braucherei, which is the traditional system of magic of the Pennsylvania Germans. As the author makes clear from the beginning, this is an entirely Christian system of magic, though many of the practices may seem quite strange to the modern reader.

Rosicrucian Cosmo-Conception, by Max Heindel

Written in 1925, this is a very different sort of book, at once deeply devout and totally radical. The Rosicrucian tradition approaches Christianity through the lens of the Esoteric tradition, especially as formulated in the nineteenth and early twentieth centuries.

Blessing Psalter of St. Arsenios of Cappadocia

An early twentieth-century Greek text, this is an excellent guide to the magical use of the psalms. Easily found online, translated into English.

ACKNOWLEDGEMENTS

It might be that someone out there could write a book like this without a great deal of help, but I could not and did not. I would therefore like to take some time to thank those who helped to make possible both this book and the books to follow in this series.

My gratitude goes first to my wife, Jennifer. Without her constant support I would barely be able to get myself out of bed in the morning, to say nothing of more complicated operations like remembering meals, paying the mortgage, or completing a book like this. And to my children as well, for their love, and for understanding—at least occasionally—why I need to sit at that boring computer and type so much.

Next, I would like to thank my friends who have supported my work over the years, and the readers and patrons of my blog and my divinatory work. Especially, that includes my longtime friend and partner in magic, Dean Smith; Erika Miller, who was among the first to read my work and offer feedback; Aaron Frazier, for his help in tracking down sources; Billy Sullivan, of the Celtic Catholic Church USA; Alistair Bate, of the Holy Celtic Church International; and Jason Spadafore, Kristopher Manghera, Chris Bilardi, and Frater Abdiel. Raise the black heart for me, fellows.

ACKNOWLEDGEMENTS

The philosophy and magical practices covered in this book draw on many sources from within the esoteric and occult traditions, orthodox Catholicism, and the Platonic traditions. As such, I am indebted to a great many authors and thinkers, both living and dead, within these traditions. Among living authors, I am especially grateful to John Michael Greer, whose influence will be obvious to anyone familiar with his work, and who has been a great help to me in my explorations of magic and esotericism for many years. In addition to Mr. Greer, I owe a great debt of gratitude to Jason Spadafore, who first confirmed my suspicion that there was more to traditional Catholicism than rote prayers and emotional manipulation.

Among those who have passed beyond this incarnation, I would like to extent my thanks to Donald Michael Kraig, Israel Regardie, Dion Fortune, Max Heindel, Eliphas Levi, Heinrich Cornelius Agrippa, and Marsilio Ficino, in reverse chronological order. Among Platonic scholars, I am especially indebted to Pierre Grimes and Wolfgang Smith, both of whom have recently departed these realms, and to Gregory Shaw, John Vervaeke, Edward Butler, and Lloyd Gerson, among living scholars. Among the saints and doctors of the Church, I have been blessed to have had as teachers Archbishop Fulton Sheen, Dorothy Day, Bonaventure, Thomas Aquinas, Francis of Assisi, John Scotus Eriugena, Augustine of Hippo (for better and for worse), and Dionysius the Areopagite (never "Pseudo"). Beyond the Church, I must also pay tribute to that golden chain of philosophers having its origin in Pythagoras and Plato, and extending through Apuleius, Maximus of Tyre, Plotinus, Porphyry of Tyre, Iamclihus, Proclus Diadouchus, Olympiodorus and Damascius. And to the spirit of Thomas Taylor, the English Platonist, without whom it may truly be said that none of us would be here: Let a libation be poured out to his genius.

I would like to extend my sincerest gratitude to Oliver, Alice, and the rest of the team at Aeon Books, without whom this would not be possible.

Finally, this book surely could not have been written without the guidance and intercession of Saint Joseph, Saint Raphael the Archangel, and Saint Synesius of Cyrene. *Ora pro me.*

Deo gratias propter omnia.

INDEX

abiding, 60
Abraham, 49, 50, 64, 65
Adam-Eve, 51
Adam, New, 51. *See also* Jesus
    of Nazareth
aeviternal things, 44
Agnus Dei (Lamb of God), 196–197
Aidan, Saint, 229
Albertus Magnus, Saint, 3
ancient city census, 52
Andrew, Saint, 229–230
angels, 15, 105
    invocation of guardian angel,
        108–110
    invoking, 105–106
    of places and communities, 110
The Angelus, 226–227
Anglican general confession, 72–73
Anthony of Padua, Saint, 230
Apostles' Creed, 76
apostolic succession, 211
Arbatel of Magic, 3
archangels, 16

The Art of War (Sun Tzu), 129
astral body, 24, 28
Astral Plane, 14, 18–20, 21, 29, 112, 113.
    See also planes of being
astrological magic, 3
Augustine of Hippo, Saint, xv
aura/sphere of sensation, 23, 26

banishing, 57
    Banishing Ritual of the Pentagram,
        57
    before, 58–59
    daily, 57–58, 61
    embodied awareness, 58–59
    and energetic purification, 57–58
    instructions for practice, 61
    movements of divine power, 60–61
    sign of the Cross, 59–60
    simple scanning exercise, 58–59
    two-week practice, 61
baptism, 175, 204
    Baptism of the Bell, 149
Bardon, F., 3

bells, 149
    Baptism of the Bell, 149
    blessing of, 150–151
Bernadette of Lourdes, Saint, 230
Bilardi, C., 239
binary thinking, 29–32
blessed oil, 146
blessing
    of bell, 150–151
    candles, 145–146
    the Cross, 152
    for natural sacramentals, 157–159
    psalms for magic and, 168–169
    ritual, 139–140
    sacramentals, 138–139
    for sacred images, 153
    traditional sacramentals, 141
Blessing Psalter of St. Arsenios
        of Cappadocia, 239
The Book of Common Prayer, 203, 208, 238
*A Book of Novenas for the Principal Feasts
        of the Year*, 163, 238
Braucherei tradition, 239
breathing, rhythmic, 38
Brigid of Kildare, Saint, 229, 230
Brother A. D. A., 238

Cadmon, A., 50
candles, 145–146
canonized saints, 162
Catherine of Siena, Saint, 230–231
cedar, 156
The Celestial Hierarchy (Dionysius), 15
chamomile, 157
chaos, 45
chastity, 112
Christian
    energy practice, 101–102
    myth and magical theology, 43–44
    spirituality, 41, 44–45
    thaumaturgy, 123
    three enemies of, 31
    tradition as magical tradition, ix
Christian magic, 3–4, 238
    Blessing Psalter of St. Arsenios
            of Cappadocia, 239
    Eucharist, 173

The Experience of the Inner Worlds,
        239
The Magic of Catholicism, 238
    origins and scope of, 169
The Red Church, 239
Rosicrucian Cosmo-Conception, 239
    sign of the Cross as ritual
            banishing, 57–58
    transubstantiation, 174
Christopher, Saint, 231
the Collect, 188
Collect for Saint Marsilio Ficino, 188
communion bread, 199
    preparation, 200–201
    recipe, 201–202
communion elements, 199–202
confession, 204–205
    Anamchara, 205–206
    confessor, 204
    "examination of conscience", 206
    ritual, 206–207
confirmation, 208–209
    self-confirmation, 209–210
Confiteor, 67
    Anglican general confession, 72–73
    evolution of soul, 68–70
    liberal catholic, 73
    nature of sin, 67–68
    ritual, 71–72, 73, 186
    Roman Catholic Confiteor, 72
    Seven Deadly Sins, 70–71
    step-by-step guide, 71–72
    traditional Confiteor prayer, 72
    weekly practice and spiritual
            balance, 73–74
consciousness, 5–7, 11, 209
consecration, 94, 111
    Immaculate Heart of Mary, 113,
            115–117
    of incense, 144
    and magical use of sacred bells,
            149–151
    Most Chaste Heart, 112, 113–115
    olive oil, 146–147
    prayers of, 194–195
    sacramentals, 138–140
    Sacred Heart of Jesus, 117–120

talisman, 173–174
theurgical path to higher planes, 111–113
three holy hearts, 111–113
tools of grace, 141
contemplative prayer, 34, 35
conversion of the soul, 83
Cornelius Agrippa, Heinrich, 3, 66
creation, 45–49
Creeds, 223
    Apostles' Creed, 76
    Nicene Creed, 190–191, 223–224
    Statement of faith of the Liberal Catholic Church, 191, 224
the Cross, 53, 152
    blessing and ritual empowerment, 152
    as ritual banishing, 57–58
    sign as ritual invocation and protection, 59–60
crown
    chakra, 88
    of glory, 89–90
Cyprian, Saint, 58, 231

daily prayers, 221. *See also* prayer book
    Glory be, 222
    Grace before meals, 222–223
    Hail Mary, 222
    Holy Spirit prayer, 222
    Lord's prayer, 195–196, 221
David, King, 64, 65
David, Saint, 231
Death, 49
    grace of happy, 88–89
    to lower self, 85–86
descent of man, 46–49
Devil, 21, 30–32
Devotional Revolution of the 1800s, xiv
The Dialogue of Divine Providence (Catherine of Siena), 230
Dion Fortune, 4, 66
Dionysius the Areopagite, xv, 13, 14, 60
divine healing ritual, 73
divine law, obedience to, 82–83
Divine Mind, xvi, xvii

Divine Plane, 14–15, 27, 28, 55, 113, 126. *See also* planes of being
divine reading. See *lectio divina*
divinization, 68

Earth, 45
energetic body/spirit, 22–23, 102–103, 186
Energetic Plane, 14, 20, 29. *See also* planes of being
energy centers, 23–24
envy, 70–71
"epiphenomenon", 11
epithymia, 25, 103
Esoteric anthropology, 68–70
Esoteric Christianity, 238
    Blessing Psalter of St. Arsenios of Cappadocia, 239
    creation, 45–49
    the Cross, 53
    descent of man, 46–49
    esoteric genesis, 45–46
    The Experience of the Inner Worlds, 239
    and foundational practices, 41
    incarnation, 49–52
    The Magic of Catholicism, 238
    mythic framework, 44–45
    mythic structure of Revelation, 54–55
    The Red Church, 239
    Rosicrucian Cosmo-Conception, 239
    Second Coming, 54–55
    soul's descent and ascent, 49–52
    statement of faith, 192, 224–225
    theology, 43
Esotericism
    Esoteric model of human person, 22–27
    genesis, 45–46
    teaching, 16
    Western, 27
    works, 66
Eternal Man, xvii, 47
Eucharist, 9, 173, 183, 192–197, 203
Eve, New, 51. *See also* Mary, Blessed Virgin
evil spirits, 21

"evolution of the soul", 69
The Experience of the Inner Worlds (Knight), 239
extemporaneous prayer, 34

faith, 86–87
Fatima prayer, 228
fir, 157
First Turning, 55
five-finger grass, 156
"folk saints", 162
Fortune, Dion. *See* Dion Fortune
Francis of Assisi, Saint, 228, 231
frankincense, 155, 156

Garden of Gethsemene, 83
gemstones, 157
general confession. *See* Confiteor
genesis, Esoteric, 45–46
George, Saint, 232
Gertrude the Great, Saint, 109, 232
gifts of the Holy Ghost, 87–88
ginger, 156
Glory be, 222
gluttony, 71
God, 45
    creative power of, 60
    as metaphor, 67–68
    uniting ourselves with, 69
    Will of, 6
    Word of, xvii
Golden Dawn, xiii, 57
Golgotha, 85, 86
grace
    of happy death, 88–89
    before meals, 222–223
greed, 70
guardian angel
    invocation of, 108–110, 185–186
    of places and communities, 110
    prayer, 109, 110, 227
Guéranger, D., 15, 108

Hades, 49
Hail Holy Queen, 79, 226. *See also* Mary, Blessed Virgin
Hail Mary, 222. *See also* Mary, Blessed Virgin
hamartia, 68
healing
    divine healing ritual, 73
    magical healing, 212–216
    oil, 147–148, 212
    Our Lady of Lourdes, 163–165
    power of kyrie, 102–104
    simpler forms of, 216
Heaven
    and Earth, 129
    Key of, 238
Heindel, M., 66, 239
Hell, 49
higher self, 69
Hildegard of Bingen, Saint, 232
Holy Chrism, 146, 148
Holy Eucharist, 9
Holy Family, 112
Holy Ghost, gifts of the, 87–88
Holy Oil, 146
    consecrated olive oil, 146–147
    Oil of Empowerment, 148–149
    Oil of Healing, 147–148
Holy Orders, 208–209
Holy Spirit prayer, 215, 222
Holy Trinity, 60, 112
Holy Water, 137, 138, 142–144
home mass, 174, 181–183
    Agnus Dei, 196–197
    charging energetic body, 186
    the Collect, 188
    communion elements, 199–202
    Confiteor ritual, 186
    consecration prayers, 194–195
    esoteric Christian statement of faith, 192
    Eucharist, 173, 183, 192–197
    fraction of the host, 196
    gloria, 186–187
    instructions, 185–197
    intercession prayers, 195
    invocation of guardian angel, 185–186
    Lord's prayer, 195–196

meditation, 190
Nicene Creed, 190–191
offertory, 193
opening, 185–187
peace of Christ, 192–193
postcommunion prayer, 197
Propers of the mass, 183, 187
selecting sacred readings, 189–190
statement of faith of Liberal Catholic Church, 191
thanksgiving, 193–194
hope, 87
host, 199. *See also* communion bread
fraction of, 196
Howe, N., 19
human microcosm. *See* microcosm
humility, 80
hyssop, 156

illumination rite, 101–102
imagination, 131–132
The Imitation of Christ (Thomas à Kempis), 66
immaculate, 113
Immaculate Conception, 51. *See also* Mary, Blessed Virgin
Immaculate Heart of Mary, 113, 115–117. *See also* Mary, Blessed Virgin
incarnation, 49–52
incense, 144
Independent Sacramental Movement (ISM), 211
intellectual body, 26
Intellectual Plane, 14, 15, 17, 27, 54. *See also* planes of being
Immaculate Heart of Mary, 113
the Sun, 126
intention, 126–128
The Interior Castle (Teresa of Avila), 66
invocation, 93–94, 105
guardian angel, 108–110, 185–186
saint, 107–108, 165
Saint Joseph for material support, 128–129
and sharing sacred stillness, 192–193

Jesus of Nazareth, xvii, 51
Jesus, Sacred Heart of, 117–120
Joan of Arc, Saint, 232–233
Johannite Gnostic tradition, 233
John the Baptist, Saint, 81, 233
John the Evangelist, Saint, 233
Joseph, Saint, 51, 112, 113–115, 128–129
Julian of Norwich, Saint, 233
Jung, C., 205
juniper, 156
Justina, 58, 231

Key of Heaven, 238
Knight, G., 239
kyrie energetic practice, 101
daily practice, 101–102
healing power of kyrie, 102–104
threefold soul, 102–104

lavender, 157
Law of Action, 134–135
Law of Correspondences, 20–21, 128–129
Law of Form, 131–132
Law of Heaven and Earth, 129–131
Law of Intention, 126–128
Law of Magic, 13
Law of the Planes, 13, 126
layered ontology. *See* planes of being
Leadbeater, C. W., 203, 238
lectio divina, 63–65
lemon balm, 156
Lesser Banishing Ritual of the Pentagram, xiii
liberal catholic Confiteor, 73
liturgical prayer, 34
The Liturgical Year (Gueranger), 15
Lord's prayer, 195–196, 221
love of neighbour, 81
lower self, 69
Luke, Saint, 17, 52, 85
lust, 70

macrocosm, 22, 102
magic, 4, 9, 125, 209
aim, 5
in Christian tradition, 3–4

Devil and evil spirits, 21
esoteric model of human person, 22–27
human microcosm, 22–27
Law of Correspondences, 20–21
Law of Magic, 13
Law of the Planes, 13
mesocosm, 27–28
metaphysics of, 11–12
planes of being, 12–21
principles of, 10
magical healing, 212–216
magical temple, opening, 95, 99
altar, 96
closing the temple, 98–99
opening ritual, 97–98
preparation, 95–97
tools and space, 95–97
magic, effective, 125
bringing magic to life, 134–135
calling on right ally, 128–129
choosing right source of power, 128–129
clearing path, 132–134
correspondences and structure of planes, 126
creating appropriate form, 131–132
imagination as vessel, 131–132
invoking Saint Joseph, 128–129
Law of Action, 134–135
Law of Correspondences, 128–129
Law of Form, 131–132
Law of Heaven and Earth, 129–131
Law of Intention, 126–128
Law of the Planes, 126
picking time and place, 129–131
power of intention, 126–128
six laws of, 125
The Magic of Catholicism (Brother A. D. A.), 238
the Magnificat, 81, 225
The Magus (Bardon), 3
man, creation of, 46–49
Marian prayers, 225
The Angelus, 226–227
Hail, Holy Queen, 226

Magnificat, 225
memorare, 226
Marsilio Ficino, Saint, 13, 14, 162, 188
Martin of Tours, Saint, 233–234
Mary, Blessed Virgin, 18, 51, 113
Collect for the Feast of the Holy Name of Mary, 188
Hail Holy Queen, 79, 226
Hail Mary, 222
Immaculate Conception, 51
Immaculate Heart of Mary, 113, 115–117
Mary-Jesus, 51
materialist philosophy, 11
Material Plane, 14, 20–21, 54. *See also* planes of being
matrimony, 207–208
meditation, 63, 66, 190
Christian tradition, 63
daily practice, 63
lectio divina, 63–65
Melangell, Saint, 234
memorare, 226
mesocosm, 27–28
St. Michael the Archangel, 144, 145, 227
microcosm, 22, 102
astral body, 24, 28
aura/sphere of sensation, 23, 26
energetic body/spirit, 22–23
energy centers, 23–24
intellectual body, 26
mesocosm, 27–28
Physical Plane, 22
Montfort, L. de, 66
morality, 68
"mortification of the flesh", 84
Most Chaste Heart, 112, 113–115
myrrh, 157
myth, 43–44

Neoplatonism, xv
Nicene Creed, 190–191, 223–224
non-canonical saints, 162
nous, 24–25, 26, 53, 103

novena, 161
   magical power and practice of, 161–162
   Our Lady of Lourdes, 163–165
   personalizing, 165
   prayer, 162–163
   ritual, 162–163
Nunc dimittis prayer, 82

offertory, 193
Oil of Empowerment, 147, 148
Oil of Healing, 147, 212
Oil of the Catechumens, 146
Oil of the Sick, 146, 148
old Roman Ritual, 137–138
orans posture, 98
ordination, 210–212
Our Lady, 18
Our Lady of Lourdes, 163–165

palo santo, 157
patchouli, 156
Patrick, Saint, 234
Paul, Saint, 234
peace of Christ, 192–193
pentagram ritual, xiii
perseverance in spiritual life, 85
Peter, Saint, 235
Philomena, Saint, 235
Physical Plane, 22, 29
pine, 157
Plane of Unity. *See* Divine Plane
planes of being, 12–13
   angels, 15
   archangels, 16
   Astral Plane, 14, 18–20, 21
   Energetic Plane, 14, 20
   esoteric teaching, 16
   evil on, 21
   five planes of being, 13–18, 27
   Intellectual Plane, 14, 15, 17, 27
   Material Plane, 14, 20–21
   Our Lady, 18
   Plane of Unity/Divine Plane, 14–15, 27, 28

Purgatory, 16
   saint, 16, 17–18
Plato, xv, xvi, 26
Pliny the Elder, xii
Pontius Pilate, 84
postcommunion prayer, 197
prayer book, 221
   The Angelus, 226–227
   consecration prayers, 194–195
   contemplative prayer, 34, 35
   Creeds, 223–224
   daily prayers, 221–223
   Esoteric Christian statement of faith, 224–225
   extemporaneous prayer, 34
   Fatima prayer, 228
   Glory be, 222
   Grace before meals, 222–223
   Guardian Angel, 110, 227
   Hail Holy Queen, 79, 226
   Hail Mary, 222
   Holy Spirit prayer, 222
   intercession prayers, 195
   Lord's prayer, 195–196, 221
   Magnificat, 225
   Marian prayers, 225–227
   memorare, 226
   Nicene Creed, 223–224
   postcommunion prayer, 197
   Prayer for the Souls in Purgatory, 228
   Prayer of Saint Francis, 228
   Prayer of the Holy Spirit, 215, 222
   Saint Michael prayer, 227
   Statement of faith of the Liberal Catholic Church, 224
prayer rule, 33
   basic prayer rule, 35
   contemplative prayer, 34, 35
   daily practice, 33–35
   daily prayer routine, 35–36
   extemporaneous prayer, 34
   instructions for practice, 35
   invocation to intercession, 35–36
   liturgical prayer, 34
   in morning, 35–36

at night, 36–37
rhythmic breathing, 38
threefold prayer, 34–35
pride, 70
proceeding, 60
Propers of the mass, 183, 187
prosphora. *See* communion bread
psalms, 167
    Christian magic, 169
    for magic and blessing, 168–169
Purgatory, 16

The Red Church (Bilardi), 239
returning, 60
Revelation, 55
rhythmic breathing, 38
ritual(s)
    Banishing Ritual of the Pentagram, 57
    blessing, 139–140, 144
    of Christian magical initiation, 111
    Confiteor, 71–72, 73, 186
    for creating traditional holy water, 142–144
    divine healing, 73
    of illumination, 101–102
    Lesser Banishing Ritual of the Pentagram, xiii
    of magical healing, 213–216
    novena, 162–163
    old Roman Ritual, 137–138
    pentagram, xiii
    of saintly invocation, 107–108
    of self-dedication, 177–180
    sign of the Cross as ritual banishing, 57–58
    temple opening, 97–98
    theurgical, 93–94, 111
    universal ritual of blessing, 139–140
Rituale Romanum, 203, 208, 237–238
Roman Catholic Confiteor, 72
Roman Ritual, old, 137–138
rosary, 75–76
    Apostles' Creed, 76
    full practice of, 76–80
    glorious mysteries, 86–90

    joyful mysteries, 80–83
    mysteries of, 80–90
    preparation, 76
    sorrowful mysteries, 83–86
rosemary, 157
roses, 155, 156
Rosicrucian Cosmo-Conception (Heindel), 66, 239

sacrament(s), 7, 173, 203, 237
    baptism, 204
    The Book of Common Prayer, 238
    A Book of Novenas for the Principal Feasts of the Year, 238
    confession, 204–205
    confirmation and holy orders, 208–209
    Esoteric Christianity and Christian magic, 238–239
    Eucharist, 9, 203
    of initiation, 208–209
    ISM, 211
    Key of Heaven, 238
    magical healing, 212–216
    as magical rites, 173–175
    magician's guide, 9–10
    matrimony, 207–208
    ordination, 210–212
    Rituale Romanum, 237–238
    sacramentals vs., 7–8
    The Science of the Sacraments, 238
    self-confirmation rite, 209–210
    self-initiations, 208
    simpler forms of healing, 216
    of unction, 212
sacramental(s), 4, 137, 237
    blessing, 138–139
    A Book of Novenas for the Principal Feasts of the Year, 238
    categories, 8–9, 137
    Esoteric Christianity and Christian magic, 238–239
    Holy Water, 137, 138
    Key of Heaven, 238
    magical framework for consecrating, 138–139

INDEX   251

natural, 138
old Roman Ritual, 137–138
preparing for practice, 140
Rituale Romanum, 237–238
Ritual of Blessing, 140
vs. sacraments, 7–8
and sacred matter, 137–138
step-by-step guide to consecrating, 139–140
traditional, 137
traditional vs. natural tools of power, 137–138
universal ritual of blessing, 139–140
sacramental magic, 4
   consciousness, 5–7
   sacramental, 7–9
   sacraments, 7–8, 9–10
   True Will, 6
   Will, 6
   Will of God, 6
sacramentals, natural, 138, 155
   blessing for, 157–159
   cedar and juniper, 156
   chamomile, 157
   fir, spruce, and pine, 157
   five-finger grass, 156
   frankincense, 155, 156
   gemstones, 157
   ginger, 156
   hyssop, 156
   lavender, 157
   lemon balm, 156
   list of, 156
   myrrh, 157
   palo santo, 157
   patchouli, 156
   rosemary, 157
   roses, 155, 156
   Saint John's wort, 156
   traditional use in Christian magic, 155–156
sacramentals, traditional, 137, 141
   bells, 149–151
   candles and fire, 145–146
   crosses, 152

   holy oil, 146–149
   holy water, 142–144
   incense, 144
   sacred images, 152–153
sacred
   flame, 145–146
   images, 152–153
   matter, 137–138
   readings, 189–190
   things, 137–140
Sacred Heart of Jesus, 117–120
saint(s), 16, 17–18, 229
   Aidan, 229
   Albertus Magnus, 3
   Andrew, 229–230
   Anthony of Padua, 230
   Augustine of Hippo, Saint, xv
   Bernadette of Lourdes, 230
   Brigid of Kildare, 229, 230
   canonized, 162
   Catherine of Sienna, 230–231
   Christopher, 231
   Cyprian, 58, 231
   David, 231
   "folk saints", 162
   Francis of Assisi, 228, 231
   George, 232
   Gertrude the Great, 109, 232
   Hildegard of Bingen, 232
   invoking, 105–108
   Joan of Arc, 232–233
   John the Baptist, 81, 233
   John the Evangelist, 233
   Joseph, 51, 112, 113–115, 128–129
   Julian of Norwich, 233
   Luke, 17, 52, 85
   Marsilio Ficino, 13, 14, 162, 188
   Martin of Tours, 233–234
   Melangell, 234
   Michael, 145, 227
   non-canonical saints, 162
   Patrick, 234
   Paul, 234
   Peter, 235
   Philomena, 235
   Teresa of Avila, 66

Therese of Lisieux, 126, 235
Thomas Aquinas, xv, 13, 14
Saint John's wort, 156
Sallust, xvi
The Science of the Sacraments (Dion Fortune), 66
The Science of the Sacraments (Leadbeater), 203, 208, 238
sciences, 5
Second Coming, 54–55
Second Vatican Council, xiv
self, 69
   -confirmation, 209–210
   -dedication rite, 177–180
   -initiations, 208
   -mastery, 84–85
serpent, 47–48
Seven Deadly Sins, 70–71, 206
Simeon, 82
sin, 67–68
sloth, 71
soul(s), 5, 27, 102
   conversion of the, 83
   descent and ascent, 49–52
   epithymia, 25, 103
   evolution of, 68–70
   nous, 24–25, 26, 103
   parts of, 24
   Prayer for the Souls in Purgatory, 228
   threefold soul, 102–104
   thymos, 25, 103
spiritual
   confession and forgiveness practice, 71–72
   perseverance, 85
   poverty, 81–82
spruce, 157
Statement of faith of the Liberal Catholic Church, 191, 224
Stoic teachings, xii
stole, 178

The Story of a Soul (Thérèse of Lisieux), 235
Strauss, W., 19
Sun Tzu, 129

talisman, 173–174
Teresa of Avila, Saint, 66
ternary thinking, 30
thanksgiving, 193–194
thaumaturgy, 93, 123
Therese of Lisieux, Saint, 126, 235
theurgy, 93–94
   of Holy Companionship, 106
   theurgical rituals, 93–94, 111
Thomas à Kempis, 66
Thomas Aquinas, Saint, xv, 13, 14
Three Books of Occult Philosophy (Cornelius Agrippa), 66
thymos, 25, 51, 103
transubstantiation, 174
Trinity, 30
True Devotion to the Blessed Virgin Mary (Montfort), 66
True Will, 6

unction, 212
Union with the will of God, 83
Universal Church, 51–52
universal ritual of blessing, 139–140

Vatican Council, Second, xiv

Western
   esotericism, 27
   Magical Tradition, xiv
Will, 6
Will of God, 6
   Union with, 83
Word of God, xvii
wrath, 71

Yahweh Elo'ah Ve'Da'ath, 126. *See* God

www.ingramcontent.com/pod-product-compliance
Ingram Content Group UK Ltd.
Pitfield, Milton Keynes, MK11 3LW, UK
UKHW022212041025
463617UK00008B/108